Book 3: Financial Reporting and Analysis

SchweserNotes™ 2019

Level I CFA®

SCHWESERNOTES™ 2019 LEVEL I CFA® BOOK 3: FINANCIAL REPORTING AND ANALYSIS

©2018 Kaplan, Inc. All rights reserved.

Published in 2018 by Kaplan, Inc.

Printed in the United States of America.

ISBN: 978-1-4754-7832-7

CONTENTS

STUDY SESSION 8—Financial Reporting and Analysis (3)

STUDY SESSION 9—Financial Reporting and Analysis (4)

LEARNING OUTCOME STATEMENTS (LOS)

STUDY SESSION 6

The topical coverage corresponds with the following CFA Institute assigned reading:
21. Financial Statement Analysis: An Introduction
The candidate should be able to:
a. describe the roles of financial reporting and financial statement analysis. (page 1)
b. describe the roles of the statement of financial position, statement of comprehensive income, statement of changes in equity, and statement of cash flows in evaluating a company's performance and financial position. (page 2)
c. describe the importance of financial statement notes and supplementary information—including disclosures of accounting policies, methods, and estimates—and management's commentary. (page 3)
d. describe the objective of audits of financial statements, the types of audit reports, and the importance of effective internal controls. (page 4)
e. identify and describe information sources that analysts use in financial statement analysis besides annual financial statements and supplementary information. (page 5)
f. describe the steps in the financial statement analysis framework. (page 6)

The topical coverage corresponds with the following CFA Institute assigned reading:
22. Financial Reporting Standards
The candidate should be able to:
a. describe the objective of financial statements and the importance of financial reporting standards in security analysis and valuation. (page 11)
b. describe roles and desirable attributes of financial reporting standard-setting bodies and regulatory authorities in establishing and enforcing reporting standards, and describe the role of the International Organization of Securities Commissions. (page 12)
c. describe the status of global convergence of accounting standards and ongoing barriers to developing one universally accepted set of financial reporting standards. (page 13)
d. describe the International Accounting Standards Board's conceptual framework, including the objective and qualitative characteristics of financial statements, required reporting elements, and constraints and assumptions in preparing financial statements. (page 14)
e. describe general requirements for financial statements under International Financial Reporting Standards (IFRS). (page 17)
f. compare key concepts of financial reporting standards under IFRS and US generally accepted accounting principles (US GAAP) reporting systems. (page 18)
g. identify characteristics of a coherent financial reporting framework and the barriers to creating such a framework. (page 18)
h. describe implications for financial analysis of differing financial reporting systems and the importance of monitoring developments in financial reporting standards. (page 19)
i. analyze company disclosures of significant accounting policies. (page 20)

STUDY SESSION 7

The topical coverage corresponds with the following CFA Institute assigned reading:
23. Understanding Income Statements
The candidate should be able to:
a. describe the components of the income statement and alternative presentation formats of that statement. (page 28)
b. describe general principles of revenue recognition and accrual accounting, specific revenue recognition applications (including accounting for long-term contracts, installment sales, barter transactions, gross and net reporting of revenue), and implications of revenue recognition principles for financial analysis. (page 30)
c. calculate revenue given information that might influence the choice of revenue recognition method. (page 30)
d. describe key aspects of the converged accounting standards for revenue recognition issued by the International Accounting Standards Board and Financial Accounting Standards Board in May 2014. (page 35)
e. describe general principles of expense recognition, specific expense recognition applications, and implications of expense recognition choices for financial analysis. (page 38)
f. describe the financial reporting treatment and analysis of non-recurring items (including discontinued operations, unusual or infrequent items) and changes in accounting policies. (page 41)
g. distinguish between the operating and non-operating components of the income statement. (page 43)
h. describe how earnings per share is calculated and calculate and interpret a company's earnings per share (both basic and diluted earnings per share) for both simple and complex capital structures. (page 45)
i. distinguish between dilutive and antidilutive securities and describe the implications of each for the earnings per share calculation. (page 45)
j. convert income statements to common-size income statements. (page 53)
k. evaluate a company's financial performance using common-size income statements and financial ratios based on the income statement. (page 54)
l. describe, calculate, and interpret comprehensive income. (page 54)
m. describe other comprehensive income and identify major types of items included in it. (page 54)

The topical coverage corresponds with the following CFA Institute assigned reading:
24. Understanding Balance Sheets
The candidate should be able to:
a. describe the elements of the balance sheet: assets, liabilities, and equity. (page 65)
b. describe uses and limitations of the balance sheet in financial analysis. (page 66)
c. describe alternative formats of balance sheet presentation. (page 66)
d. distinguish between current and non-current assets and current and non-current liabilities. (page 67)
e. describe different types of assets and liabilities and the measurement bases of each. (page 68)
f. describe the components of shareholders' equity. (page 76)

g. convert balance sheets to common-size balance sheets and interpret common-size balance sheets. (page 78)

h. calculate and interpret liquidity and solvency ratios. (page 80)

The topical coverage corresponds with the following CFA Institute assigned reading:

25. Understanding Cash Flow Statements

The candidate should be able to:

a. compare cash flows from operating, investing, and financing activities and classify cash flow items as relating to one of those three categories given a description of the items. (page 90)

b. describe how non-cash investing and financing activities are reported. (page 91)

c. contrast cash flow statements prepared under International Financial Reporting Standards (IFRS) and US generally accepted accounting principles (US GAAP). (page 92)

d. distinguish between the direct and indirect methods of presenting cash from operating activities and describe arguments in favor of each method. (page 92)

e. describe how the cash flow statement is linked to the income statement and the balance sheet. (page 94)

f. describe the steps in the preparation of direct and indirect cash flow statements, including how cash flows can be computed using income statement and balance sheet data. (page 97)

g. convert cash flows from the indirect to direct method. (page 105)

h. analyze and interpret both reported and common-size cash flow statements. (page 108)

i. calculate and interpret free cash flow to the firm, free cash flow to equity, and performance and coverage cash flow ratios. (page 110)

The topical coverage corresponds with the following CFA Institute assigned reading:

26. Financial Analysis Techniques

The candidate should be able to:

a. describe tools and techniques used in financial analysis, including their uses and limitations. (page 121)

b. classify, calculate, and interpret activity, liquidity, solvency, profitability, and valuation ratios. (page 127)

c. describe relationships among ratios and evaluate a company using ratio analysis. (page 137)

d. demonstrate the application of DuPont analysis of return on equity and calculate and interpret effects of changes in its components. (page 140)

e. calculate and interpret ratios used in equity analysis and credit analysis. (page 144)

f. explain the requirements for segment reporting and calculate and interpret segment ratios. (page 148)

g. describe how ratio analysis and other techniques can be used to model and forecast earnings. (page 149)

STUDY SESSION 8

The topical coverage corresponds with the following CFA Institute assigned reading:

27. Inventories

The candidate should be able to:

a. distinguish between costs included in inventories and costs recognised as expenses in the period in which they are incurred. (page 156)

b. describe different inventory valuation methods (cost formulas). (page 157)

c. calculate and compare cost of sales, gross profit, and ending inventory using different inventory valuation methods and using perpetual and periodic inventory systems. (page 158)

d. calculate and explain how inflation and deflation of inventory costs affect the financial statements and ratios of companies that use different inventory valuation methods. (page 163)

e. explain LIFO reserve and LIFO liquidation and their effects on financial statements and ratios. (page 166)

f. convert a company's reported financial statements from LIFO to FIFO for purposes of comparison. (page 166)

g. describe the measurement of inventory at the lower of cost and net realisable value. (page 171)

h. describe implications of valuing inventory at net realisable value for financial statements and ratios. (page 173)

i. describe the financial statement presentation of and disclosures relating to inventories. (page 173)

j. explain issues that analysts should consider when examining a company's inventory disclosures and other sources of information. (page 174)

k. calculate and compare ratios of companies, including companies that use different inventory methods. (page 175)

l. analyze and compare the financial statements of companies, including companies that use different inventory methods. (page 175)

The topical coverage corresponds with the following CFA Institute assigned reading:

28. Long-Lived Assets

The candidate should be able to:

a. distinguish between costs that are capitalised and costs that are expensed in the period in which they are incurred. (page 189)

b. compare the financial reporting of the following types of intangible assets: purchased, internally developed, acquired in a business combination. (page 191)

c. explain and evaluate how capitalising versus expensing costs in the period in which they are incurred affects financial statements and ratios. (page 193)

d. describe the different depreciation methods for property, plant, and equipment and calculate depreciation expense. (page 196)

e. describe how the choice of depreciation method and assumptions concerning useful life and residual value affect depreciation expense, financial statements, and ratios. (page 199)

f. describe the different amortisation methods for intangible assets with finite lives and calculate amortisation expense. (page 200)

g. describe how the choice of amortisation method and assumptions concerning useful life and residual value affect amortisation expense, financial statements, and ratios. (page 201)

h. describe the revaluation model. (page 202)

i. explain the impairment of property, plant, and equipment and intangible assets. (page 204)

j. explain the derecognition of property, plant, and equipment and intangible assets. (page 206)

k. explain and evaluate how impairment, revaluation, and derecognition of property, plant, and equipment and intangible assets affect financial statements and ratios. (page 207)

l. describe the financial statement presentation of and disclosures relating to property, plant, and equipment and intangible assets. (page 210)

m. analyze and interpret financial statement disclosures regarding property, plant, and equipment and intangible assets. (page 211)

n. compare the financial reporting of investment property with that of property, plant, and equipment. (page 212)

o. explain and evaluate how leasing rather than purchasing assets affects financial statements and ratios. (page 213)

p. explain and evaluate how finance leases and operating leases affect financial statements and ratios from the perspective of both the lessor and the lessee. (page 213)

The topical coverage corresponds with the following CFA Institute assigned reading:

29. Income Taxes

The candidate should be able to: ·

a. describe the differences between accounting profit and taxable income and define key terms, including deferred tax assets, deferred tax liabilities, valuation allowance, taxes payable, and income tax expense. (page 225)

b. explain how deferred tax liabilities and assets are created and the factors that determine how a company's deferred tax liabilities and assets should be treated for the purposes of financial analysis. (page 227)

c. calculate the tax base of a company's assets and liabilities. (page 228)

d. calculate income tax expense, income taxes payable, deferred tax assets, and deferred tax liabilities, and calculate and interpret the adjustment to the financial statements related to a change in the income tax rate. (page 231)

e. evaluate the effect of tax rate changes on a company's financial statements and ratios. (page 234)

f. distinguish between temporary and permanent differences in pre-tax accounting income and taxable income. (page 237)

g. describe the valuation allowance for deferred tax assets—when it is required and what effect it has on financial statements. (page 238)

h. explain recognition and measurement of current and deferred tax items. (page 239)

i. analyze disclosures relating to deferred tax items and the effective tax rate reconciliation and explain how information included in these disclosures affects a company's financial statements and financial ratios. (page 239)

j. identify the key provisions of and differences between income tax accounting under International Financial Reporting Standards (IFRS) and US generally accepted accounting principles (GAAP). (page 243)

The topical coverage corresponds with the following CFA Institute assigned reading:
30. Non-Current (Long-term) Liabilities
The candidate should be able to:
a. determine the initial recognition, initial measurement and subsequent measurement of bonds. (page 252)
b. describe the effective interest method and calculate interest expense, amortisation of bond discounts/premiums, and interest payments. (page 253)
c. explain the derecognition of debt. (page 259)
d. describe the role of debt covenants in protecting creditors. (page 260)
e. describe the financial statement presentation of and disclosures relating to debt. (page 261)
f. explain motivations for leasing assets instead of purchasing them. (page 262)
g. distinguish between a finance lease and an operating lease from the perspectives of the lessor and the lessee. (page 263)
h. determine the initial recognition, initial measurement, and subsequent measurement of finance leases. (page 264)
i. compare the disclosures relating to finance and operating leases. (page 271)
j. compare the presentation and disclosure of defined contribution and defined benefit pension plans. (page 271)
k. calculate and interpret leverage and coverage ratios. (page 273)

STUDY SESSION 9

The topical coverage corresponds with the following CFA Institute assigned reading:
31. Financial Reporting Quality
The candidate should be able to:
a. distinguish between financial reporting quality and quality of reported results (including quality of earnings, cash flow, and balance sheet items). (page 281)
b. describe a spectrum for assessing financial reporting quality. (page 282)
c. distinguish between conservative and aggressive accounting. (page 283)
d. describe motivations that might cause management to issue financial reports that are not high quality. (page 285)
e. describe conditions that are conducive to issuing low-quality, or even fraudulent, financial reports. (page 285)
f. describe mechanisms that discipline financial reporting quality and the potential limitations of those mechanisms. (page 286)
g. describe presentation choices, including non-GAAP measures, that could be used to influence an analyst's opinion. (page 287)
h. describe accounting methods (choices and estimates) that could be used to manage earnings, cash flow, and balance sheet items. (page 288)
i. describe accounting warning signs and methods for detecting manipulation of information in financial reports. (page 292)

The topical coverage corresponds with the following CFA Institute assigned reading:
32. Financial Statement Analysis: Applications
The candidate should be able to:
a. evaluate a company's past financial performance and explain how a company's strategy is reflected in past financial performance. (page 301)

b. forecast a company's future net income and cash flow. (page 302)
c. describe the role of financial statement analysis in assessing the credit quality of a potential debt investment. (page 303)
d. describe the use of financial statement analysis in screening for potential equity investments. (page 304)
e. explain appropriate analyst adjustments to a company's financial statements to facilitate comparison with another company. (page 305)

READING
21

Financial Statement Analysis: An Introduction

Study Session 6

EXAM FOCUS

This introduction may be useful to those who have no previous experience with financial statements. While the income statement, balance sheet, and statement of cash flows are covered in detail in subsequent readings, candidates should pay special attention here to the other sources of information for financial analysis. The nature of the audit report is important, as is the information that is contained in the footnotes to financial statements, proxy statements, Management's Discussion and Analysis, and the supplementary schedules. A useful framework enumerating the steps in financial statement analysis is presented.

MODULE 21.1: FINANCIAL STATEMENT ROLES

Video covering this content is available online.

LOS 21.a: Describe the roles of financial reporting and financial statement analysis.

CFA® Program Curriculum, Volume 3, page 6

Financial reporting refers to the way companies show their financial performance to investors, creditors, and other interested parties by preparing and presenting financial statements. According to the *IASB Conceptual Framework for Financial Reporting 2010*:

> "The objective of general purpose financial reporting is to provide financial information about the reporting entity that is useful to existing and potential investors, lenders, and other creditors in making decisions about providing resources to the entity. Those decisions involve buying, selling or holding equity and debt instruments, and providing or settling loans and other forms of credit."

The role of **financial statement analysis** is to use the information in a company's financial statements, along with other relevant information, to make economic decisions. Examples of such decisions include whether to invest in the company's securities or recommend them to investors and whether to extend trade or bank credit to the company. Analysts use financial statement data to evaluate a company's past performance and current financial position in order to form opinions about the company's ability to earn profits and generate cash flow in the future.

PROFESSOR'S NOTE

This topic review deals with financial analysis for external users. Management also performs financial analysis in making everyday decisions. However, management may rely on internal financial information that is likely maintained in a different format and unavailable to external users.

LOS 21.b: Describe the roles of the statement of financial position, statement of comprehensive income, statement of changes in equity, and statement of cash flows in evaluating a company's performance and financial position.

CFA® Program Curriculum, Volume 3, page 11

The **balance sheet** (also known as the *statement of financial position or statement of financial condition*) reports the firm's financial position at a point in time. The balance sheet consists of three elements:

1. *Assets* are the resources controlled by the firm.

2. *Liabilities* are amounts owed to lenders and other creditors.

3. *Owners' equity* is the residual interest in the net assets of an entity that remains after deducting its liabilities.

Transactions are measured so that the fundamental **accounting equation** holds:

assets = liabilities + owners' equity

The **statement of comprehensive income** reports all changes in equity except for shareholder transactions (e.g., issuing stock, repurchasing stock, and paying dividends). The **income statement** (also known as the *statement of operations* or the *profit and loss statement*) reports on the financial performance of the firm over a period of time. The elements of the income statement include revenues, expenses, and gains and losses.

- *Revenues* are inflows from delivering or producing goods, rendering services, or other activities that constitute the entity's ongoing major or central operations.

- *Expenses* are outflows from delivering or producing goods or services that constitute the entity's ongoing major or central operations.

- *Other income* includes gains that may or may not arise in the ordinary course of business.

The income statement can be combined with "other comprehensive income" and presented as a single statement of comprehensive income. Alternatively, the income statement and the statement of comprehensive income can be presented separately.

The **statement of changes in equity** reports the amounts and sources of changes in equity investors' investment in the firm over a period of time.

The **statement of cash flows** reports the company's cash receipts and payments. These cash flows are classified as follows:

- *Operating cash flows* include the cash effects of transactions that involve the normal business of the firm.

- *Investing cash flows* are those resulting from the acquisition or sale of property, plant, and equipment; of a subsidiary or segment; of securities; and of investments in other firms.

- *Financing cash flows* are those resulting from issuance or retirement of the firm's debt and equity securities and include dividends paid to stockholders.

MODULE 21.2: FOOTNOTES, AUDIT, AND ANALYSIS

Video covering this content is available online.

LOS 21.c: Describe the importance of financial statement notes and supplementary information—including disclosures of accounting policies, methods, and estimates—and management's commentary.

CFA® Program Curriculum, Volume 3, page 24

Financial statement notes (footnotes) include disclosures that provide further details about the information summarized in the financial statements. Footnotes allow users to improve their assessments of the amount, timing, and uncertainty of the estimates reported in the financial statements. Footnotes:

- Discuss the basis of presentation such as the fiscal period covered by the statements and the inclusion of consolidated entities.

- Provide information about accounting methods, assumptions, and estimates used by management.

- Provide additional information on items such as business acquisitions or disposals, legal actions, employee benefit plans, contingencies and commitments, significant customers, sales to related parties, and segments of the firm.

Management's commentary [also known as management's report, operating and financial review, and **management's discussion and analysis** (MD&A)] is one of the most useful sections of the annual report. In this section, management discusses a variety of issues. IFRS guidance recommends that management commentary address the nature of the business, management's objectives, the company's past performance, the performance measures used, and the company's key relationships, resources, and risks. Analysts must be aware that some parts of management's commentary may be unaudited.

For publicly held firms in the United States, the SEC requires that MD&A discuss trends and identify significant events and uncertainties that affect the firm's liquidity, capital resources, and results of operations. MD&A must also discuss:

- Effects of inflation and changing prices if material.

- Impact of off-balance-sheet obligations and contractual obligations such as purchase commitments.

- Accounting policies that require significant judgment by management.

- Forward-looking expenditures and divestitures.

LOS 21.d: Describe the objective of audits of financial statements, the types of audit reports, and the importance of effective internal controls.

CFA® Program Curriculum, Volume 3, page 27

An **audit** is an independent review of an entity's financial statements. Public accountants conduct audits and examine the financial reports and supporting records. The objective of an audit is to enable the auditor to provide an opinion on the fairness and reliability of the financial statements.

The independent certified public accounting firm employed by the Board of Directors is responsible for seeing that the financial statements conform to the applicable accounting standards. The auditor examines the company's accounting and internal control systems, confirms assets and liabilities, and generally tries to determine that there are no material errors in the financial statements. The auditor's report is an important source of information.

The **standard auditor's opinion** contains three parts and states that:

1. Whereas the financial statements are prepared by management and are its responsibility, the auditor has performed an independent review.

2. Generally accepted auditing standards were followed, thus providing *reasonable assurance* that the financial statements contain no material errors.

3. The auditor is satisfied that the statements were prepared in accordance with accepted accounting principles and that the principles chosen and estimates made are reasonable. The auditor's report must also contain additional explanation when accounting methods have not been used consistently between periods.

An *unqualified opinion* (also known as a clean opinion) indicates that the auditor believes the statements are free from material omissions and errors. If the statements make any exceptions to the accounting principles, the auditor may issue a *qualified opinion* and explain these exceptions in the audit report. The auditor can issue an *adverse opinion* if the statements are not presented fairly or are materially nonconforming with accounting standards. If the auditor is unable to express an opinion (e.g., in the case of a scope limitation), a *disclaimer of opinion* is issued.

The auditor's opinion will also contain an explanatory paragraph when a material loss is probable but the amount cannot be reasonably estimated. These "uncertainties" may relate to the *going concern assumption* (the assumption that the

Study Session 6
Cross-Reference to CFA Institute Assigned Reading #21 – Financial Statement Analysis: An Introduction

Study Session 6

firm will continue to operate for the foreseeable future), the valuation or realization of asset values, or to litigation. This type of disclosure may be a signal of serious problems and may call for close examination by the analyst.

Internal controls are the processes by which the company ensures that it presents accurate financial statements. Internal controls are the responsibility of management. For publicly traded firms in the United States, the auditor must express an opinion on the firm's internal controls. The auditor can provide this opinion separately or as the fourth element of the standard opinion.

LOS 21.e: Identify and describe information sources that analysts use in financial statement analysis besides annual financial statements and supplementary information.

CFA® Program Curriculum, Volume 3, page 29

Besides the annual financial statements, an analyst should examine a company's *quarterly or semiannual reports*. These interim reports typically update the major financial statements and footnotes but are not necessarily audited.

Securities and Exchange Commission (SEC) filings are available from EDGAR (Electronic Data Gathering, Analysis, and Retrieval System, *www.sec.gov*). These include Form 8-K, which a company must file to report events such as acquisitions and disposals of major assets or changes in its management or corporate governance. Companies' annual and quarterly financial statements are also filed with the SEC (Form 10-K and Form 10-Q, respectively).

Proxy statements are issued to shareholders when there are matters that require a shareholder vote. These statements, which are also filed with the SEC and available from EDGAR, are a good source of information about the election of (and qualifications of) board members, compensation, management qualifications, and the issuance of stock options.

Corporate reports and *press releases* are written by management and are often viewed as public relations or sales materials. Not all of the material is independently reviewed by outside auditors. Such information can often be found on the company's website. Firms often provide **earnings guidance** before the financial statements are released. Once an earnings announcement is made, a conference call may be held whereby senior management is available to answer questions.

An analyst should also review pertinent information on economic conditions and the company's industry and compare the company to its competitors. The necessary information can be acquired from trade journals, statistical reporting services, and government agencies.

LOS 21.f: Describe the steps in the financial statement analysis framework.

CFA® Program Curriculum, Volume 3, page 30

The **financial statement analysis framework**[1] consists of six steps:

Step 1: State the objective and context. Determine what questions the analysis seeks to answer, the form in which this information needs to be presented, and what resources and how much time are available to perform the analysis.

Step 2: Gather data. Acquire the company's financial statements and other relevant data on its industry and the economy. Ask questions of the company's management, suppliers, and customers, and visit company sites.

Step 3: Process the data. Make any appropriate adjustments to the financial statements. Calculate ratios. Prepare exhibits such as graphs and common-size balance sheets.

Step 4: Analyze and interpret the data. Use the data to answer the questions stated in the first step. Decide what conclusions or recommendations the information supports.

Step 5: Report the conclusions or recommendations. Prepare a report and communicate it to its intended audience. Be sure the report and its dissemination comply with the Code and Standards that relate to investment analysis and recommendations.

Step 6: Update the analysis. Repeat these steps periodically and change the conclusions or recommendations when necessary.

MODULE QUIZ 21.1, 21.2

To best evaluate your performance, enter your quiz answers online.

1. Which of the following statements *least accurately* describes a role of financial statement analysis?
    A. Use the information in financial statements to make economic decisions.
    B. Provide reasonable assurance that the financial statements are free of material errors.
    C. Evaluate an entity's financial position and past performance to form opinions about its future ability to earn profits and generate cash flow.

2. A firm's financial position at a specific point in time is reported in the:
    A. balance sheet.
    B. income statement.
    C. cash flow statement.

---

1. Hennie van Greuning and Sonja Brajovic Bratanovic, *Analyzing and Managing Banking Risk: Framework for Assessing Corporate Governance and Financial Risk*, International Bank for Reconstruction and Development, April 2003, p. 300.

3. Information about accounting estimates, assumptions, and methods chosen for reporting is *most likely* found in:
   A. the auditor's opinion.
   B. financial statement notes.
   C. Management's Discussion and Analysis.

4. If an auditor finds that a company's financial statements have made a specific exception to applicable accounting principles, she is *most likely* to issue a:
   A. dissenting opinion.
   B. cautionary note.
   C. qualified opinion.

5. Information about elections of members to a company's Board of Directors is *most likely* found in:
   A. a 10-Q filing.
   B. a proxy statement.
   C. footnotes to the financial statements.

6. Which of these steps is *least likely* to be a part of the financial statement analysis framework?
   A. State the purpose and context of the analysis.
   B. Determine whether the company's securities are suitable for the client.
   C. Adjust the financial statement data and compare the company to its industry peers.

KEY CONCEPTS

LOS 21.a

The role of financial reporting is to provide a variety of users with useful information about a company's performance and financial position.

The role of financial statement analysis is to use the data from financial statements to support economic decisions.

LOS 21.b

The statement of financial position (balance sheet) shows assets, liabilities, and owners' equity at a point in time.

The statement of comprehensive income shows the results of a firm's business activities over the period. Revenues, the cost of generating those revenues, and the resulting profit or loss are presented on the income statement.

The statement of changes in equity reports the amount and sources of changes in the equity owners' investment in the firm.

The statement of cash flows shows the sources and uses of cash over the period.

LOS 21.c

Important information about accounting methods, estimates, and assumptions is disclosed in the footnotes to the financial statements and supplementary schedules. These disclosures also contain information about segment results, commitments and contingencies, legal proceedings, acquisitions or divestitures, issuance of stock options, and details of employee benefit plans.

Management's commentary (management's discussion and analysis) contains an overview of the company and important information about business trends, future capital needs, liquidity, significant events, and significant choices of accounting methods requiring management judgment.

LOS 21.d

The objective of audits of financial statements is to provide an opinion on the statements' fairness and reliability.

The auditor's opinion gives evidence of an independent review of the financial statements that verifies that appropriate accounting principles were used, that standard auditing procedures were used to establish reasonable assurance that the statements contain no material errors, and that management's report on the company's internal controls has been reviewed.

An auditor can issue an unqualified (clean) opinion if the statements are free from material omissions and errors, a qualified opinion that notes any exceptions to accounting principles, an adverse opinion if the statements are not presented fairly in the auditor's opinion, or a disclaimer of opinion if the auditor is unable to express an opinion.

A company's management is responsible for maintaining an effective internal control system to ensure the accuracy of its financial statements.

LOS 21.e

Along with the annual financial statements, important information sources for an analyst include a company's quarterly and semiannual reports, proxy statements, press releases, and earnings guidance, as well as information on the industry and peer companies from external sources.

LOS 21.f

The framework for financial analysis has six steps:

1. State the objective of the analysis.
2. Gather data.
3. Process the data.
4. Analyze and interpret the data.
5. Report the conclusions or recommendations.
6. Update the analysis.

ANSWER KEY FOR MODULE QUIZ

Module Quiz 21.1, 21.2

1. **B**   This statement describes the role of an auditor, rather than the role of an analyst. The other responses describe the role of financial statement analysis. (Module 21.1, LOS 21.a)

2. **A**   The balance sheet reports a company's financial position as of a specific date. The income statement, cash flow statement, and statement of changes in owners' equity show the company's performance during a specific period. (Module 21.1, LOS 21.b)

3. **B**   Information about accounting methods and estimates is contained in the footnotes to the financial statements. (Module 21.2, LOS 21.c)

4. **C**   An auditor will issue a qualified opinion if the financial statements make any exceptions to applicable accounting standards and will explain the effect of these exceptions in the auditor's report. (Module 21.2, LOS 21.d)

5. **B**   Proxy statements contain information related to matters that come before shareholders for a vote, such as elections of board members. (Module 21.2, LOS 21.e)

6. **B**   Determining the suitability of an investment for a client is not one of the six steps in the financial statement analysis framework. The analyst would only perform this function if he also had an advisory relationship with the client. Stating the objective and processing the data are two of the six steps in the framework. The others are gathering the data, analyzing the data, updating the analysis, and reporting the conclusions. (Module 21.2, LOS 21.f)

READING
22

Financial Reporting Standards

EXAM FOCUS

This topic review covers accounting standards: why they exist, who issues them, and who enforces them. Know the difference between the roles of private standard-setting bodies and government regulatory authorities and be able to name the most important organizations of both kinds. Become familiar with the framework for International Financial Reporting Standards (IFRS), including qualitative characteristics, constraints and assumptions, and features for preparing financial statements. Be able to identify barriers to convergence of national accounting standards (such as U.S. GAAP) with IFRS, key differences between the IFRS and U.S. GAAP frameworks, and elements of and barriers to creating a coherent financial reporting network.

MODULE 22.1: STANDARDS OVERVIEW

Video covering this content is available online.

LOS 22.a: Describe the objective of financial statements and the importance of financial reporting standards in security analysis and valuation.

CFA® Program Curriculum, Volume 3, page 44

According to the IASB *Conceptual Framework for Financial Reporting 2010*, the objective of financial reporting is to provide information about the firm to current and potential investors and creditors that is useful for making their decisions about investing in or lending to the firm.

The conceptual framework is used in the development of accounting standards. Given the variety and complexity of possible transactions and the estimates and assumptions a firm must make when presenting its performance, financial statements could potentially take any form if reporting standards did not exist.

Thus, financial reporting standards are needed to provide consistency by narrowing the range of acceptable responses.

Reporting standards ensure that transactions are reported by firms similarly. However, standards must remain flexible and allow discretion to management to properly describe the economics of the firm.

Financial reporting is not designed solely for valuation purposes; however, it does provide important inputs for valuation purposes.

LOS 22.b: Describe roles and desirable attributes of financial reporting standard-setting bodies and regulatory authorities in establishing and enforcing reporting standards, and describe the role of the International Organization of Securities Commissions.

CFA® Program Curriculum, Volume 3, page 47

Standard-setting bodies are professional organizations of accountants and auditors that establish financial reporting standards. **Regulatory authorities** are government agencies that have the legal authority to enforce compliance with financial reporting standards.

The two primary standard-setting bodies are the *Financial Accounting Standards Board* (FASB) and the *International Accounting Standards Board* (IASB). In the United States, the FASB sets forth Generally Accepted Accounting Principles (GAAP). Outside the United States, the IASB establishes International Financial Reporting Standards (IFRS). Other national standard-setting bodies exist as well. Many of them (including the FASB) are working toward convergence with IFRS. Some of the older IASB standards are referred to as International Accounting Standards (IAS).

Desirable attributes of standard-setters:

- Observe high professional standards.
- Have adequate authority, resources, and competencies to accomplish its mission.
- Have clear and consistent standard-setting processes.
- Guided by a well-articulated framework.
- Operate independently while still seeking input from stakeholders.
- Should not be compromised by special interests.
- Decisions are made in the public interest.

Regulatory authorities, such as the *Securities and Exchange Commission* (SEC) in the United States and the *Financial Conduct Authority* in the United Kingdom, are established by national governments. Figure 22.1 summarizes the SEC's filing requirements for publicly traded companies in the United States. These filings, which are available from the SEC website (*www.sec.gov*), are arguably the most important source of information for the analysis of publicly traded firms.

Most national authorities belong to the **International Organization of Securities Commissions (IOSCO)**. The three objectives of financial market regulation according to IOSCO[1] are to (1) protect investors; (2) ensure the fairness, efficiency, and transparency of markets; and (3) reduce systemic risk. Because of the increasing globalization of securities markets, IOSCO has a goal of uniform financial regulations across countries.

Figure 22.1: Securities and Exchange Commission Required Filings

Form S-1. Registration statement filed prior to the sale of new securities to the public. The registration statement includes audited financial statements, risk assessment, underwriter identification, and the estimated amount and use of the offering proceeds.

Form 10-K. Required annual filing that includes information about the business and its management, audited financial statements and disclosures, and disclosures about legal matters involving the firm. Information required in Form 10-K is similar to that which a firm typically provides in its annual report to shareholders. However, a firm's annual report is not a substitute for the required 10-K filing. Equivalent SEC forms for foreign issuers in the U.S. markets are Form 40-F for Canadian companies and Form 20-F for other foreign issuers.

Form 10-Q. U.S. firms are required to file this form quarterly, with updated financial statements (unlike Form 10-K, these statements do not have to be audited) and disclosures about certain events such as significant legal proceedings or changes in accounting policy. Non-U.S. companies are typically required to file the equivalent Form 6-K semiannually.

Form DEF-14A. When a company prepares a proxy statement for its shareholders prior to the annual meeting or other shareholder vote, it also files the statement with the SEC as Form DEF-14A.

Form 8-K. Companies must file this form to disclose material events including significant asset acquisitions and disposals, changes in management or corporate governance, or matters related to its accountants, its financial statements, or the markets in which its securities trade.

Form 144. A company can issue securities to certain qualified buyers without registering the securities with the SEC but must notify the SEC that it intends to do so.

Forms 3, 4, and 5 involve the beneficial ownership of securities by a company's officers and directors. Analysts can use these filings to learn about purchases and sales of company securities by corporate insiders.

LOS 22.c: Describe the status of global convergence of accounting standards and ongoing barriers to developing one universally accepted set of financial reporting standards.

CFA® Program Curriculum, Volume 3, page 56

The European Union requires IFRS financial reporting by publicly listed companies. In most major countries that have not fully adopted IFRS, accounting standard setters are attempting to converge their standards with IFRS. Many aspects of U.S. GAAP and IFRS, for example, have converged over the past decade, and the Securities and Exchange Commission no longer requires IFRS reporting firms to reconcile their financial statements to U.S. GAAP. Although no further projects related to U.S. GAAP/IFRS convergence are scheduled as of year-end 2017, IFRS convergence efforts are ongoing in many other countries.

One barrier to convergence (developing one universally accepted set of accounting standards) is simply that different standard-setting bodies and the regulatory authorities of different countries can and do disagree on the best treatment of

---

1. International Organization of Securities Commissions, "Objectives and Principles of Securities Regulation," June 2010.

a particular item or issue. Other barriers result from the political pressures that regulatory bodies face from business groups and others who will be affected by changes in reporting standards.

MODULE QUIZ 22.1

To best evaluate your performance, enter your quiz answers online.

1. The objective of financial reporting, according to the IASB framework, is to:
    A. provide information about the firm to current and potential investors.
    B. decide the acceptable standards for presenting financial performance.
    C. minimize management discretion in presenting the financial results of a firm.

2. Standard-setting bodies are responsible for:
    A. establishing financial reporting standards only.
    B. establishing and enforcing standards for financial reporting.
    C. enforcing compliance with financial reporting standards only.

3. Which of the following organizations is *least likely* involved with enforcing compliance with financial reporting standards?
    A. Financial Conduct Authority.
    B. Securities and Exchange Commission.
    C. International Accounting Standards Board.

4. Dawn Czerniak is writing an article about international financial reporting standards. In her article she states, "Despite strong support from business groups for a universally accepted set of financial reporting standards, disagreements among the standard-setting bodies and regulatory authorities of various countries remain a barrier to developing one." Czerniak's statement is:
    A. correct.
    B. incorrect, because business groups have not supported a uniform set of financial reporting standards.
    C. incorrect, because disagreements among national standard-setting bodies and regulatory agencies have not been a barrier to developing a universal set of standards.

Video covering this content is available online.

MODULE 22.2: IFRS AND U.S. GAAP

LOS 22.d: Describe the International Accounting Standards Board's conceptual framework, including the objective and qualitative characteristics of financial statements, required reporting elements, and constraints and assumptions in preparing financial statements.

CFA® Program Curriculum, Volume 3, page 60

The ideas on which the IASB bases its standards are expressed in the "Conceptual Framework for Financial Reporting" that the organization adopted in 2010. The IASB framework details the qualitative characteristics of financial statements and specifies the required reporting elements. The framework also notes certain constraints and assumptions that are involved in financial statement preparation.

At the center of the IASB Conceptual Framework is the objective to provide financial information that is useful in making decisions about providing resources to an entity. The resource providers include investors, lenders, and other creditors. Users of financial statements need information about the firm's performance, financial position, and cash flow.

Qualitative Characteristics

There are two fundamental characteristics that make financial information useful: relevance and faithful representation.[2]

■ *Relevance.* Financial statements are relevant if the information in them can influence users' economic decisions or affect users' evaluations of past events or forecasts of future events. To be relevant, information should have predictive value, confirmatory value (confirm prior expectations), or both. Materiality is an aspect of relevance.[3]

■ *Faithful representation.* Information that is faithfully representative is complete, neutral (absence of bias), and free from error.

There are four characteristics that enhance relevance and faithful representation: comparability, verifiability, timeliness, and understandability.

■ *Comparability.* Financial statement presentation should be consistent among firms and across time periods.

■ *Verifiability.* Independent observers, using the same methods, obtain similar results.

■ *Timeliness.* Information is available to decision makers before the information is stale.

■ *Understandability.* Users with a basic knowledge of business and accounting and who make a reasonable effort to study the financial statements should be able to readily understand the information the statements present. Useful information should not be omitted just because it is complicated.

Required Reporting Elements

The elements of financial statements are the by-now familiar groupings of assets, liabilities, and owners' equity (for measuring financial position) and income and expenses (for measuring performance). The Conceptual Framework describes each of these elements:[4]

■ *Assets.* Resources controlled as a result of past transactions that are expected to provide future economic benefits.

■ *Liabilities.* Obligations as a result of past events that are expected to require an outflow of economic resources.

---

2. *Conceptual Framework for Financial Reporting (2010).* paragraphs QC5-18.
3. Ibid., paragraphs QC19-34
4. Ibid., paragraphs 4.4-4.23.

■ *Equity.* The owners' residual interest in the assets after deducting the liabilities.

■ *Income.* An increase in economic benefits, either increasing assets or decreasing liabilities in a way that increases owners' equity (but not including contributions by owners). Income includes revenues and gains.

■ *Expenses.* Decreases in economic benefits, either decreasing assets or increasing liabilities in a way that decreases owners' equity (but not including distributions to owners). Losses are included in expenses.

An item should be *recognized* in its financial statement element if a future economic benefit from the item (flowing to or from the firm) is probable and the item's value or cost can be measured reliably.

The amounts at which items are reported in the financial statement elements depend on their **measurement base**. Measurement bases include *historical cost* (the amount originally paid for the asset), *amortized cost* (historical cost adjusted for depreciation, amortization, depletion, and impairment), *current cost* (the amount the firm would have to pay today for the same asset), *net realizable value* (the estimated selling price of the asset in the normal course of business minus the selling costs), *present value* (the discounted value of the asset's expected future cash flows), and *fair value* (the price at which an asset could be sold, or a liability transferred, in an orderly transaction between willing parties).

PROFESSOR'S NOTE

In the next Study Sessions, we will discuss these measurement bases in more detail and the situations in which each is appropriate.

Constraints and Assumptions

According to the Conceptual Framework, there is cost-benefit tradeoff of the enhancing characteristics.[5] Accordingly, the benefit that users gain from the information should be greater than the cost of presenting it. Another constraint, not specifically mentioned in the Conceptual Framework, is the fact that non-quantifiable information about a company (its reputation, brand loyalty, capacity for innovation, etc.) cannot be captured directly in financial statements.

Two important underlying assumptions of financial statements are *accrual accounting* and *going concern.*[6] Accrual accounting means that financial statements should reflect transactions at the time they actually occur, not necessarily when cash is paid. Going concern assumes the company will continue to exist for the foreseeable future. If this is not the case, then presenting the company's financial position fairly requires a number of adjustments (e.g., its inventory or other assets may only be worth their liquidation values).

---

5.   Ibid., paragraphs QC35-39.

6.   Ibid., paragraphs OB17 and 4.1.

LOS 22.e: Describe general requirements for financial statements under International Financial Reporting Standards (IFRS).

CFA® Program Curriculum, Volume 3, page 66

International Accounting Standard (IAS) No. 1 defines which financial statements are required and how they must be presented. The **required financial statements** are:

- Balance sheet (statement of financial position).
- Statement of comprehensive income.
- Cash flow statement.
- Statement of changes in owners' equity.
- Explanatory notes, including a summary of accounting policies.

The general **features for preparing financial statements** are stated in IAS No. 1:

- *Fair presentation*, defined as faithfully representing the effects of the entity's transactions and events according to the standards for recognizing assets, liabilities, revenues, and expenses.
- *Going concern basis*, meaning the financial statements are based on the assumption that the firm will continue to exist unless its management intends to (or must) liquidate it.
- *Accrual basis* of accounting is used to prepare the financial statements other than the statement of cash flows.
- *Consistency* between periods in how items are presented and classified, with prior-period amounts disclosed for comparison.
- *Materiality*, meaning the financial statements should be free of misstatements or omissions that could influence the decisions of users of financial statements.
- *Aggregation* of similar items and separation of dissimilar items.
- *No offsetting* of assets against liabilities or income against expenses unless a specific standard permits or requires it.
- *Reporting frequency* must be at least annually.
- *Comparative information* for prior periods should be included unless a specific standard states otherwise.

Also stated in IAS No. 1 are the **structure and content of financial statements**:

- Most entities should present a *classified balance sheet* showing current and noncurrent assets and liabilities.
- *Minimum information* is required on the face of each financial statement and in the notes. For example, the face of the balance sheet must show specific items such as cash and cash equivalents, plant, property and equipment, and inventories. Items listed on the face of the comprehensive income statement must include revenue, profit or loss, tax expense, and finance costs, among others.
- *Comparative information* for prior periods should be included unless a specific standard states otherwise.

LOS 22.f: Compare key concepts of financial reporting standards under IFRS and US generally accepted accounting principles (US GAAP) reporting systems.

CFA® Program Curriculum, Volume 3, page 71

U.S. GAAP consists of standards issued by the FASB, along with numerous other pronouncements and interpretations. Like the IASB, the FASB has a framework for preparing and presenting financial statements. The two organizations have made significant progress toward a common framework, but the two frameworks still differ in several respects.

- The IASB framework lists income and expenses as elements related to performance, while the FASB framework includes revenues, expenses, gains, losses, and comprehensive income.

- The FASB defines an asset as a future economic benefit, whereas the IASB defines it as a resource from which a future economic benefit is expected to flow. Also, the FASB uses the word *probable* in its definition of assets and liabilities, while IASB uses the word *probable* in the context of revenue and expense recognition.

- The FASB does not allow the upward valuation of most assets.

Analysts will need to interpret financial statements that are prepared under different standards. In many cases, however, a company will present a **reconciliation statement** showing what its financial results would have been under an alternative reporting system. For example, firms that list their shares in the United States but do not use U.S. GAAP or IFRS are required to reconcile their financial statements with U.S. GAAP. For IFRS firms listing their shares in the United States, reconciliation is no longer required.

Even if a unified framework emerges, special reporting standards that apply to particular industries (e.g., insurance and banking) will continue to exist.

MODULE 22.3: FINANCIAL REPORTING FRAMEWORK

Video covering this content is available online.

LOS 22.g: Identify characteristics of a coherent financial reporting framework and the barriers to creating such a framework.

CFA® Program Curriculum, Volume 3, page 72

A coherent financial reporting framework is one that fits together logically. Such a framework should be transparent, comprehensive, and consistent.

- *Transparency*—Full disclosure and fair presentation reveal the underlying economics of the company to the financial statement user.

- *Comprehensiveness*—All types of transactions that have financial implications should be part of the framework, including new types of transactions that emerge.

- *Consistency*—Similar transactions should be accounted for in similar ways across companies, geographic areas, and time periods.

Barriers to creating a coherent financial reporting framework include issues related to valuation, standard setting, and measurement.

- *Valuation*—Measurement bases for valuation that require little judgment, such as historical cost, may be less relevant than a basis like fair value that requires more judgment.

- *Standard setting*—Three approaches to standard setting are a "principles-based" approach that relies on a broad framework, a "rules-based" approach that gives specific guidance about how to classify transactions, and an "objectives-oriented" approach that blends the other two approaches. IFRS is largely a principles-based approach. U.S. GAAP has traditionally been more rules-based, but the common conceptual framework is moving toward an objectives-oriented approach.

- *Measurement*—Another trade-off in financial reporting is between properly valuing the elements at one point in time (as on the balance sheet) and properly valuing the changes between points in time (as on the income statement). An "asset/liability" approach, which standard setters have largely used, focuses on balance sheet valuation. A "revenue/expense" approach would tend to place more significance on the income statement.

LOS 22.h: Describe implications for financial analysis of differing financial reporting systems and the importance of monitoring developments in financial reporting standards.

CFA® Program Curriculum, Volume 3, page 74

As financial reporting standards continue to evolve, analysts need to monitor how these developments will affect the financial statements they use. An analyst should be aware of new products and innovations in the financial markets that generate new types of transactions. These might not fall neatly into the existing financial reporting standards. The analyst can use the financial reporting framework as a guide for evaluating what effect new products or transactions might have on financial statements.

To keep up to date on the evolving standards, an analyst can monitor professional journals and other sources, such as the IASB (*www.ifrs.org*) and FASB (*www.fasb.org*) websites. CFA Institute produces position papers on financial reporting issues through the CFA Institute Centre for Financial Market Integrity.

Finally, analysts must monitor company disclosures for significant accounting standards and estimates.

LOS 22.i: Analyze company disclosures of significant accounting policies.

CFA® Program Curriculum, Volume 3, page 79

Companies that prepare financial statements under IFRS or U.S. GAAP must disclose their accounting policies and estimates in the footnotes. Significant policies and estimates that require management judgement are also addressed in Management's Discussion and Analysis (management commentary). An analyst should use these disclosures to evaluate what policies are discussed, whether they cover all the relevant data in the financial statements, which policies required management to make estimates, and whether the disclosures and estimates have changed since the prior period.

Another disclosure that is required for public companies is the likely impact of implementing recently issued accounting standards. Management can discuss the impact of adopting a new standard, conclude that the standard does not apply or will not affect the financial statements materially, or state that they are still evaluating the effects of the new standards. Analysts should be aware of the uncertainty this last statement implies.

MODULE QUIZ 22.2, 22.3

To best evaluate your performance, enter your quiz answers online.

1. According to the IASB Conceptual Framework, the fundamental qualitative characteristics that make financial statements useful are:
   A. verifiability and timeliness.
   B. relevance and faithful representation.
   C. understandability and relevance.

2. Which of the following *most accurately* lists a required reporting element that is used to measure a company's financial position and one that is used to measure a company's performance?

	Position	Performance
A.	Assets	Liabilities
B.	Income	Expenses
C.	Liabilities	Income

3. International Accounting Standard (IAS) No. 1 *least likely* requires which of the following?
   A. Neither assets and liabilities, nor income and expenses, may be offset unless required or permitted by a financial reporting standard.
   B. Audited financial statements and disclosures, along with updated information about the firm and its management, must be filed at least quarterly.
   C. Fair presentation of financial statements means faithfully representing the firm's events and transactions according to the financial reporting standards.

4. Which of the following statements about the FASB conceptual framework, as compared to the IASB conceptual framework, is *most accurate*?
    A. The FASB framework allows for upward revaluations of tangible, long-lived assets.
    B. The FASB framework and IASB framework are now fully converged.
    C. The FASB framework lists revenue, expenses, gains, losses, and comprehensive income related to financial performance.

5. Rules-based and principles-based approaches to standard setting are:
    A. each used for specific industries.
    B. examples of coherent financial reporting frameworks.
    C. an example of barriers to creating a coherent financial reporting framework.

6. Which is *least likely* one of the conclusions about the impact of a change in financial reporting standards that might appear in management's discussion and analysis?
    A. Management has chosen not to implement the new standard.
    B. Management is currently evaluating the impact of the new standard.
    C. The new standard will not have a material impact on the company's financial statements.

KEY CONCEPTS

LOS 22.a

The objective of financial statements is to provide economic decision makers with useful information about a firm's financial performance and changes in financial position.

Reporting standards are designed to ensure that different firms' statements are comparable to one another and to narrow the range of reasonable estimates on which financial statements are based. This aids users of the financial statements who rely on them for information about the company's activities, profitability, and creditworthiness.

LOS 22.b

Standard-setting bodies are private sector organizations that establish financial reporting standards. The two primary standard-setting bodies are the International Accounting Standards Board (IASB) and, in the United States, the Financial Accounting Standards Board (FASB).

Regulatory authorities are government agencies that enforce compliance with financial reporting standards. Regulatory authorities include the Securities and Exchange Commission (SEC) in the United States and the Financial Services Authority (FSA) in the United Kingdom. Many national regulatory authorities belong to the International Organization of Securities Commissions (IOSCO).

LOS 22.c

Efforts to achieve convergence of local accounting standards with IFRS are underway in most major countries that have not adopted IFRS.

Barriers to developing one universally accepted set of financial reporting standards include differences of opinion among standard-setting bodies and regulatory authorities from different countries and political pressure within countries from groups affected by changes in reporting standards.

LOS 22.d

The IFRS "Conceptual Framework for Financial Reporting" defines the fundamental and enhancing qualitative characteristics of financial statements, specifies the required reporting elements, and notes the constraints and assumptions involved in preparing financial statements.

- The fundamental characteristics of financial statements are relevance and faithful representation. The enhancing characteristics include comparability, verifiability, timeliness, and understandability.

- Elements of financial statements are assets, liabilities, and owners' equity (for measuring financial position) and income and expenses (for measuring performance).

■ Constraints on financial statement preparation include cost versus benefit and the difficulty of capturing non-quantifiable information in financial statements.

■ The two primary assumptions that underlie the preparation of financial statements are the accrual basis and the going concern assumption.

LOS 22.e

Required financial statements are the balance sheet, comprehensive income statement, cash flow statement, statement of changes in owners' equity, and explanatory notes.

The general features of financial statements according to IAS No. 1 are:

■ Fair presentation.

■ Going concern.

■ Accrual accounting.

■ Consistency.

■ Materiality.

■ Aggregation.

■ No offsetting.

■ Reporting frequency.

■ Comparative information.

Other presentation requirements include a classified balance sheet and specific minimum information that must be reported in the notes and on the face of the financial statements.

LOS 22.f

The IASB and FASB frameworks are similar but are moving towards convergence. Some of the remaining differences are:

■ The IASB lists income and expenses as performance elements, while the FASB lists revenues, expenses, gains, losses, and comprehensive income.

■ There are minor differences in the definition of assets. Also, the FASB uses the word *probable* when defining assets and liabilities.

■ The FASB does not allow the upward revaluation of most assets.

Firms that list their shares in the United States but do not use U.S. GAAP or IFRS are required to reconcile their financial statements with U.S. GAAP. For IFRS firms listing their shares in the United States, reconciliation is no longer required.

LOS 22.g

A coherent financial reporting framework should exhibit transparency, comprehensiveness, and consistency.

Barriers to creating a coherent framework include issues of valuation, standard setting, and measurcmcnt.

LOS 22.h

An analyst should be aware of evolving financial reporting standards and new products and innovations that generate new types of transactions.

LOS 22.i

Under IFRS and U.S. GAAP, companies must disclose their accounting policies and estimates in the footnotes and MD&A. Public companies are also required to disclose the likely impact of recently issued accounting standards on their financial statements.

ANSWER KEY FOR MODULE QUIZZES

Module Quiz 22.1

1. **A** The IASB Conceptual Framework states that the objective of financial reporting is to provide information about the firm to current and potential investors that is useful for making decisions about investing in or lending to the firm. (LOS 22.a)

2. **A** Standard-setting bodies are private-sector organizations that establish financial reporting standards. Enforcement is the responsibility of regulatory authorities. (LOS 22.b)

3. **C** The IASB is a standard-setting body. The Securities and Exchange Commission (in the United States) and the Financial Conduct Authority (in the United Kingdom) are regulatory authorities. (LOS 22.b)

4. **B** Political pressure from business groups and other interest groups who are affected by financial reporting standards has been a barrier to developing a universally accepted set of financial reporting standards. Disagreements among national standard-setting bodies and regulatory agencies have also been a barrier. (LOS 22.c)

Module Quiz 22.2, 22.3

1. **B** The fundamental qualitative characteristics are relevance and faithful representation. Verifiability, timeliness, and understandability are enhancing qualitative characteristics. (Module 22.2, LOS 22.d)

2. **C** Balance sheet reporting elements (assets, liabilities, and owners' equity) measure a company's financial position. Income statement reporting elements (income, expenses) measure its financial performance. (Module 22.2, LOS 22.d)

3. **B** According to IAS No. 1, financial statements must be presented at least *annually*. Fair presentation is one of the IAS No. 1 principles for preparing financial statements. The ban against offsetting is one of the IAS No. 1 principles for presenting financial statements. (Module 22.2, LOS 22.e)

4. **C** The FASB framework lists revenues, expenses, gains, losses, and comprehensive income. The IASB framework only lists income and expenses. (Module 22.2, LOS 22.f)

5. **C** One of the barriers to creating a coherent financial reporting framework is that standard setting bodies may take a rules-based, principles-based, or objectives-based approach to standard setting. (Module 22.3, LOS 22.g)

6. **A** Management can discuss the impact of adopting the new standard, conclude that it does not apply or will have no material impact, or state that they are still evaluating the potential impact. (Module 22.3, LOS 22.i)

READING 23

Understanding Income Statements

EXAM FOCUS

Now we're getting to the heart of the matter. Since forecasts of future earnings, and therefore estimates of firm value, depend crucially on understanding a firm's income statement, everything in this topic review is important. Some of the items requiring calculation include depreciation, COGS, and inventory under different cost flow assumptions, as well as basic and diluted EPS. The separation of items into operating and non-operating categories is important when estimating recurring income as a first step in forecasting future firm earnings. Note that questions regarding the effect on financial ratios of the choice of accounting method and of accounting estimates are one common way to test your understanding of the material on those topics presented here.

MODULE 23.1: INCOME STATEMENT OVERVIEW

Video covering this content is available online.

The income statement reports the revenues and expenses of the firm over a period of time. The income statement is sometimes referred to as the "statement of operations," the "statement of earnings," or the "profit and loss statement." The income statement equation is:

revenues − expenses = net income

Under IFRS, the income statement can be combined with "other comprehensive income" and presented as a single statement of comprehensive income. Alternatively, the income statement and the statement of comprehensive income can be presented separately. Presentation is similar under U.S. GAAP.

Investors examine a firm's income statement for valuation purposes while lenders examine the income statement for information about the firm's ability to make the promised interest and principal payments on its debt.

LOS 23.a: Describe the components of the income statement and alternative presentation formats of that statement.

CFA® Program Curriculum, Volume 3, page 95

Revenues are the amounts reported from the sale of goods and services in the normal course of business. Revenue less adjustments for estimated returns and allowances is known as **net revenue**.

PROFESSOR'S NOTE

The terms "revenue" and "sales" are sometimes used synonymously. However, sales is just one component of revenue in many firms. In some countries, revenues are referred to as "turnover."

Expenses are the amounts incurred to generate revenue and include cost of goods sold, operating expenses, interest, and taxes. Expenses are grouped together by their nature or function. Presenting all depreciation expense from manufacturing and administration together in one line of the income statement is an example of grouping by nature of the expense. Combining all costs associated with manufacturing (e.g., raw materials, depreciation, labor, etc.) as cost of goods sold is an example of grouping by function. Grouping expenses by function is sometimes referred to as the cost of sales method.

PROFESSOR'S NOTE

Firms can present columnar data in chronological order from left-to-right or vice versa. Also, some firms present expenses as negative numbers while other firms use parentheses to signify expenses. Still other firms present expenses as positive numbers with the assumption that users know that expenses are subtracted in the income statement. Watch for these different treatments on the exam.

The income statement also includes **gains and losses**, which result in an increase (gains) or decrease (losses) of economic benefits. Gains and losses may or may not result from ordinary business activities. For example, a firm might sell surplus equipment used in its manufacturing operation that is no longer needed. The difference between the sales price and book value is reported as a gain or loss on the income statement. Summarizing, net income is equal to income (revenues + gains) minus expenses (including losses). Thus, the components can be rearranged as follows:

net income = revenues − ordinary expenses + other income − other expense + gains − losses

If a firm has a controlling interest in a subsidiary, the pro rata share of the subsidiary's income not owned by the parent is reported in parent's income statement as the **noncontrolling interest** (also known as **minority interest** or **minority owners' interest**). The noncontrolling interest is subtracted in arriving at net income because the parent is reporting all of the subsidiary's revenue and expense.

Presentation Formats

A firm can present its income statement using a single-step or multi-step format. In a single-step statement, all revenues are grouped together and all expenses are grouped together. A multi-step format includes *gross profit*, revenues minus cost of goods sold.

Figure 23.1 is an example of a multi-step income statement format for the BHG Company.

Figure 23.1: Multi-Step Income Statement

BHG Company Income Statement For the year ended December 31, 20X7	
Revenue	$579,312
Cost of goods sold	(362,520)
Gross profit	216,792
Selling, general, and administrative expense	(109,560)
Depreciation expense	(69,008)
Operating profit	38,224
Interest expense	(2,462)
Income before tax	35,762
Provision for income taxes	(14,305)
Income from continuing operations	21,457
Earnings (losses) from discontinued operations, net of tax	1,106
Net income	$22,563

Gross profit is the amount that remains after the direct costs of producing a product or service are subtracted from revenue. Subtracting operating expenses, such as selling, general, and administrative expenses, from gross profit results in another subtotal known as **operating profit** or operating income. For nonfinancial firms, operating profit is profit before financing costs, income taxes, and non-operating items are considered. Subtracting interest expense and income taxes from operating profit results in the firm's net income, sometimes referred to as "earnings" or the "bottom line."

PROFESSOR'S NOTE

Interest expense is usually considered an operating expense for financial firms.

MODULE 23.2: PERCENTAGE OF COMPLETION

Video covering this content is available online.

LOS 23.b: Describe general principles of revenue recognition and accrual accounting, specific revenue recognition applications (including accounting for long-term contracts, installment sales, barter transactions, gross and net reporting of revenue), and implications of revenue recognition principles for financial analysis.

LOS 23.c: Calculate revenue given information that might influence the choice of revenue recognition method.

CFA® Program Curriculum, Volume 3, page 99

Under the accrual method of accounting, revenue is recognized when earned and expenses are recognized when incurred. The important point to remember is that accrual accounting does not necessarily coincide with the receipt or payment of cash. Consequently, firms can manipulate net income by recognizing revenue earlier or later or by delaying or accelerating the recognition of expenses.

PROFESSOR'S NOTE

The revenue recognition principles listed here are based on IAS 18. This accounting standard has been replaced by IFRS 15, which we discuss later in this topic review. However, the IAS 18 standards, and examples based on them, remain in the Level I curriculum for this exam season.

According to the International Accounting Standards Board (IASB), revenue is recognized from the sale of goods when:[1]

1. The risk and reward of ownership is transferred.

2. There is no continuing control or management over the goods sold.

3. Revenue can be reliably measured.

4. There is a probable flow of economic benefits.

5. The cost can be reliably measured.

For services rendered, revenue is recognized when:[2]

1. The amount of revenue can be reliably measured.

2. There is a probable flow of economic benefits.

3. The stage of completion can be measured.

4. The cost incurred and cost of completion can be reliably measured.

According to the Financial Accounting Standards Board (FASB), revenue is recognized in the income statement when (a) realized or realizable and (b) earned.[3]

---

1. IAS No. 18, *Revenue*, paragraph 14.

2. IAS No. 18, *Revenue*, paragraph 20.

3. FASB Accounting Standards Codification, section 605-10-25.

©2018 Kaplan, Inc.

The Securities and Exchange Commission (SEC) provides additional guidance by listing four criteria to determine whether revenue should be recognized:[4]

1. There is evidence of an arrangement between the buyer and seller.

2. The product has been delivered or the service has been rendered.

3. The price is determined or determinable.

4. The seller is reasonably sure of collecting money.

If a firm receives cash before revenue recognition is complete, the firm reports it as *unearned revenue*. Unearned revenue is reported on the balance sheet as a liability. The liability is reduced in the future as the revenue is earned. For example, a magazine publisher typically receives subscription payments in advance of delivery. When payments are received, both assets (cash) and liabilities (unearned revenue) increase. As the magazines are delivered, the publisher recognizes revenue on the income statement and the liability is reduced.

Specific Revenue Recognition Applications

Revenue is usually recognized at delivery using the revenue recognition criteria previously discussed. However, in some cases, revenue may be recognized before delivery occurs or even after delivery takes place.

Long-Term Contracts

The percentage-of-completion method and the completed-contract method are used for contracts that extend beyond one accounting period, often contracts related to construction projects.

In certain cases involving service contracts or licensing agreements, the firm may simply recognize revenue equally over the term of the contract or agreement.

When the outcome of a long-term contract can be reliably estimated, the **percentage-of-completion method** is used under both IFRS and U.S. GAAP. Accordingly, revenue, expense, and therefore profit, are recognized as the work is performed. The percentage of completion is measured by the total cost incurred to date divided by the total expected cost of the project.

Under International Financial Reporting Standards (IFRS), if the firm cannot reliably measure the outcome of the project, revenue is recognized to the extent of contract costs, costs are expensed when incurred, and profit is recognized only at completion. Under U.S. GAAP, the **completed-contract method** is used when the outcome of the project cannot be reliably estimated. Accordingly, revenue, expense, and profit are recognized only when the contract is complete.

If a loss is expected, the loss must be recognized immediately under IFRS and U.S. GAAP.

---

4.   SEC Staff Accounting Bulletin 101.

EXAMPLE: Percentage of completion method for long-term contracts

Wildon Properties has a contract to build a hotel for $2,000,000. Payment for this contract will be received in equal installments at the end of each of the next four years. A reliable estimate of the total cost of this contract is $1,600,000.

Wildon incurred costs of $400,000 during the first year and $500,000 during the second year. The estimate of the project's total cost had not changed during the second year. Calculate the revenue and profit to be recognized in each of the first two years.

Answer:

Because Wildon has a reliable estimate of the project's costs, the percentage-of-completion method of revenue recognition is appropriate. The percentage of the project that was completed through the first two years is:

Year 1: $400,000 / $1,600,000 = 25%

Year 2: ($400,000 + $500,000) / $1,600,000 = 56.25%

Wildon may recognize revenue and estimated profit in the first two years that reflect the percentage of the project that has been completed.

Year 1 revenue: 25% × $2,000,000 = $500,000

Year 1 profit: $500,000 revenue − $400,000 cost = $100,000

Year 2 revenue: 56.25% × $2,000,000 − $500,000 recognized in Year 1 = $625,000

Year 2 profit: $625,000 revenue − $500,000 cost = $125,000

> **PROFESSOR'S NOTE**
>
> In this example, revenue recognized in Year 2 could have been calculated as the total expected profit times the percentage of the project completed in Year 2: ($500,000 / $1,600,000) × $2,000,000 = $625,000. However, this shortcut only works when the estimate of total cost has not changed. For example, if the estimated total cost had increased to $1,800,000, the percentage of completion through Year 2 would have been ($400,000 + $500,000) / $1,800,000 = 50%, and Year 2 revenue would have been 50% × $2,000,000 − $500,000 recognized in Year 1 = $500,000. In this case, using the percentage completed during Year 2 would produce an incorrect value: ($500,000 / $1,800,000) × $2,000,000 = $555,556.

EXAMPLE: Long-term contracts when outcome cannot be estimated reliably

A construction firm has a contract to build a hotel for $40 million. The firm does not believe it can reliably estimate the total cost of the project over its life. In the first year of the project, the firm incurred construction costs of $6.4 million. At the completion of the project, total construction costs totaled $32 million. Calculate the revenue and profit the firm should recognize for the first year and at the completion of the project, both under IFRS and under U.S. GAAP.

Total Costs to date

─────────────────── × Sales price

Total Projected Cost

Answer:

Under IFRS, if the outcome of a project cannot be estimated reliably, revenue and expenses are recognized over the project's life but no profit may be recorded until the project is completed. In the first year of this project, the firm would report the $6.4 million of expenses and recognize revenue in the same amount, resulting in zero profit for the first year. On completion of the project, the firm would recognize the entire profit of $40 million – $32 million = $8 million. Revenue recognized in the final year of the project is $40 million minus any revenue recognized in earlier periods.

Under U.S. GAAP, if the outcome of a project cannot be estimated reliably, the firm would use the completed contract method of revenue recognition. No revenue, expense, or profit would be recognized in the first year of this project. On completion of the project, the firm would recognize the entire $40 million of revenue, $32 million of expenses, and $8 million of profit.

 PROFESSOR'S NOTE

In the first year using the completed contract method, the $6.4 million of construction costs would be reflected in a balance sheet asset for construction in progress. This may be thought of as similar to work-in-process inventory for a manufacturing firm.

As compared to the completed contract method, the percentage-of-completion method is more aggressive since revenue is reported sooner. Also, the percentage-of-completion method is more subjective because it involves cost estimates. However, the percentage-of-completion method provides smoother earnings and results in better matching of revenues and expenses over time. Cash flows are the same under both methods.

MODULE 23.3: INSTALLMENT SALES

Video covering this content is available online.

An **installment sale** occurs when a firm finances a sale and payments are expected to be received over an extended period. Under U.S. GAAP, if collectibility is certain, revenue is recognized at the time of sale using the normal revenue recognition criteria. If collectibility cannot be reasonably estimated, the **installment method** is used. If collectibility is highly uncertain, the **cost recovery method** is used.

Under the installment method, profit is recognized as cash is collected. Profit is equal to the cash collected during the period multiplied by the total expected profit as a percentage of sales. Under the cost recovery method, profit is recognized only when cash collected exceeds costs incurred. Both the installment and cost recovery methods are typically used only for sales of real estate.

The effects of using the installment and the cost recovery methods are illustrated in the following example.

Real estate Payment

Rev – is – present value of future Payment

> **EXAMPLE: Revenue recognition under the installment and cost recovery methods**
>
> Assume that BBB Property Corp. sells a piece of land for $1,000. The original cost of the land was $800. Collections received by BBB for the sale are as follows:
>
> **BBB Installment Collections**
>
> | Year | 20X5 | 20X6 | 20X7 | Total |
> |------|------|------|------|-------|
> | Collections | $400 | $400 | $200 | $1,000 |
>
> Determine BBB's profit under the installment and cost recovery methods.
>
> **Answer:**
>
> Total expected profit as a percentage of sales is 20% [($1,000 − $800) / $1,000]. Under the installment method, BBB will report profit in 20X5 and 20X6 of $80 [$400 × 20%] each year. In 20X7, BBB will report profit of $40 [$200 × 20%].
>
> Under the cost recovery method, the collections received during 20X5 and 20X6 are applied to the recovery of costs. In 20X7, BBB will report $200 of profit.

Under IFRS, the discounted present value of the installment payments is recognized at the time of sale. The difference between the installment payments and the discounted present value is recognized as interest over time. If the outcome of the project cannot be reliably estimated, revenue recognition under IFRS is similar to the cost recovery method.

Barter Transactions

In a **barter transaction** (or **non-monetary exchange**), two parties exchange goods or services without cash payment. A **round-trip transaction** involves the sale of goods to one party with the simultaneous purchase of almost identical goods from the same party. The underlying issue with these transactions is whether revenue should be recognized. In the late 1990s, several internet companies increased their revenue significantly by "buying" equal values of advertising space on each others' websites.

According to U.S. GAAP, revenue from a barter transaction can be recognized at fair value only if the firm has historically received cash payments for such goods and services and can use this historical experience to determine fair value. Otherwise, the revenue is recorded at the carrying value of the asset surrendered.[5]

Under IFRS, revenue from barter transactions must be based on the fair value of revenue from similar nonbarter transactions with unrelated parties.[6]

---

5. FASB ASC paragraph 605-20-25-14 (Revenue Recognition-Services-Recognition-Advertising Barter Services).

6. IASB, SIC Interpretation 31, Revenue – Barter Transactions Involving Advertising Services, paragraph 5.

Gross and Net Reporting of Revenue

Under **gross revenue reporting**, the selling firm reports sales revenue and cost of goods sold separately. Under **net revenue reporting**, only the difference in sales and cost is reported. While profit is the same, sales are higher using gross revenue reporting.

For example, consider a travel agent who arranges a first-class ticket for a customer flying to Singapore. The ticket price is $10,000, and the travel agent receives a $1,000 commission. Using gross reporting, the travel agent would report $10,000 of revenue, $9,000 of expense, and $1,000 of profit. Using net reporting, the travel agent would simply report $1,000 of revenue and no expense.

The following criteria must be met in order to use gross revenue reporting under U.S. GAAP.[7] The firm must:

- Be the primary obligor under the contract.
- Bear the inventory risk and credit risk.
- Be able to choose its supplier.
- Have reasonable latitude to establish the price.

Implications for Financial Analysis

As noted previously, firms can recognize revenue before delivery, at the time of delivery, or after delivery takes place, as appropriate. Different revenue recognition methods can be used within the firm. Firms disclose their revenue recognition policies in the financial statement footnotes.

Users of financial information must consider two points when analyzing a firm's revenue: (1) how conservative are the firm's revenue recognition policies (recognizing revenue sooner rather than later is more aggressive), and (2) the extent to which the firm's policies rely on judgment and estimates.

LOS 23.d: Describe key aspects of the converged accounting standards for revenue recognition issued by the International Accounting Standards Board and Financial Accounting Standards Board in May 2014.

CFA® Program Curriculum, Volume 3, page 112

In May 2014, IASB and FASB issued converged standards for revenue recognition. The new standards take a principles-based approach to revenue recognition issues. The central principle is that a firm should recognize revenue when it has transferred a good or service to a customer. This is consistent with the familiar accrual accounting principle that revenue should be recognized when earned.

---

7. FASB ASC Section 605-45-45 [Revenue Recognition-Principal Agent Considerations-Other Presentation Matters].

The converged standards identify a five-step process[8] for recognizing revenue:

1. Identify the contract(s) with a customer.

2. Identify the separate or distinct performance obligations in the contract.

3. Determine the transaction price.

4. Allocate the transaction price to the performance obligations in the contract.

5. Recognize revenue when (or as) the entity satisfies a performance obligation.

The standard defines a **contract** as an agreement between two or more parties that specifies their obligations and rights. Collectability must be probable for a contract to exist, but "probable" is defined differently under IFRS and U.S. GAAP so an identical activity could still be accounted for differently by IFRS and U.S. GAAP reporting firms.

A **performance obligation** is a promise to deliver a distinct good or service. A "distinct" good or service is one that meets the following criteria:

■ The customer can benefit from the good or service on its own or combined with other resources that are readily available.

■ The promise to transfer the good or service can be identified separately from any other promises.

A **transaction price** is the amount a firm expects to receive from a customer in exchange for transferring a good or service to the customer. A transaction price is usually a fixed amount but can also be variable, for example, if it includes a bonus for early delivery.

A firm should recognize revenue only when it is highly probable they will not have to reverse it. For example, a firm may need to recognize a liability for a refund obligation (and an offsetting asset for the right to returned goods) if revenue from a sale cannot be estimated reliably.

For long-term contracts, revenue is recognized based on a firm's progress toward completing a performance obligation. This treatment is consistent with the percentage-of-completion method currently in use, although the new standards do not call it that.

Required disclosures under the converged standards include:

■ Contracts with customers by category.

■ Assets and liabilities related to contracts, including balances and changes.

■ Outstanding performance obligations and the transaction prices allocated to them.

■ Management judgments used to determine the amount and timing of revenue recognition, including any changes to those judgments.

For many transactions, revenue recognition under the converged standards will be little changed. Industries that are expected to be affected most are those that often sell bundles of goods and services, such as the software and telecommunications industries.

---

8. IFRS 15 *Revenue From Contracts With Customers*.

MODULE QUIZ 23.1, 23.2, 23.3

To best evaluate your performance, enter your quiz answers online.

1. For a nonfinancial firm, are depreciation expense and interest expense included or excluded from operating expenses in the income statement?

Depreciation expense	Interest expense
A. Included	Included
B. Included	Excluded
C. Excluded	Included

2. Are income taxes and cost of goods sold examples of expenses classified by nature or classified by function in the income statement?

Income taxes	Cost of goods sold
A. Nature	Function
B. Function	Nature
C. Function	Function

3. Which of the following is *least likely* a condition necessary for revenue recognition?
   A. Cash has been collected.
   B. The goods have been delivered.
   C. The price has been determined.

4. Which principle requires that cost of goods sold be recognized in the same period in which the sale of the related inventory is recorded?
   A. Going concern.
   B. Certainty.
   C. Matching.

5. AAA has a contract to build a building for $100,000 with an estimated time to completion of three years. A reliable cost estimate for the project is $60,000. In the first year of the project, AAA incurred costs totaling $24,000. How much profit should AAA report at the end of the first year under the percentage-of-completion method and the completed-contract method?

Percentage-of-completion	Completed-contract
A. $16,000	$0
B. $16,000	$40,000
C. $40,000	$0

6. A manufacturing firm sells a large amount of precision parts and provides financing to the buyer at its usual credit terms. The firm should recognize revenue from this transaction:
   A. at the time of the sale.
   B. using the installment method.
   C. proportionally as payments are received.

7. According to converged accounting standards issued in May 2014, the first step in the revenue recognition process is to:
   A. determine the price.
   B. identify the contract.
   C. identify the obligations.

Video covering this
content is available
online.

MOD~ 23.4: EXPENSE RECOGNITION

~ibe general principles of expense recognition, specific
~n applications, and implications of expense recognition
~l analysis.

CFA® Program Curriculum, Volume 3, page 116

~om revenue to calculate net income. According to the
~es in economic benefits during the accounting period in
~etions of assets or incurrence of liabilities that result in
~ those relating to distributions to equity participants.[9]

~prepared on a cash basis, neither revenue
~ion would be an issue. The firm would simply
~evenue and cash payments as expense.

~al method of accounting, expense recognition is based on the
~principle whereby expenses to generate revenue are recognized in the
~e period as the revenue. Inventory provides a good example. Assume inventory
is purchased during the fourth quarter of one year and sold during the first quarter
of the following year. Using the matching principle, both the revenue and the
expense (cost of goods sold) are recognized in the first quarter, when the inventory
is sold, not the period in which the inventory was purchased.

Not all expenses can be directly tied to revenue generation. These costs are known
as **period costs**. Period costs, such as administrative costs, are expensed in the
period incurred.

Inventory Expense Recognition

If a firm can identify exactly which items were sold and which items remain in
inventory, it can use the **specific identification** method. For example, an auto dealer
records each vehicle sold or in inventory by its identification number.

Under the **first-in, first-out** (FIFO) method, the first item purchased is assumed
to be the first item sold. The cost of inventory acquired first (beginning inventory
and early purchases) is used to calculate the cost of goods sold for the period. The
cost of the most recent purchases is used to calculate ending inventory. FIFO is
appropriate for inventory that has a limited shelf life. For example, a food products
company will sell its oldest inventory first to keep the inventory on hand fresh.

Under the **last-in, first-out** (LIFO) method, the last item purchased is assumed to
be the first item sold. The cost of inventory most recently purchased is assigned to
the cost of goods sold for the period. The costs of beginning inventory and earlier
purchases are assigned to ending inventory. LIFO is appropriate for inventory that
does not deteriorate with age. For example, a coal distributor will sell coal off the
top of the pile.

---

9.   IASB *Framework for the Preparation and Presentation of Financial Statements*, paragraph 4.25(b).

In the United States, LIFO is popular because of its income tax benefits. In an inflationary environment, LIFO results in higher cost of goods sold. Higher cost of goods sold results in lower taxable income and, therefore, lower income taxes.

The **weighted average cost** method makes no assumption about the physical flow of the inventory. It is popular because of its ease of use. The cost per unit is calculated by dividing cost of available goods by total units available, and this average cost is used to determine both cost of goods sold and ending inventory. Average cost results in cost of goods sold and ending inventory values between those of LIFO and FIFO.

FIFO and average cost are permitted under both U.S. GAAP and IFRS. LIFO is allowed under U.S. GAAP but is prohibited under IFRS.

Figure 23.2 summarizes the effects of the inventory methods.

Figure 23.2: Inventory Method Comparison

Method	Assumption	Cost of Goods Sold Consists of...	Ending Inventory Consists of...
FIFO (U.S. and IFRS)	The items first purchased are the first to be sold.	first purchased	most recent purchases
LIFO (U.S. only)	The items last purchased are the first to be sold.	last purchased	earliest purchases
Weighted average cost (U.S. and IFRS)	Items sold are a mix of purchases.	average cost of all items	average cost of all items

PROFESSOR'S NOTE

We will illustrate how to calculate inventory and cost of goods sold using each of these three cost flow assumptions in our topic review of Inventories.

Depreciation Expense Recognition

The cost of long-lived assets must also be matched with revenues. Long-lived assets are expected to provide economic benefits beyond one accounting period. The allocation of cost over an asset's life is known as depreciation (tangible assets), depletion (natural resources), or amortization (intangible assets). Most firms use the **straight-line depreciation** method for financial reporting purposes. The straight-line method recognizes an equal amount of depreciation expense each period. However, most assets generate more benefits in the early years of their economic life and fewer benefits in the later years. In this case, an *accelerated depreciation method* is more appropriate for matching the expenses to revenues.

In the early years of an asset's life, the straight-line method will result in lower depreciation expense as compared to an accelerated method. Lower expense results in higher net income. In the later years of the asset's life, the effect is reversed, and straight-line depreciation results in higher expense and lower net income compared to accelerated methods.

Straight-line depreciation (SL) allocates an equal amount of depreciation each year over the asset's useful life as follows:

$$\text{SL depreciation expense} = \frac{\text{cost} - \text{residual value}}{\text{useful life}}$$

Accelerated depreciation speeds up the recognition of depreciation expense in a systematic way to recognize more depreciation expense in the early years of the asset's life and less depreciation expense in the later years of its life. Total depreciation expense over the life of the asset will be the same as it would be if straight-line depreciation were used.

The **declining balance method** (DB) applies a constant rate of depreciation to an asset's (declining) book value each year.

> **PROFESSOR'S NOTE**
>
> The declining balance method is also known as the diminishing balance method.

The most common declining balance method is *double-declining balance* (DDB), which applies two times the straight-line rate to the declining balance. If an asset's life is ten years, the straight-line rate is 1/10 or 10%, and the DDB rate would be 2/10 or 20%.

$$\text{DDB depreciation} = \left(\frac{2}{\text{useful life}}\right)(\text{cost} - \text{accumulated depreciation})$$

DB does not explicitly use the asset's residual value in the calculations, but depreciation ends once the estimated residual value has been reached. If the asset is expected to have no residual value, the DB method will never fully depreciate it, so the DB method is typically changed to straight-line at some point in the asset's life.

> **PROFESSOR'S NOTE**
>
> We will illustrate how to calculate depreciation expense in our topic review of Long-Lived Assets.

Amortization Expense Recognition

Amortization is the allocation of the cost of an intangible asset (such as a franchise agreement) over its useful life. Amortization expense should match the proportion of the asset's economic benefits used during the period. Most firms use the straight-line method to calculate annual amortization expense for financial reporting. Straight-line amortization is calculated exactly like straight-line depreciation.

Intangible assets with indefinite lives (e.g., goodwill) are not amortized. However, they must be tested for impairment at least annually. If the asset value is impaired, an expense equal to the impairment amount is recognized on the income statement.

Bad Debt Expense and Warranty Expense Recognition

If a firm sells goods or services on credit or provides a warranty to the customer, the matching principle requires the firm to estimate bad debt expense and/or warranty expense. By doing so, the firm is recognizing the expense in the period of the sale, rather than a later period.

Implications for Financial Analysis

Like revenue recognition, expense recognition requires a number of estimates. Since estimates are involved, it is possible for firms to delay or accelerate the recognition of expenses. Delayed expense recognition increases current net income and is therefore more aggressive.

Analysts must consider the underlying reasons for a change in an expense estimate. If a firm's bad debt expense has recently decreased, did the firm lower its expense estimate because its collection experience improved, or was the expense decreased to manipulate net income?

Analysts should also compare a firm's estimates to those of other firms within the firm's industry. If a firm's warranty expense is significantly less than that of a peer firm, is the lower warranty expense a result of higher quality products, or is the firm's expense recognition more aggressive than that of the peer firm?

Firms disclose their accounting policies and significant estimates in the financial statement footnotes and in the management discussion and analysis (MD&A) section of the annual report.

LOS 23.f: Describe the financial reporting treatment and analysis of non-recurring items (including discontinued operations, unusual or infrequent items) and changes in accounting policies.

CFA® Program Curriculum, Volume 3, page 125

Non-Recurring Items

Discontinued operations. A *discontinued operation* is one that management has decided to dispose of, but either has not yet done so, or has disposed of in the current year after the operation had generated income or losses. To be accounted for as a discontinued operation, the business—in terms of assets, operations, and investing and financing activities—must be physically and operationally distinct from the rest of the firm.

The date when the company develops a formal plan for disposing of an operation is referred to as the *measurement date*, and the time between the measurement period and the actual disposal date is referred to as the *phaseout period*. Any income or loss from discontinued operations is reported separately in the income statement, net of tax, after income from continuing operations. Any past income statements presented must be restated, separating the income or loss from the discontinued operations. On the measurement date, the company will accrue any estimated loss during the phaseout period and any estimated loss on the sale of the business. Any expected gain on the disposal cannot be reported until after the sale is completed.

Analytical implications: The analysis is straightforward. Discontinued operations do not affect net income from continuing operations. Discontinued operations should be excluded by the analyst when forecasting future earnings. The actual event of discontinuing a business segment or selling assets may provide information about the future cash flows of the firm, however.

Unusual or infrequent items. The definition of these items is obvious—these events are either unusual in nature or infrequent in occurrence. Examples of items that could be considered unusual or infrequent include:

■ Gains or losses from the sale of assets or part of a business, if these activities are not a firm's ordinary operations.

■ Impairments, write-offs, write-downs, and restructuring costs.

Unusual or infrequent items are included in income from continuing operations and are reported before tax.

Analytical implications: Even though unusual or infrequent items affect net income from continuing operations, an analyst may want to review them to determine whether they truly should be included when forecasting future firm earnings. Some companies appear to be accident-prone and have "unusual or infrequent" losses every year or every few years.

Extraordinary items. Under U.S. GAAP, historically, an *extraordinary item* was a material transaction or event that was *both* unusual *and* infrequent in occurrence. Extraordinary items were reported separately in the income statement, net of tax, after income from continuing operations. For periods beginning after December 15, 2015, U.S. GAAP no longer allows items to be treated as extraordinary. IFRS also does not allow items to be treated as extraordinary.

Changes in Accounting Policies

Accounting changes include changes in accounting principles, changes in accounting estimates, and prior-period adjustments.

A **change in accounting principle** refers to a change from one GAAP or IFRS method to another (e.g., a change in inventory accounting from LIFO to FIFO). A change in accounting principle requires **retrospective application**. Accordingly, all of the prior-period financial statements currently presented are restated to reflect the change. Retrospective application enhances the comparability of the financial statements over time.

 PROFESSOR'S NOTE

Under U.S. GAAP, a firm that changes to LIFO from another inventory cost method does not apply the change retrospectively, but instead uses the carrying value of inventory as the first LIFO layer. This exception to retrospective application is described in the topic review of Inventories.

Generally, a **change in accounting estimate** is the result of a change in management's judgment, usually due to new information. For example, management may change the estimated useful life of an asset because new information indicates the asset has a longer or shorter life than originally expected. A change in estimate is applied prospectively and does not require the restatement of prior financial statements.

Analytical implications: Accounting estimate changes typically do not affect cash flow. An analyst should review changes in accounting estimates to determine the impact on future operating results.

A change from an incorrect accounting method to one that is acceptable under GAAP or IFRS or the correction of an accounting error made in previous financial statements is reported as a **prior-period adjustment**. Prior-period adjustments are made by restating results for all prior periods presented in the current financial statements. Disclosure of the nature of the adjustment and its effect on net income is also required.

Analytical implications: Prior-period adjustments usually involve errors or new accounting standards and do not typically affect cash flow. Analysts should review adjustments carefully because errors may indicate weaknesses in the firm's internal controls.

LOS 23.g: Distinguish between the operating and non-operating components of the income statement.

CFA® Program Curriculum, Volume 3, page 130

Operating and nonoperating transactions are usually reported separately in the income statement. For a nonfinancial firm, nonoperating transactions may result from investment income and financing expenses. For example, a nonfinancial firm may receive dividends and interest from investments in other firms. The investment income and any gains and losses from the sale of these securities are not a part of the firm's normal business operations. Interest expense is based on the firm's capital structure, which is also independent of the firm's operations. Conversely, for a financial firm, investment income and financing expenses are usually considered operating activities.

MODULE QUIZ 23.4

To best evaluate your performance, enter your quiz answers online.

1. When accounting for inventory, are the first-in, first-out (FIFO) and last-in, first-out (LIFO) cost flow assumptions permitted under U.S. GAAP?

	FIFO	LIFO
A.	Yes	Yes
B.	Yes	No
C.	No	Yes

2. Which of the following *best* describes the impact of depreciating equipment with a useful life of 6 years using the declining balance method as compared to the straight-line method?
   A. Total depreciation expense will be higher over the life of the equipment.
   B. Depreciation expense will be higher in the first year.
   C. Scrapping the equipment after five years will result in a larger loss.

3. CC Corporation reported the following inventory transactions (in chronological order) for the year:

Purchase	Sales
40 units at $30	13 units at $35
20 units at $40	35 units at $45
90 units at $50	60 units at $60

   Assuming inventory at the beginning of the year was zero, calculate the year-end inventory using FIFO and LIFO.

	FIFO	LIFO
A.	$5,220	$1,040
B.	$2,100	$1,280
C.	$2,100	$1,040

4. At the beginning of the year, Triple W Corporation purchased a new piece of equipment to be used in its manufacturing operation. The cost of the equipment was $25,000. The equipment is expected to be used for 4 years and then sold for $4,000. Depreciation expense to be reported for the second year using the double-declining-balance method is *closest* to:
   A. $5,250.
   B. $6,250.
   C. $7,000.

5. Changing an accounting estimate:
   A. is reported prospectively.
   B. requires restatement of all prior-period statements presented in the current financial statements.
   C. is reported by adjusting the beginning balance of retained earnings for the cumulative effect of the change.

6. Which of the following transactions would *most likely* be reported below income from continuing operations, net of tax?
   A. Gain or loss from the sale of equipment used in a firm's manufacturing operation.
   B. A change from the accelerated method of depreciation to the straight-line method.
   C. The operating income of a physically and operationally distinct division that is currently for sale, but not yet sold.

7. Which of the following statements about nonrecurring items is *least accurate*?
   A. Discontinued operations are reported net of taxes at the bottom of the income statement before net income.
   B. Unusual or infrequent items are reported before taxes above net income from continuing operations.
   C. A change in accounting principle is reported in the income statement net of taxes after extraordinary items and before net income.

8. Which of the following is *least likely* considered a nonoperating transaction from the perspective of a manufacturing firm?
   A. Dividends received from available-for-sale securities.
   B. Interest expense on subordinated debentures.
   C. Accruing bad debt expense for goods sold on credit.

MODULE 23.5: EPS AND DILUTIVE SECURITIES

Video covering this content is available online.

LOS 23.h: Describe how earnings per share is calculated and calculate and interpret a company's earnings per share (both basic and diluted earnings per share) for both simple and complex capital structures.

LOS 23.i: Distinguish between dilutive and antidilutive securities and describe the implications of each for the earnings per share calculation.

CFA® Program Curriculum, Volume 3, page 131

Earnings per share (EPS) is one of the most commonly used corporate profitability performance measures for publicly-traded firms (nonpublic companies are not required to report EPS data). EPS is reported only for shares of common stock (also known as ordinary stock).

A company may have either a simple or complex capital structure:

- A **simple capital structure** is one that contains *no* potentially dilutive securities. A simple capital structure contains only common stock, nonconvertible debt, and nonconvertible preferred stock.

- A **complex capital structure** contains *potentially dilutive securities* such as options, warrants, or convertible securities.

All firms with complex capital structures must report both *basic* and *diluted* EPS. Firms with simple capital structures report only basic EPS.

Basic EPS

The basic EPS calculation does not consider the effects of any dilutive securities in the computation of EPS.

$$\text{basic EPS} = \frac{\text{net income} - \text{preferred dividends}}{\text{weighted average number of common shares outstanding}}$$

The current year's preferred dividends are subtracted from net income because EPS refers to the per-share earnings *available to common shareholders*. Net income minus preferred dividends is the income available to common stockholders. Common stock dividends are *not* subtracted from net income because they are a part of the net income available to common shareholders.

The **weighted average number of common shares** is the number of shares outstanding during the year, weighted by the portion of the year they were outstanding.

Effect of Stock Dividends and Stock Splits

A **stock dividend** is the distribution of additional shares to each shareholder in an amount proportional to their current number of shares. If a 10% stock dividend is paid, the holder of 100 shares of stock would receive 10 additional shares.

A **stock split** refers to the division of each "old" share into a specific number of "new" (post-split) shares. The holder of 100 shares will have 200 shares after a 2-for-1 split or 150 shares after a 3-for-2 split.

The important thing to remember is that each shareholder's proportional ownership in the company is unchanged by either of these events. Each shareholder has more shares but the same percentage of the total shares outstanding.

PROFESSOR'S NOTE

For our purposes here, a stock dividend and a stock split are two ways of doing the same thing. For example, a 50% stock dividend and a 3-for-2 stock split both result in three "new" shares for every two "old" shares. Stock dividends and stock splits are explained further in the Equity Investments topic area.

EXAMPLE: Weighted average shares outstanding

Johnson Company has 10,000 shares outstanding at the beginning of the year. On April 1, Johnson issues 4,000 new shares. On July 1, Johnson distributes a 10% stock dividend. On September 1, Johnson repurchases 3,000 shares. Calculate Johnson's weighted average number of shares outstanding for the year, for its reporting of basic earnings per share.

Answer:

Shares outstanding are weighted by the portion of the year the shares were outstanding. Any shares that were outstanding before the 10% stock dividend must be adjusted for it. Transactions that occur after the stock dividend do not need to be adjusted.

PROFESSOR'S NOTE

Think of the shares before the stock dividend as "old" shares and shares after the stock dividend as "new" shares that each represent ownership of a smaller portion of the company, in this example 10/11ths of that of an old (pre-stock dividend) share. The weighted average number of shares for the year will be in new shares.

Shares outstanding on January 1: $10,000 \times 1.10 \times 12/12$ of the year = 11,000

Shares issued April 1: $4,000 \times 1.10 \times 9/12$ of the year = 3,300

Shares repurchased September 1: $-3,000 \times 4/12$ of the year = $\underline{-1,000}$

Weighted average shares outstanding = 13,300

EXAMPLE: Basic earnings per share

Johnson Company has net income of $10,000, paid $1,000 cash dividends to its preferred shareholders, and paid $1,750 cash dividends to its common shareholders. Calculate Johnson's basic EPS using the weighted average number of shares from the previous example.

Answer:

$$\text{Basic EPS} = \frac{\text{net income} - \text{pref. div.}}{\text{wt. avg. shares of common}} = \frac{\$10,000 - \$1,000}{13,300} = \$0.68$$

 PROFESSOR'S NOTE

Remember, the payment of a cash dividend on common shares is not considered in the calculation of EPS.

Things to know about the weighted average shares outstanding calculation:

■ The weighting system is days outstanding divided by the number of days in a year, but on the exam, the monthly approximation method will probably be used.

■ Shares issued enter into the computation from the date of issuance.

■ Reacquired shares are excluded from the computation from the date of reacquisition.

■ Shares sold or issued in a purchase of assets are included from the date of issuance.

■ A stock split or stock dividend is applied to all shares outstanding prior to the split or dividend and to the beginning-of-period weighted average shares. A stock split or stock dividend adjustment is not applied to any shares issued or repurchased after the split or dividend date.

Diluted EPS

Before calculating diluted EPS, it is necessary to understand the following terms:

■ **Dilutive securities** are stock options, warrants, convertible debt, or convertible preferred stock that would *decrease* EPS if exercised or converted to common stock.

■ **Antidilutive securities** are stock options, warrants, convertible debt, or convertible preferred stock that would *increase* EPS if exercised or converted to common stock.

The numerator of the basic EPS equation contains income available to common shareholders (net income less preferred dividends). In the case of diluted EPS, if there are dilutive securities, then the numerator must be adjusted as follows:

■ If convertible preferred stock is dilutive (meaning EPS will fall if it is converted to common stock), the convertible preferred dividends must be added to earnings available to common shareholders.

■ If convertible bonds are dilutive, then the bonds' after-tax interest expense is not considered an interest expense for diluted EPS. Hence, interest expense multiplied by (1 – the tax rate) must be added back to the numerator.

PROFESSOR'S NOTE

Interest paid on bonds is typically tax deductible for the firm. If convertible bonds are converted to stock, the firm saves the interest cost but loses the tax deduction. Thus, only the after-tax interest savings are added back to income available to common shareholders.

The basic EPS denominator is the weighted average number of shares. When the firm has dilutive securities outstanding, the denominator is the basic EPS denominator adjusted for the equivalent number of common shares that would be created by the conversion of all dilutive securities outstanding (convertible bonds, convertible preferred shares, warrants, and options), with each one considered separately to determine if it is dilutive.

If a dilutive security was issued during the year, the increase in the weighted average number of shares for diluted EPS is based on only the portion of the year the dilutive security was outstanding.

Dilutive stock options or warrants increase the number of common shares outstanding in the denominator for diluted EPS. There is no adjustment to the numerator.

The **diluted EPS equation** is:

diluted EPS =

$$\frac{\text{adjusted income available for common shares}}{\text{weighted-average common and potential common shares outstanding}}$$

where *adjusted income available for common shares* is:

net income – preferred dividends

+ dividends on convertible preferred stock

+ after-tax interest on convertible debt

Therefore, diluted EPS is:

diluted EPS =

$$\frac{\left[\begin{smallmatrix}\text{net} \\ \text{income}\end{smallmatrix} - \begin{smallmatrix}\text{preferred} \\ \text{dividends}\end{smallmatrix}\right] + \left[\begin{smallmatrix}\text{convertible} \\ \text{preferred} \\ \text{dividends}\end{smallmatrix}\right] + \left[\begin{smallmatrix}\text{convertible} \\ \text{debt} \\ \text{interest}\end{smallmatrix}\right](1-t)}{\left(\begin{smallmatrix}\text{weighted} \\ \text{average} \\ \text{shares}\end{smallmatrix}\right) + \left(\begin{smallmatrix}\text{shares from} \\ \text{converstion of} \\ \text{conv. pfd. shares}\end{smallmatrix}\right) + \left(\begin{smallmatrix}\text{shares from} \\ \text{conversion of} \\ \text{conv. debt}\end{smallmatrix}\right) + \left(\begin{smallmatrix}\text{shares} \\ \text{issuable from} \\ \text{stock options}\end{smallmatrix}\right)}$$

The effect of conversion to common shares is included in the calculation of diluted EPS for a given security only if it is, in fact, dilutive. If a firm has more than one potentially dilutive security outstanding, each potentially dilutive security must be examined separately to determine if it is actually dilutive (i.e., would reduce EPS if converted to common stock).

EXAMPLE 1: EPS with convertible preferred stock

During 20X6, ZZZ reported net income of $4,350,000 and had 2,000,000 shares of common stock outstanding for the entire year. ZZZ's 7%, $5,000,000 par value preferred stock is convertible into common stock at a conversion rate of 1.1 shares for every $10 of par value. Compute basic and diluted EPS.

Answer:

Step 1: Calculate 20X6 basic EPS:

$$\text{basic EPS} = \frac{\$4,350,000 - (0.07)(\$5,000,000)}{2,000,000} = \$2.00$$

Step 2: Calculate diluted EPS:

- Compute the increase in common stock outstanding if the preferred stock is converted to common stock at the beginning of 20X6: ($5,000,000 / $10) × 1.1 = 550,000 shares.

- If the convertible preferred shares were converted to common stock, there would be no preferred dividends paid. Therefore, you should add back the convertible preferred dividends that had previously been subtracted from net income in the numerator.

  Compute diluted EPS as if the convertible preferred stock were converted into common stock:

$$\text{diluted EPS} = \frac{\text{net. inc.} - \text{pref. div.} + \text{convert. pref. dividends}}{\text{wt. avg. shares} + \text{convert. pref. common shares}}$$

$$\text{diluted EPS} = \frac{\$4,350,000}{2,000,000 + 550,000} = \$1.71$$

- Check to see if diluted EPS is less than basic EPS ($1.71 < $2.00). If the answer is yes, the preferred stock is dilutive and must be included in diluted EPS as computed above. If the answer is no, the preferred stock is antidilutive and conversion effects are not included in diluted EPS.

A quick way to check whether convertible preferred stock is dilutive is to divide the preferred dividend by the number of shares that will be created if the preferred stock is converted. For ZZZ: $\dfrac{\$5,000,000 \times 0.07}{550,000}$ = $0.64. Since this is less than basic EPS, the convertible preferred is dilutive.

EXAMPLE 2: EPS with convertible debt

During 20X6, YYY Corp. had earnings available to common shareholders of $2,500,000 and had 1,000,000 shares of common stock outstanding for the entire year, for basic EPS of $2.50. During 20X5, YYY issued 2,000, $1,000 par, 5% bonds for $2,000,000 (issued at par). Each of these bonds is convertible to 120 shares of common stock. The tax rate is 30%. Compute the 20X6 diluted EPS.

Answer:

Compute the increase in common stock outstanding if the convertible debt is converted to common stock at the beginning of 20X6:

shares issuable for debt conversion = (2,000)(120) = 240,000 shares

If the convertible debt is considered converted to common stock at the beginning of 20X6, then there would be no interest expense related to the convertible debt. Therefore, it is necessary to increase YYY's after-tax net income for the after-tax effect of the decrease in interest expense:

increase in income = [(2,000)($1,000)(0.05)] (1 − 0.30) = $70,000

Compute diluted EPS as if the convertible debt were common stock:

$$\text{diluted EPS} = \frac{\text{net. inc.} - \text{pref. div.} + \text{convert. int. } (1 - t)}{\text{wt. avg. shares} + \text{convertible debt shares}}$$

$$\text{diluted EPS} = \frac{\$2,500,000 + \$70,000}{1,000,000 + 240,000} = \$2.07$$

Check to make sure that *diluted EPS is less than basic EPS* ($2.07 < $2.50). If diluted EPS is more than the basic EPS, the convertible bonds are *antidilutive* and should not be treated as common stock in computing diluted EPS.

A quick way to determine whether the convertible debt is dilutive is to calculate its per share impact by:

$$\frac{\text{convertible debt interest } (1 - t)}{\text{convertible debt shares}}$$

If this per share amount is greater than basic EPS, the convertible debt is antidilutive, and the effects of conversion should not be included when calculating diluted EPS.

If this per share amount is less than basic EPS, the convertible debt is dilutive, and the effects of conversion should be included in the calculation of diluted EPS.

For YYY:

$$\frac{\$70,000}{240,000} = \$0.29$$

The company's basic EPS is $2.50, so the convertible debt is dilutive, and the effects of conversion should be included in the calculation of diluted EPS.

Stock options and warrants are dilutive only when their exercise prices are less than the average market price of the stock over the year. If the options or warrants are dilutive, use the **treasury stock method** to calculate the number of shares used in the denominator.

■ The treasury stock method assumes that the funds received by the company from the exercise of the options would be used to hypothetically purchase shares of the company's common stock in the market at the average market price.

■ The net increase in the number of shares outstanding (the adjustment to the denominator) is the number of shares created by exercising the options less the number of shares hypothetically repurchased with the proceeds of exercise.

EXAMPLE 3: EPS with stock options

During 20X6, XXX reported earnings available to common shareholders of $1,200,000 and had 500,000 shares of common stock outstanding for the entire year, for basic EPS of $2.40. XXX has 100,000 stock options (or warrants) outstanding the entire year. Each option allows its holder to purchase one share of common stock at $15 per share. The average market price of XXX's common stock during 20X6 is $20 per share. Compute diluted EPS.

Answer:

Number of common shares created if the options are exercised:	100,000 shares
Cash inflow if the options are exercised ($15/share)(100,000):	$1,500,000
Number of shares that can be purchased with these funds is: $1,500,000 / $20	75,000 shares
Net increase in common shares outstanding from the exercise of the stock options (100,000 – 75,000)	25,000 shares

$$\text{diluted EPS} \ = \ \frac{\$1,200,000}{500,000 + 25,000} \ = \ \$2.29$$

A quick way to calculate the net increase in common shares from the potential exercise of stock options or warrants when the exercise price is less than the average market price is:

$$\left[\frac{AMP - EP}{AMP} \right] \times N$$

where:

AMP = average market price over the year
EP   = exercise price of the options or warrants
N   = number of common shares that the options and warrants can be converted into

For XXX: $\dfrac{\$20 - \$15}{\$20} \times 100,000 \text{ shares} \ = \ 25,000 \text{ shares}$

MODULE QUIZ 23.5

To best evaluate your performance, enter your quiz answers online.

1. The Hall Corporation had 100,000 shares of common stock outstanding at the beginning of the year. Hall issued 30,000 shares of common stock on May 1. On July 1, the company issued a 10% stock dividend. On September 1, Hall issued 1,000, 10% bonds, each convertible into 21 shares of common stock. What is the weighted average number of shares to be used in computing basic and diluted EPS, assuming the convertible bonds are dilutive?

	Average shares, basic	Average shares, dilutive
A.	132,000	139,000
B.	132,000	146,000
C.	139,000	146,000

2. Given the following information, how many shares should be used in computing diluted EPS?
    - 300,000 shares outstanding.
    - 100,000 warrants exercisable at $50 per share.
    - Average share price is $55.
    - Year-end share price is $60.

    A. 9,091.
    B. 90,909.
    C. 309,091.

3. An analyst gathered the following information about a company:
    - 100,000 common shares outstanding from the beginning of the year.
    - Earnings of $125,000.
    - 1,000, 7%, $1,000 par bonds convertible into 25 shares each, outstanding as of the beginning of the year.
    - The tax rate is 40%.

    The company's diluted EPS is *closest* to:
    A. $1.22.
    B. $1.25.
    C. $1.34.

4. An analyst has gathered the following information about a company:
    - 50,000 common shares outstanding from the beginning of the year.
    - Warrants outstanding all year on 50,000 shares, exercisable at $20 per share.
    - Stock is selling at year-end for $25.
    - The average price of the company's stock for the year was $15.

    How many shares should be used in calculating the company's diluted EPS?
    A. 16,667.
    B. 50,000.
    C. 66,667.

MODULE 23.6: COMMON-SIZE INCOME STATEMENTS

LOS 23.j: Convert income statements to common-size income statements.

CFA® Program Curriculum, Volume 3, page 141

A vertical **common-size income statement** expresses each category of the income statement as a percentage of revenue. The common-size format standardizes the income statement by eliminating the effects of size. This allows for comparison of income statement items over time (time-series analysis) and across firms (cross-sectional analysis). For example, the following are year-end income statements of industry competitors North Company and South Company:

	North Co.	South Co.
Revenue	$75,000,000	$3,500,000
Cost of goods sold	52,500,000	700,000
Gross profit	$22,500,000	$2,800,000
Administrative expense	11,250,000	525,000
Research expense	3,750,000	700,000
Operating profit	$7,500,000	$1,575,000

Notice that North is significantly larger and more profitable than South when measured in absolute dollars. North's gross profit is $22,500,000, as compared to South's gross profit of $2,800,000. Similarly, North's operating profit of $7,500,000 is significantly greater than South's operating profit of $1,575,000.

Once we convert the income statements to common-size format, we can see that South is the more profitable firm on a relative basis. South's gross profit of 80% and operating profit of 45% are significantly greater than North's gross profit of 30% and operating profit of 10%.

	North Co.	South Co.
Revenue	100%	100%
Cost of goods sold	70%	20%
Gross profit	30%	80%
Administrative expense	15%	15%
Research expense	5%	20%
Operating profit	10%	45%

Common-size analysis can also be used to examine a firm's strategy. South's higher gross profit margin may be the result of technologically superior products. Notice that South spends more on research than North on a relative basis. This may allow South to charge a higher price for its products.

In most cases, expressing expenses as a percentage of revenue is appropriate. One exception is income tax expense. Tax expense is more meaningful when expressed as a percentage of pretax income. The result is known as the **effective tax rate**.

LOS 23.k: Evaluate a company's financial performance using common-size income statements and financial ratios based on the income statement.

CFA® Program Curriculum, Volume 3, page 141

Margin ratios can be used to measure a firm's profitability quickly. **Gross profit margin** is the ratio of gross profit (revenue minus cost of goods sold) to revenue (sales).

$$\text{gross profit margin } = \frac{\text{gross profit}}{\text{revenue}}$$

Gross profit margin can be increased by raising prices or reducing production costs. A firm might be able to increase prices if its products can be differentiated from other firms' products as a result of factors such as brand names, quality, technology, or patent protection. This was illustrated in the previous example whereby South's gross profit margin was higher than North's.

Another popular margin ratio is **net profit margin**. Net profit margin is the ratio of net income to revenue.

$$\text{net profit margin } = \frac{\text{net income}}{\text{revenue}}$$

Net profit margin measures the profit generated after considering all expenses. Like gross profit margin, net profit margin should be compared over time and with the firm's industry peers.

Any subtotal found in the income statement can be expressed as a percentage of revenue. For example, operating profit divided by revenue is known as **operating profit margin**. Pretax accounting profit divided by revenue is known as **pretax margin**.

LOS 23.l: Describe, calculate, and interpret comprehensive income.

LOS 23.m: Describe other comprehensive income and identify major types of items included in it.

CFA® Program Curriculum, Volume 3, page 145

At the end of each accounting period, the net income of the firm is added to stockholders' equity through an account known as **retained earnings**. Therefore, any transaction that affects the income statement (net income) will also affect stockholders' equity.

Recall that net income is equal to revenue minus expenses. **Comprehensive income** is a more inclusive measure that includes all changes in equity except for owner contributions and distributions. That is, comprehensive income is the sum of net income and **other comprehensive income**. Other comprehensive income includes transactions that are *not* included in net income, such as:

1. Foreign currency translation gains and losses.

2. Adjustments for minimum pension liability.

3. Unrealized gains and losses from cash flow hedging derivatives.

4. Unrealized gains and losses from available-for-sale securities.

Available-for-sale securities are investment securities that are not expected to be held to maturity or sold in the near term. Available-for-sale securities are reported on the balance sheet at fair value. The unrealized gains and losses (the changes in fair value before the securities are sold) are not reported in the income statement but are reported directly in stockholders' equity as a component of other comprehensive income.

Effective in 2018, IFRS treatment of financial instruments no longer includes the available-for-sale classification. However, firms can still choose, at the time of purchase, to treat an equity securities investment as "financial assets measured at fair value through other comprehensive income."

Under IFRS, firms can choose to report certain long-lived assets at fair value rather than historical cost. In this case, the changes in fair value are also included in other comprehensive income.

EXAMPLE: Calculating comprehensive income

Calculate comprehensive income for Triple C Corporation using the selected financial statement data found in the following table.

Triple C Corporation – Selected Financial Statement Data	
Net income	$1,000
Dividends received from available-for-sale securities	60
Unrealized loss from foreign currency translation	(15)
Dividends paid	(110)
Reacquire common stock	(400)
Unrealized gain from cash flow hedge	30
Unrealized loss from available-for-sale securities	(10)
Realized gain on sale of land	65

Answer:

Net income	$1,000
Unrealized loss from foreign currency translation	(15)
Unrealized gain from cash flow hedge	30
Unrealized loss from available-for-sale securities	(10)
Comprehensive income	$1,005

The dividends received for available-for-sale securities and the realized gain on the sale of land are already included in net income. Dividends paid and the reacquisition of common stock are transactions with shareholders, so they are not included in comprehensive income.

Because firms have some flexibility of including or excluding transactions from net income, analysts must examine comprehensive income when comparing financial performance with other firms.

MODULE QUIZ 23.6

To best evaluate your performance, enter your quiz answers online.

1. A vertical common-size income statement expresses each category of the income statement as a percentage of:
    A. assets.
    B. gross profit.
    C. revenue.

2. Which of the following would *most likely* result in higher gross profit margin, assuming no fixed costs?
    A. A 10% increase in the number of units sold.
    B. A 5% decrease in production cost per unit.
    C. A 7% decrease in administrative expenses.

3. Which of the following transactions affects owners' equity but does not affect net income?
    A. Foreign currency translation gain.
    B. Repaying the face amount on a bond issued at par.
    C. Dividends received from available-for-sale securities.

4. Which of the following is *least likely* to be included when calculating comprehensive income?
    A. Unrealized loss from cash flow hedging derivatives.
    B. Unrealized gain from available-for-sale securities.
    C. Dividends paid to common shareholders.

KEY CONCEPTS

LOS 23.a

The income statement shows an entity's revenues, expenses, gains and losses during a reporting period.

A multi-step income statement provides a subtotal for gross profit and a single step income statement does not. Expenses on the income statement can be grouped by the nature of the expense items or by their function, such as with expenses grouped into cost of goods sold.

LOS 23.b

Revenue is recognized when earned and expenses are recognized when incurred.

Methods for accounting for long-term contracts include:

■ Percentage-of-completion—recognizes revenue in proportion to costs incurred.

■ Completed-contract—recognizes revenue only when the contract is complete.

Revenue recognition methods for installment sales are:

■ Normal revenue recognition at time of sale if collectibility is reasonably assured.

■ Installment sales method if collectibility cannot be reasonably estimated.

■ Cost recovery method if collectibility is highly uncertain.

Revenue from barter transactions can only be recognized if its fair value can be estimated from historical data on similar non-barter transactions.

Gross revenue reporting shows sales and cost of goods sold, while net revenue reporting shows only the difference between sales and cost of goods sold and should be used when the firm is acting essentially as a selling agent and does not stock inventory, take credit risk, or have control over supplier and price.

LOS 23.c

A firm using a revenue recognition method that is aggressive will inflate current period earnings at a minimum and perhaps inflate overall earnings. Because of the estimates involved, the percentage-of-completion method is more aggressive than the completed-contract method. Also, the installment method is more aggressive than the cost recovery method.

LOS 23.d

Converged accounting standards issued in May 2014 take a principles-based approach to revenue recognition. These standards identify a five-step process for recognizing revenue:

1. Identify the contract(s) with a customer.

2. Identify the performance obligations in the contract.

3. Determine the transaction price.

4. Allocate the transaction price to the performance obligations in the contract.

5. Recognize revenue when (or as) the entity satisfies a performance obligation.

LOS 23.e

The matching principle requires that firms match revenues recognized in a period with the expenses required to generate them. One application of the matching principle is seen in accounting for inventory, with cost of goods sold as the cost of units sold from inventory that are included in current-period revenue. Other costs, such as depreciation of fixed assets or administrative overhead, are period costs and are taken without regard to revenues generated during the period.

Depreciation methods:

- Straight-line: Equal amount of depreciation expense in each year of the asset's useful life.

- Declining balance: Apply a constant rate of depreciation to the declining book value until book value equals residual value.

Inventory valuation methods:

- FIFO: Inventory reflects cost of most recent purchases, COGS reflects cost of oldest purchases.

- LIFO: COGS reflects cost of most recent purchases, inventory reflects cost of oldest purchases.

- Average cost: Unit cost equals cost of goods available for sale divided by total units available and is used for both COGS and inventory.

- Specific identification: Each item in inventory is identified and its historical cost is used for calculating COGS when the item is sold.

Intangible assets with limited lives should be amortized using a method that reflects the flow over time of their economic benefits. Intangible assets with indefinite lives (e.g., goodwill) are not amortized.

Users of financial data should analyze the reasons for any changes in estimates of expenses and compare these estimates with those of peer companies.

LOS 23.f

Results of discontinued operations are reported below income from continuing operations, net of tax, from the date the decision to dispose of the operations is made. These results are segregated because they likely are non-recurring and do not affect future net income.

Unusual or infrequent items are reported before tax and above income from continuing operations. An analyst should determine how "unusual" or "infrequent" these items really are for the company when estimating future earnings or firm value.

Changes in accounting standards, changes in accounting methods applied, and corrections of accounting errors require retrospective restatement of all prior-period financial statements included in the current statement. A change in an accounting estimate, however, is applied prospectively (to subsequent periods) with no restatement of prior-period results.

LOS 23.g

Operating income is generated from the firm's normal business operations. For a nonfinancial firm, income that results from investing or financing transactions is classified as non-operating income, while it is operating income for a financial firm since its business operations include investing in and financing securities.

LOS 23.h

$$\text{basic EPS} = \frac{\text{net income} - \text{preferred dividends}}{\text{weighted average number of common shares outstanding}}$$

When a company has potentially dilutive securities, it must report diluted EPS.

For any convertible preferred stock, convertible debt, warrants, or stock options that are dilutive, the calculation of diluted EPS is:

$$\text{diluted EPS} = \frac{\left[\begin{array}{c}\text{net}\\\text{income}\end{array} - \begin{array}{c}\text{preferred}\\\text{dividends}\end{array}\right] + \left[\begin{array}{c}\text{convertible}\\\text{preferred}\\\text{dividends}\end{array}\right] + \left[\begin{array}{c}\text{convertible}\\\text{debt}\\\text{interest}\end{array}\right](1-t)}{\left(\begin{array}{c}\text{weighted}\\\text{average}\\\text{shares}\end{array}\right) + \left(\begin{array}{c}\text{shares from}\\\text{converstion of}\\\text{conv. pfd. shares}\end{array}\right) + \left(\begin{array}{c}\text{shares from}\\\text{conversion of}\\\text{conv. debt}\end{array}\right) + \left(\begin{array}{c}\text{shares}\\\text{issuable from}\\\text{stock options}\end{array}\right)}$$

LOS 23.i

A dilutive security is one that, if converted to its common stock equivalent, would decrease EPS. An antidilutive security is one that would not reduce EPS if converted to its common stock equivalent.

LOS 23.j

A vertical common-size income statement expresses each item as a percentage of revenue. The common-size format standardizes the income statement by eliminating the effects of size. Common-size income statements are useful for trend analysis and for comparisons with peer firms.

LOS 23.k

Common-size income statements are useful in examining a firm's business strategies.

Two popular profitability ratios are gross profit margin (gross profit / revenue) and net profit margin (net income / revenue). A firm can often achieve higher profit margins by differentiating its products from the competition.

LOS 23.l

Comprehensive income is the sum of net income and other comprehensive income. It measures all changes to equity other than those from transactions with shareholders.

LOS 23.m

Transactions with shareholders, such as dividends paid and shares issued or repurchased, are not reported on the income statement.

Other comprehensive income includes other transactions that affect equity but do not affect net income, including:

■ Gains and losses from foreign currency translation.

■ Pension obligation adjustments.

■ Unrealized gains and losses from cash flow hedging derivatives.

■ Unrealized gains and losses on available-for-sale securities.

©2018 Kaplan, Inc.

ANSWER KEY FOR MODULE QUIZZES

Module Quiz 23.1, 23.2, 23.3

1. **B** Depreciation is included in the computation of operating expenses. Interest expense is a financing cost. Thus, it is excluded from operating expenses. (Module 23.1, LOS 23.a)

2. **A** Income taxes are expenses grouped together by their nature. Cost of goods sold includes a number of expenses related to the same function, the production of inventory. (Module 23.1, LOS 23.a)

3. **A** In order to recognize revenue, the seller must know the sales price and be reasonably sure of collection, and must have delivered the goods or rendered the service. Actual collection of cash is not required. (Module 23.2, LOS 23.b)

4. **C** The matching principle requires that the expenses incurred to generate the revenue be recognized in the same accounting period as the revenue. (Module 23.2, LOS 23.b)

5. **A** $24,000 / $60,000 = 40% of the project completed. 40% of $100,000 = $40,000 revenue. $40,000 revenue – $24,000 cost = $16,000 profit for the period. No profit would be reported in the first year using the completed contract method. (Module 23.2, LOS 23.b, 23.c)

6. **A** For credit sales to its customers, the firm can recognize revenue at the time of the sale. The installment method would be appropriate if collectability could not be estimated reliably, and the cost recovery method would be appropriate if collectability was highly uncertain. (Module 23.3, LOS 23.b, 23.c)

7. **B** The five steps in revenue recognition under the converged standards are:
    1. Identify the contract or contracts with the customer.
    2. Identify the performance obligations in the contract(s).
    3. Determine a transaction price.
    4. Allocate the transaction price to the performance obligations.
    5. Recognize revenue when/as the performance obligations have been satisfied.

    (Module 23.3, LOS 23.d)

Module Quiz 23.4

1. **A** LIFO and FIFO are both permitted under U.S. GAAP. LIFO is prohibited under IFRS. (LOS 23.e)

2. **B** Accelerated depreciation will result in higher depreciation in the early years and lower depreciation in the later years compared to the straight-line method. Total depreciation expense will be the same under both methods. The book value would be higher in the later years using straight-line depreciation, so the loss from scrapping the equipment under an accelerated method is less compared to the straight-line method. (LOS 23.e)

3. **B** 108 units were sold (13 + 35 + 60) and 150 units were available for sale (beginning inventory of 0 plus purchases of 40 + 20 + 90), so there are 150 – 108 = 42 units in ending inventory. Under FIFO, units from the last batch purchased would remain in inventory: 42 × $50 = $2,100. Under LIFO, the first 42 units purchased would be in inventory: (40 × $30) + (2 × $40) = $1,280. (LOS 23.e)

4. **B** Year 1: (2 / 4) × 25,000 = $12,500. Year 2: (2 / 4) × (25,000 – 12,500) = $6,250. (LOS 23.e)

5. **A** A change in an accounting estimate is reported prospectively. No restatement of prior period statements is necessary. (LOS 23.f)

6. **C** A physically and operationally distinct division that is currently for sale is treated as a discontinued operation. The income from the division is reported net of tax below income from continuing operations. Changing a depreciation method is a change of accounting principle, which is applied retrospectively and will change operating income. (LOS 23.f)

7. **C** A change in accounting principle requires retrospective application; that is, all prior period financial statements currently presented are restated to reflect the change. (LOS 23.f)

8. **C** Bad debt expense is an operating expense. The other choices are nonoperating items from the perspective of a manufacturing firm. (LOS 23.g)

Module Quiz 23.5

1. **A** The new stock is weighted by 8 / 12. The bonds are weighted by 4 / 12 and are not affected by the stock dividend.

    Basic shares = {[100,000 × (12 / 12)] + [30,000 × (8 / 12)]} × 1.10
    = 132,000

    Diluted shares = 132,000 + [21,000 × (4 / 12)] = 139,000

    (LOS 23.h, 23.i)

2. **C** Since the exercise price of the warrants is less than the average share price, the warrants are dilutive. Using the treasury stock method to determine the denominator impact:

    $$\frac{\$55 - \$50}{\$55} \times 100,000 \text{ shares} = 9,091 \text{ shares}$$

Thus, the denominator will increase by 9,091 shares to 309,091 shares. The question asks for the total, not just the impact of the warrants. (LOS 23.h, 23.i)

3. **B** First, calculate basic EPS $= \dfrac{\$125,000}{100,000} = \$1.25$.

Next, check if the convertible bonds are dilutive:

numerator impact $= (1,000 \times 1,000 \times 0.07) \times (1 - 0.4) = \$42,000$

denominator impact $= (1,000 \times 25) = 25,000$ shares

per share impact $= \dfrac{\$42,000}{25,000 \text{ shares}} = \$1.68$

Since $1.68 is greater than the basic EPS of $1.25, the bonds are antidilutive. Thus, diluted EPS = basic EPS = $1.25.

(LOS 23.h, 23.i)

4. **B** The warrants in this case are antidilutive. The average price per share of $15 is less than the exercise price of $20. The year-end price per share is not relevant. The denominator consists of only the common stock for basic EPS. (LOS 23.h, 23.i)

Module Quiz 23.6

1. **C** Each category of the income statement is expressed as a percentage of revenue (sales). (LOS 23.j)

2. **B** A 5% decrease in per unit production cost will increase gross profit by lowering cost of goods sold. Assuming no fixed costs, gross profit margin will remain the same if sale quantities increase. Administrative expenses are not included in gross profit margin. (LOS 23.k)

3. **A** A foreign currency translation gain is not included in net income but the gain increases owners' equity. Dividends received are reported in the income statement. The repayment of principal does not affect owners' equity. (LOS 23.l, 23.m)

4. **C** Comprehensive income includes all changes in equity except transactions with shareholders. Therefore, dividends paid to common shareholders are not included in comprehensive income. (LOS 23.l, 23.m)

The following is a review of the Financial Reporting and Analysis (2) principles designed to address the learning outcome statements set forth by CFA Institute. Cross-Reference to CFA Institute Assigned Reading #24.

READING 24

Understanding Balance Sheets

EXAM FOCUS

While the income statement presents a picture of a firm's economic activities over a period of time, its balance sheet is a snapshot of its financial and physical assets and its liabilities at a point in time. Just as with the income statement, understanding balance sheet accounts, how they are valued, and what they represent, is also crucial to the financial analysis of a firm. Again, different choices of accounting methods and different accounting estimates will affect a firm's financial ratios, and an analyst must be careful to make the necessary adjustments in order to compare two or more firms. Special attention should be paid to the method by which each balance sheet item is calculated and how changes in balance sheet values relate to the income statement and to shareholders' equity. The next Study Session includes more detailed information on several balance sheet accounts, including inventories, long-lived assets, deferred taxes, and long-term liabilities.

MODULE 24.1: BALANCE SHEET INTRODUCTION

LOS 24.a: Describe the elements of the balance sheet: assets, liabilities, and equity.

Video covering this content is available online.

CFA® Program Curriculum, Volume 3, page 162

The **balance sheet** (also known as the statement of financial position or statement of financial condition) reports the firm's financial position at a point in time. The balance sheet consists of assets, liabilities, and equity.

Assets: Resources controlled as a result of past transactions that are expected to provide future economic benefits.

Liabilities: Obligations as a result of past events that are expected to require an outflow of economic resources.

Equity: The owners' residual interest in the assets after deducting the liabilities. Equity is also referred to as stockholders' equity, shareholders' equity, or owners' equity. Analysts sometimes refer to equity as "net assets."

A financial statement item should be recognized if a future economic benefit from the item (flowing to or from the firm) is *probable* and the item's value or cost can be measured reliably.

MODULE 24.2: ASSETS AND LIABILITIES

Video covering this content is available online.

LOS 24.b: Describe uses and limitations of the balance sheet in financial analysis.

CFA® Program Curriculum, Volume 3, page 162

The balance sheet can be used to assess a firm's liquidity, solvency, and ability to make distributions to shareholders. From the firm's perspective, **liquidity** is the ability to meet short-term obligations and **solvency** is the ability to meet long-term obligations.

The balance sheet elements (assets, liabilities, and equity) should not be interpreted as market value or intrinsic value. For most firms, the balance sheet consists of a mixture of values. For example, some assets are reported at historical cost, some are reported at amortized cost, and others may be reported at fair value. There are numerous valuation bases. Even if the balance sheet was reported at fair value, the value may have changed since the balance sheet date. Also, there are a number of assets and liabilities that do not appear on the balance sheet but certainly have value. For example, the value of a firm's employees and reputation is not reported on the balance sheet.

LOS 24.c: Describe alternative formats of balance sheet presentation.

CFA® Program Curriculum, Volume 3, page 165

Both IFRS and U.S. GAAP require firms to separately report their current assets and noncurrent assets and current and noncurrent liabilities. The current/ noncurrent format is known as a **classified balance sheet** and is useful in evaluating liquidity.

Under IFRS, firms can choose to use a **liquidity-based format** if the presentation is more relevant and reliable. Liquidity-based presentations, which are often used in the banking industry, present assets and liabilities in the order of liquidity.

MODULE QUIZ 24.1, 24.2

To best evaluate your performance, enter your quiz answers online.

1. Which of the following is *most likely* an essential characteristic of an asset?
   A. An asset is tangible.
   B. An asset is obtained at a cost.
   C. An asset provides future benefits.

©2018 Kaplan, Inc.

2. Which of the following statements about analyzing the balance sheet is *most accurate*?
   A. The value of the firm's reputation is reported on the balance sheet at amortized cost.
   B. Shareholders' equity is equal to the intrinsic value of the firm.
   C. The balance sheet can be used to measure the firm's capital structure.

3. Century Company's balance sheet follows:

Century Company Balance Sheet (in millions)		
	20X7	20X6
Current assets	$340	$280
Noncurrent assets	660	630
Total assets	$1,000	$910
Current liabilities	$170	$110
Noncurrent liabilities	50	50
Total liabilities	$220	$160
Equity	$780	$750
Total liabilities and equity	$1,000	$910

Century's balance sheet presentation is known as:
   A. a classified balance sheet.
   B. a liquidity-based balance sheet.
   C. an account form balance sheet.

MODULE 24.3: CURRENT ASSETS AND LIABILITIES

LOS 24.d: Distinguish between current and non-current assets and current and non-current liabilities.

Video covering this content is available online.

CFA® Program Curriculum, Volume 3, page 165

Current assets include cash and other assets that will likely be converted into cash or used up within one year or one operating cycle, whichever is greater. The **operating cycle** is the time it takes to produce or purchase inventory, sell the product, and collect the cash. Current assets are usually presented in the order of their liquidity, with cash being the most liquid. Current assets reveal information about the operating activities of the firm.

Current liabilities are obligations that will be satisfied within one year or one operating cycle, whichever is greater. More specifically, a liability that meets any of the following criteria is considered current:

■ Settlement is expected during the normal operating cycle.

■ Settlement is expected within one year.

- Held primarily for trading purposes.

- There is not an unconditional right to defer settlement for more than one year.

Current assets minus current liabilities equals **working capital**. Not enough working capital may indicate liquidity problems. Too much working capital may be an indication of inefficient use of assets.

Noncurrent assets do not meet the definition of current assets because they will not be converted into cash or used up within one year or operating cycle. Noncurrent assets provide information about the firm's investing activities, which form the foundation upon which the firm operates.

Noncurrent liabilities do not meet the criteria of current liabilities. Noncurrent liabilities provide information about the firm's long-term financing activities.

LOS 24.e: Describe different types of assets and liabilities and the measurement bases of each.

CFA® Program Curriculum, Volume 3, page 167

Current Assets

Current assets include cash and other assets that will be converted into cash or used up within one year or operating cycle, whichever is greater.

Cash and cash equivalents. Cash equivalents are short-term, highly liquid investments that are readily convertible to cash and near enough to maturity that interest rate risk is insignificant. Examples of cash equivalents include Treasury bills, commercial paper, and money market funds. Cash and equivalents are considered financial assets. Generally, financial assets are reported on the balance sheet at amortized cost or fair value. For cash equivalents, either measurement base should result in about the same value.

Marketable securities. Marketable securities are financial assets that are traded in a public market and whose value can be readily determined. Examples include Treasury bills, notes, bonds, and equity securities. Details of the investment are disclosed in the financial footnotes. Measurement bases for marketable securities will be discussed later in this topic review.

Accounts receivable. Accounts receivable (also known as trade receivables) are financial assets that represent amounts owed to the firm by customers for goods or services sold on credit. Accounts receivable are reported at **net realizable value**, which is based on estimated **bad debt expense**. Bad debt expense increases the **allowance for doubtful accounts**, a contra-asset account. A **contra account** is used to reduce the value of its controlling account. Thus, gross receivables less the allowance for doubtful accounts is equal to accounts receivable at net realizable value, the amount the firm expects to collect. When receivables are "written off" (removed from the balance sheet because they are uncollectible), both gross receivables and the allowance account are reduced.

Firms are required to disclose significant concentrations of credit risk, including customer, geographic, and industry concentrations.

Analyzing receivables relative to sales can reveal collection problems. The allowance for doubtful accounts should also be considered relative to the level and growth rate of sales. Firms can underestimate bad debt expense, thereby increasing reported earnings.

Inventories. Inventories are goods held for sale to customers or used in manufacture of goods to be sold. Manufacturing firms separately report inventories of raw materials, work-in-process, and finished goods.

The costs included in inventory include purchase cost, conversion costs, and other costs necessary to bring the inventory to its present location and condition. Costs that are excluded from inventory include abnormal waste, including material, labor, and manufacturing overhead. Storage costs (unless they are necessary as a part of the production process), administrative overhead, and selling costs are also excluded.

Standard costing and the retail method are used by some firms to measure inventory costs. **Standard costing**, often used by manufacturing firms, involves assigning predetermined amounts of materials, labor, and overhead to goods produced. Firms that use the **retail method** measure inventory at retail prices and then subtract gross profit in order to determine cost.

Using different cost flow assumptions (also known as cost flow methods), firms assign inventory costs to the income statement (cost of goods sold). As discussed in the topic review of Understanding Income Statements, FIFO and average cost are permitted under both IFRS and U.S. GAAP. LIFO is permitted under U.S. GAAP but is prohibited under IFRS.

Inventories are reported at the lower of cost or net realizable value under IFRS, and under U.S. GAAP for companies that use inventory cost methods other than LIFO or retail. Net realizable value is equal to the selling price less any completion costs and disposal (selling) costs. Under U.S. GAAP, companies using LIFO or the retail method report inventories at the lower of cost or market. Market is usually equal to replacement cost; however, market cannot be greater than net realizable value or less than net realizable value less a normal profit margin. If net realizable value (IFRS) or market (U.S. GAAP) is less than the inventory's carrying value, the inventory is written down and a loss is recognized in the income statement. If there is a subsequent recovery in value, the inventory can be written back up under IFRS. No write-up is allowed under U.S. GAAP; the firm simply reports greater profit when the inventory is sold.

PROFESSOR'S NOTE

Inventories are described in more detail in the next Study Session.

Other current assets. Other current assets are amounts that may not be material if shown separately; thus, the items are combined into a single amount. Examples include prepaid expenses and deferred tax assets. **Prepaid expenses** are operating costs that have been paid in advance. As the costs are actually incurred, an expense is recognized in the income statement and prepaid expenses (an asset) decrease. For example, if a firm makes an annual rent payment of $400,000 at the beginning of the year, an asset (cash) decreases and another asset (prepaid rent) increases by the amount of the payment. At the end of three months, one-quarter of the prepaid rent has been used. At this point, the firm will recognize $100,000 of rent expense in its income statement and reduce assets (prepaid rent) by $100,000.

As we will discuss in our topic review of Income Taxes, deferred taxes are the result of temporary differences between financial reporting income and tax reporting income. **Deferred tax assets** are created when the amount of taxes payable exceeds the amount of income tax expense recognized in the income statement. This can occur when expenses or losses are recognized in the income statement before they are tax deductible, or when revenues or gains are taxable before they are recognized in the income statement. Eventually, the deferred tax asset will reverse when the expense is deducted for tax purposes or the revenue is recognized in the income statement. Deferred tax assets can also be created from unused tax losses.

Current Liabilities

Current liabilities are obligations that will be satisfied within one year or operating cycle, whichever is greater.

Accounts payable. Accounts payable (also known as trade payables) are amounts the firm owes to suppliers for goods or services purchased on credit. Analyzing payables relative to purchases can signal credit problems with suppliers.

Notes payable and current portion of long-term debt. Notes payable are obligations in the form of promissory notes owed to creditors and lenders. Notes payable can also be reported as noncurrent liabilities if their maturities are greater than one year. The current portion of long-term debt is the principal portion of debt due within one year or operating cycle, whichever is greater.

Accrued liabilities. Accrued liabilities (accrued expenses) are expenses that have been recognized in the income statement but are not yet contractually due. Accrued liabilities result from the accrual method of accounting, under which expenses are recognized as incurred. For example, consider a firm that is required to make annual year-end interest payments of $100,000 on an outstanding bank loan. At the end of March, the firm would recognize one-quarter ($25,000) of the total interest expense in its income statement and an accrued liability would be increased by the same amount, even though the liability is not actually due until the end of the year.

Some firms include income tax payable as an accrued liability. **Taxes payable** are current taxes that have been recognized in the income statement but have not yet been paid. Other examples of accrued liabilities include interest payable, wages payable, and accrued warranty expense.

Unearned revenue. Unearned revenue (also known as unearned income, deferred revenue, or deferred income) is cash collected in advance of providing goods and services. For example, a magazine publisher receives subscription payments in advance of delivery. When payment is received, assets (cash) and liabilities (unearned revenue) increase by the same amount. As the magazines are delivered, the publisher recognizes revenue in the income statement and reduces the liability.

When analyzing liquidity, keep in mind that unearned revenue does not require a future outflow of cash like accounts payable. Also, unearned revenue may be an indication of future growth as the revenue will ultimately be recognized in the income statement.

MODULE 24.4: NONCURRENT ASSETS AND LIABILITIES

Video covering this content is available online.

Property, plant, and equipment. Property, plant, and equipment (PP&E) are tangible assets used in the production of goods and services. PP&E includes land and buildings, machinery and equipment, furniture, and natural resources. Under IFRS, PP&E can be reported using the **cost model** or the **revaluation model**. Under U.S. GAAP, only the cost model is allowed.

Under the cost model, PP&E other than land is reported at amortized cost (historical cost minus accumulated depreciation, amortization, depletion, and impairment losses). Land is not depreciated because it has an indefinite life. **Historical cost** includes the purchase price plus any cost necessary to get the asset ready for use, such as delivery and installation costs. As discussed in the topic review of Understanding Income Statements, there are several depreciation methods (e.g., straight-line and declining balance methods) used to allocate the cost to the income statement over time. Thus, the balance sheet and income statement are affected by the depreciation method and related estimates (i.e., salvage value and useful life of assets).

Also under the cost model, PP&E must be tested for **impairment**. An asset is impaired if its carrying value exceeds the **recoverable amount**. Under IFRS, the recoverable amount of an asset is the greater of fair value less any selling costs, or the asset's **value in use**. Value in use is the present value of the asset's future cash flow stream. If impaired, the asset is written down to its recoverable amount and a loss is recognized in the income statement. Loss recoveries are allowed under IFRS but not under U.S. GAAP.

Under the revaluation model, PP&E is reported at fair value less any accumulated depreciation. Changes in fair value are reflected in shareholders' equity and may be recognized in the income statement in certain circumstances.

> **PROFESSOR'S NOTE**
>
> The revaluation model will be discussed in more detail in the topic review of Long-Lived Assets.

Investment property. Under IFRS, investment property includes assets that generate rental income or capital appreciation. U.S. GAAP does not have a specific definition of investment property. Under IFRS, investment property can either be reported at amortized cost (just like PP&E) or fair value. Under the **fair value model**, any change in fair value is recognized in the income statement.

> **MODULE QUIZ 24.3, 24.4**
>
> *To best evaluate your performance, enter your quiz answers online.*
>
> 1. Which of the following would *most likely* result in a current liability?
>   A. Possible warranty claims.
>   B. Future operating lease payments.
>   C. Estimated income taxes for the current year.

2. How should the proceeds received from the advance sale of tickets to a sporting event be treated by the seller, assuming the tickets are nonrefundable?
   A. Unearned revenue is recognized to the extent that costs have been incurred.
   B. Revenue is recognized to the extent that costs have been incurred.
   C. Revenue is deferred until the sporting event is held.

3. Which of the following inventory valuation methods is required by the accounting standard-setting bodies?
   A. Lower of cost or net realizable value.
   B. Weighted average cost.
   C. First-in, first-out.

4. Under IFRS, a firm may report the value of property, plant, and equipment using:
   A. only the cost model.
   B. the cost model or the fair value model.
   C. the cost model or the revaluation model.

MODULE 24.5: INTANGIBLE ASSETS

Video covering this content is available online.

Intangible assets are non-monetary assets that lack physical substance. Securities are not considered intangible assets. Intangible assets are either identifiable or unidentifiable. **Identifiable intangible assets** can be acquired separately or are the result of rights or privileges conveyed to their owner. Examples of identifiable intangibles are patents, trademarks, and copyrights. **Unidentifiable intangible assets** cannot be acquired separately and may have an unlimited life. The best example of an unidentifiable intangible asset is goodwill.

Under IFRS, identifiable intangibles that are *purchased* can be reported on the balance sheet using the cost model or the revaluation model, although the revaluation model can only be used if an active market for the intangible asset exists. Both models are basically the same as the measurement models used for PP&E. Under U.S. GAAP, only the cost model is allowed.

Except for certain legal costs, intangible assets that are *created internally*, such as research and development costs, are expensed as incurred under U.S. GAAP. Under IFRS, a firm must identify the research stage (discovery of new scientific or technical knowledge) and the development stage (using research results to plan or design products). Under IFRS, the firm must expense costs incurred during the research stage but can capitalize costs incurred during the development stage.

Finite-lived intangible assets are amortized over their useful lives and tested for impairment in the same way as PP&E. The amortization method and useful life estimates are reviewed at least annually. Intangible assets with infinite lives are not amortized, but are tested for impairment at least annually.

Under IFRS and U.S. GAAP, all of the following should be expensed as incurred:

■ Start-up and training costs.

■ Administrative overhead.

■ Advertising and promotion costs.

- Relocation and reorganization costs.
- Termination costs.

Some analysts choose to eliminate intangible assets for analytical purposes. However, analysts should consider the value to the firm of each intangible asset before making any adjustments.

Goodwill. Goodwill is the excess of purchase price over the fair value of the identifiable net assets (assets minus liabilities) acquired in a business acquisition. Acquirers are often willing to pay more than the fair value of the target's identifiable net assets because the target may have assets that are not reported on its balance sheet. For example, the target's reputation and customer loyalty certainly have value; however, the value is not quantifiable. Also, the target may have research and development assets that remain off-balance-sheet because of current accounting standards. Finally, part of the acquisition price may reflect perceived synergies from the business combination. For example, the acquirer may be able to eliminate duplicate facilities and reduce payroll as a result of the acquisition.

PROFESSOR'S NOTE

Occasionally the purchase price of an acquisition is less than fair value of the identifiable net assets. In this case, the difference is immediately recognized as a gain in the acquirer's income statement.

Goodwill is only created in a purchase acquisition. Internally generated goodwill is expensed as incurred.

Goodwill is not amortized but must be tested for impairment at least annually. If impaired, goodwill is reduced and a loss is recognized in the income statement. The impairment loss does not affect cash flow. As long as goodwill is not impaired, it can remain on the balance sheet indefinitely.

Since goodwill is not amortized, firms can manipulate net income upward by allocating more of the acquisition price to goodwill and less to the identifiable assets. The result is less depreciation and amortization expense, resulting in higher net income.

Accounting goodwill should not be confused with economic goodwill. Economic goodwill derives from the expected future performance of the firm, while accounting goodwill is the result of past acquisitions.

When computing ratios, analysts should eliminate goodwill from the balance sheet and goodwill impairment charges from the income statement for comparability. Also, analysts should evaluate future acquisitions in terms of the price paid relative to the earning power of the acquired assets.

MODULE 24.6: MARKETABLE SECURITIES

Video covering this content is available online.

Financial instruments are contracts that give rise to both a financial asset of one entity and a financial liability or equity instrument of another entity.[1] Financial instruments can be found on the asset side and the liability side of the balance sheet.

---

1. IAS 32, *Financial Instruments*: Presentation, paragraph 11.

Financial assets include investment securities (stocks and bonds), derivatives, loans, and receivables.

Financial instruments are measured at historical cost, amortized cost, or fair value. Financial assets measured at cost include unquoted equity investments (whereby fair value cannot be reliably measured) and loans to and receivables from other entities.

Financial assets measured at amortized cost are known as held-to-maturity securities. **Held-to-maturity securities** are debt securities acquired with the intent to be held to maturity. Amortized cost is equal to the original issue price minus any principal payments, plus any amortized discount or minus any amortized premium, minus any impairment losses. Subsequent changes in market value are ignored.

Financial assets measured at fair value, also known as **mark-to-market** accounting, include trading securities, available-for-sale securities, and derivatives.

Trading securities (also known as held-for-trading securities) are debt and equity securities acquired with the intent to profit over the near term. Trading securities are reported on the balance sheet at fair value, and the unrealized gains and losses (changes in market value before the securities are sold) are recognized in the income statement. Unrealized gains and losses are also known as holding period gains and losses. **Derivative instruments** are treated the same as trading securities.

Available-for-sale securities are debt and equity securities that are not expected to be held to maturity or traded in the near term. Like trading securities, available-for-sale securities are reported on the balance sheet at fair value. However, any unrealized gains and losses are not recognized in the income statement, but are reported in other comprehensive income as a part of shareholders' equity. Although under IFRS the available-for-sale classification no longer exists, firms may still elect at the time of purchase to account for equity securities this way.

For all three classifications of securities, dividend and interest income and realized gains and losses (actual gains or losses when the securities are sold) are recognized in the income statement.

Figure 24.1 summarizes the different classifications and measurement bases of financial assets.

Figure 24.1 Financial Asset Classifications and Measurement Bases

Historical Cost	Amortized Cost	Fair Value
Unlisted equity investments	Held-to-maturity securities	Trading securities
Loans and receivables		Available-for-sale securities
		Derivatives

> **EXAMPLE:** Classification of investment securities
>
> Triple D Corporation, a U.S. GAAP reporting firm, purchased a 6% bond, at par, for $1,000,000 at the beginning of the year. Interest rates have recently increased and the market value of the bond declined $20,000. Determine the bond's effect on Triple D's financial statements under each classification of securities.

Answer:

If the bond is classified as a *held-to-maturity* security, the bond is reported on the balance sheet at $1,000,000. Interest income of $60,000 [$1,000,000 × 6%] is reported in the income statement.

If the bond is classified as a *trading* security, the bond is reported on the balance sheet at $980,000. The $20,000 unrealized loss and $60,000 of interest income are both recognized in the income statement.

If the bond is classified as an *available-for-sale* security, the bond is reported on the balance sheet at $980,000. Interest income of $60,000 is recognized in the income statement. The $20,000 unrealized loss is not recognized in the income statement. Rather, it is reported as a change in stockholders' equity.

Non-Current Liabilities

Long-term financial liabilities. Financial liabilities include bank loans, notes payable, bonds payable, and derivatives. If the financial liabilities are not issued at face amount, the liabilities are usually reported on the balance sheet at amortized cost. Amortized cost is equal to the issue price minus any principal payments, plus any amortized discount or minus any amortized premium.

In some cases, financial liabilities are reported at fair value. Examples include held-for-trading liabilities such as a short position in a stock (which may be classified as a short-term liability), derivative liabilities, and non-derivative liabilities with exposures hedged by derivatives.

Deferred tax liabilities. Deferred tax liabilities are amounts of income taxes payable in future periods as a result of taxable temporary differences. Deferred tax liabilities are created when the amount of income tax expense recognized in the income statement is greater than taxes payable. This can occur when expenses or losses are tax deductible before they are recognized in the income statement. A good example is when a firm uses an accelerated depreciation method for tax purposes and the straight-line method for financial reporting. Deferred tax liabilities are also created when revenues or gains are recognized in the income statement before they are taxable. For example, a firm often recognizes the earnings of a subsidiary before any distributions (dividends) are made. Eventually, deferred tax liabilities will reverse when the taxes are paid.

MODULE QUIZ 24.5, 24.6

To best evaluate your performance, enter your quiz answers online.

1. SF Corporation has created employee goodwill by reorganizing its retirement benefit package. An independent management consultant estimated the value of the goodwill at $2 million. In addition, SF recently purchased a patent that was developed by a competitor. The patent has an estimated useful life of five years. Should SF report the goodwill and patent on its balance sheet?

	Goodwill	Patent
A.	Yes	No
B.	No	Yes
C.	No	No

2. At the beginning of the year, Parent Company purchased all 500,000 shares of Sub Incorporated for $15 per share. Just before the acquisition date, Sub's balance sheet reported net assets of $6 million. Parent determined the fair value of Sub's property and equipment was $1 million higher than reported by Sub. What amount of goodwill should Parent report as a result of its acquisition of Sub?
   A. $0.
   B. $500,000.
   C. $1,500,000.

Use the following information to answer Questions 3 and 4.

At the beginning of the year, Company P purchased 1,000 shares of Company S for $80 per share. During the year, Company S paid a dividend of $4 per share. At the end of the year, Company S's share price was $75.

3. What amount should Company P report on its balance sheet at year-end if the investment in Company S is considered a trading security, and what amount should be reported if the investment is considered an available-for-sale security?

	Trading	Available-for-sale
A.	$75,000	$75,000
B.	$75,000	$80,000
C.	$80,000	$80,000

4. What amount of investment income should Company P recognize in its income statement if the investment in Company S is considered trading, and what amount should be recognized if the investment is considered available-for-sale?

	Trading	Available-for-sale
A.	($1,000)	($1,000)
B.	($1,000)	$4,000
C.	($5,000)	$4,000

Video covering this content is available online.

MODULE 24.7: SHAREHOLDERS' EQUITY AND RATIOS

LOS 24.f: Describe the components of shareholders' equity.

CFA® Program Curriculum, Volume 3, page 192

Owners' equity is the residual interest in assets that remains after subtracting an entity's liabilities. Owners' equity includes contributed capital, preferred stock, treasury stock, retained earnings, non-controlling interest, and accumulated other comprehensive income.

Contributed capital (also known as issued capital) is the amount contributed by equity shareholders.

The **par value** of common stock is a stated or legal value. Par value has no relationship to fair value. Some common shares are even issued without a par value. When par value exists, it is reported separately in stockholders' equity. In that case,

©2018 Kaplan, Inc.

the total proceeds from issuing an equity security are the par value of the issued shares plus "additional paid-in capital."

Also disclosed is the number of common shares that are authorized, issued, and outstanding. **Authorized shares** are the number of shares that may be sold under the firm's articles of incorporation. **Issued shares** are the number of shares that have actually been sold to shareholders. The number of **outstanding shares** is equal to the issued shares less shares that have been reacquired by the firm (i.e., treasury stock).

Preferred stock has certain rights and privileges not conferred by common stock. For example, preferred shareholders are paid dividends at a specified rate, usually expressed as a percentage of par value, and have priority over the claims of the common shareholders in the event of liquidation.

Preferred stock can be classified as debt or equity, depending on the terms. For example, perpetual preferred stock that is non-redeemable is considered equity. However, preferred stock that calls for *mandatory redemption* in fixed amounts is considered a financial liability.

Noncontrolling interest (minority interest) is the minority shareholders' pro-rata share of the net assets (equity) of a subsidiary that is not wholly owned by the parent.

Retained earnings are the undistributed earnings (net income) of the firm since inception, the cumulative earnings that have not been paid out to shareholders as dividends.

Treasury stock is stock that has been reacquired by the issuing firm but not yet retired. Treasury stock reduces stockholders' equity. It does not represent an investment in the firm. Treasury stock has no voting rights and does not receive dividends.

Accumulated other comprehensive income includes all changes in stockholders' equity except for transactions recognized in the income statement (net income) and transactions with shareholders, such as issuing stock, reacquiring stock, and paying dividends.

As discussed in the topic review of Understanding Income Statements, comprehensive income aggregates net income and certain special transactions that are not reported in the income statement but that affect stockholders' equity. These special transactions comprise what is known as "other comprehensive income." Comprehensive income is equal to net income plus other comprehensive income.

PROFESSOR'S NOTE

It is easy to confuse the two terms "comprehensive income" and "accumulated other comprehensive income." Comprehensive income is an income measure over a period of time. It includes net income and other comprehensive income for the period. Accumulated other comprehensive income does not include net income but is a component of stockholders' equity at a point in time.

The **statement of changes in stockholders' equity** summarizes all transactions that increase or decrease the equity accounts for the period. The statement includes transactions with shareholders and reconciles the beginning and ending balance of each equity account, including capital stock, additional paid-in-capital, retained earnings, and accumulated other comprehensive income. In addition, the components of accumulated other comprehensive income are disclosed (i.e., unrealized gains and losses from available-for-sale securities, cash flow hedging derivatives, foreign currency translation, and adjustments for minimum pension liability).

A statement of changes in stockholders' equity is illustrated in Figure 24.2.

Figure 24.2:   Sample Statement of Changes in Stockholders' Equity

	Common Stock	Retained Earnings (in thousands)	Accumulated Other Comprehensive Income (loss)	Total
Beginning balance	$49,234	$26,664	($406)	$75,492
Net income		6,994		6,994
Net unrealized loss on available-for-sale securities			(40)	(40)
Net unrealized loss on cash flow hedges			(56)	(56)
Minimum pension liability			(26)	(26)
Cumulative translation adjustment			42	42
Comprehensive income				6,914
Issuance of common stock	1,282			1,282
Repurchases of common stock	(6,200)			(6,200)
Dividends		(2,360)		(2,360)
Ending balance	$44,316	$31,298	($486)	$75,128

LOS 24.g: Convert balance sheets to common-size balance sheets and interpret common-size balance sheets.

CFA® Program Curriculum, Volume 3, page 196

A vertical **common-size balance sheet** expresses each item of the balance sheet as a percentage of total assets. The common-size format standardizes the balance sheet by eliminating the effects of size. This allows for comparison over time (time-series analysis) and across firms (cross-sectional analysis). For example, following are the balance sheets of industry competitors East Company and West Company.

	East	West
Cash	$2,300	$1,500
Accounts receivable	3,700	1,100
Inventory	5,500	900
Current assets	11,500	3,500
Plant and equipment	32,500	11,750
Goodwill	1,750	0
Total assets	$45,750	$15,250
Current liabilities	$10,100	$1,000
Long-term debt	26,500	5,100
Total liabilities	36,600	6,100
Equity	9,150	9,150
Total liabilities & equity	$45,750	$15,250

East is obviously the larger company. By converting the balance sheets to common-size format, we can eliminate the size effect.

	East	West
Cash	5%	10%
Accounts receivable	8%	7%
Inventory	12%	6%
Current assets	25%	23%
Plant and equipment	71%	77%
Goodwill	4%	0%
Total assets	100%	100%
Current liabilities	22%	7%
Long-term debt	58%	33%
Total liabilities	80%	40%
Equity	20%	60%
Total liabilities & equity	100%	100%

East's investment in current assets of 25% of total assets is slightly higher than West's current assets of 23%. However, East's current liabilities of 22% of total assets are significantly higher than West's current liabilities of 7%. Thus, East is less liquid and may have more difficulty paying its current obligations when due. However, West's superior working capital position may not be an efficient use of resources. The investment returns on working capital are usually lower than the returns on long-term assets.

A closer look at current assets reveals that East reports less cash as a percentage of assets than West. In fact, East does not have enough cash to satisfy its current liabilities without selling more inventory and collecting receivables. East's inventories of 12% of total assets are higher than West's inventories of 6%. Carrying higher inventories may be an indication of inventory obsolescence. Further analysis of inventory is necessary.

Not only are East's current liabilities higher than West's, but East's long-term debt of 58% of total assets is much greater than West's long-term debt of 33%. Thus, East may have trouble satisfying its long-term obligations since its capital structure consists of more debt.

Common-size analysis can also be used to examine a firm's strategies. East appears to be growing through acquisitions since it is reporting goodwill. West is growing internally since no goodwill is reported. It could be that East is financing the acquisitions with debt.

LOS 24.h: Calculate and interpret liquidity and solvency ratios.

CFA® Program Curriculum, Volume 3, page 204

Balance sheet ratios compare balance sheet items only. Balance sheet ratios, along with common-size analysis, can be used to evaluate a firm's liquidity and solvency. The results should be compared over time (time-series analysis) and across firms (cross-sectional analysis).

PROFESSOR'S NOTE

Ratio analysis is covered in more detail in the topic review of Financial Analysis Techniques.

Liquidity ratios measure the firm's ability to satisfy its short-term obligations as they come due. Liquidity ratios include the current ratio, the quick ratio, and the cash ratio.

$$\text{current ratio} = \frac{\text{current assets}}{\text{current liabilities}}$$

$$\text{quick ratio} = \frac{\text{cash} + \text{marketable securities} + \text{receivables}}{\text{current liabilities}}$$

$$\text{cash ratio} = \frac{\text{cash} + \text{marketable securities}}{\text{current liabilities}}$$

Although all three ratios measure the firm's ability to pay current liabilities, they should be considered collectively. For example, assume Firm A has a higher current ratio but a lower quick ratio as compared to Firm B. This is the result of higher inventory as compared to Firm B. The quick ratio (also known as the acid-test ratio) is calculated by excluding inventory from current assets. Similar analysis can be performed by comparing the quick ratio and the cash ratio. The cash ratio is calculated by excluding inventory and receivables.

Solvency ratios measure the firm's ability to satisfy its long-term obligations. Solvency ratios include the long-term debt-to-equity ratio, the total debt-to-equity ratio, the debt ratio, and the financial leverage ratio.

$$\text{long-term debt-to-equity} = \frac{\text{long-term debt}}{\text{total equity}}$$

$$\text{total debt-to-equity} = \frac{\text{total debt}}{\text{total equity}}$$

$$\text{debt ratio} = \frac{\text{total debt}}{\text{total assets}}$$

$$\text{financial leverage} = \frac{\text{total assets}}{\text{total equity}}$$

All four ratios measure solvency but they should be considered collectively. For example, Firm A might have a higher long-term debt-to-equity ratio but a lower total debt-to-equity ratio as compared to Firm B. This is an indication that Firm B is utilizing more short-term debt to finance itself.

When calculating solvency ratios, debt is considered to be any interest bearing obligation. On the other hand, the financial leverage ratio captures the impact of all obligations, both interest bearing and non-interest bearing.

Analysts must understand the limitations of balance sheet ratio analysis:

■ Comparisons with peer firms are limited by differences in accounting standards and estimates.

■ Lack of homogeneity as many firms operate in different industries.

■ Interpretation of ratios requires significant judgment.

■ Balance sheet data are only measured at a single point in time.

 MODULE QUIZ 24.7

To best evaluate your performance, enter your quiz answers online.

1. Miller Corporation has 160,000 shares of common stock authorized. There are 92,000 shares issued and 84,000 shares outstanding. How many shares of treasury stock does Miller own?
   A. 8,000.
   B. 68,000.
   C. 76,000.

2. Selected data from Alpha Company's balance sheet at the end of the year follows:

Investment in Beta Company, at fair value	$150,000
Deferred taxes	$86,000
Common stock, $1 par value	$550,000
Preferred stock, $100 par value	$175,000
Retained earnings	$893,000
Accumulated other comprehensive income	$46,000

   The investment in Beta Company had an original cost of $120,000. Assuming the investment in Beta is classified as available-for-sale, Alpha's total owners' equity at year-end is *closest* to:
   A. $1,618,000.
   B. $1,664,000.
   C. $1,714,000.

3. A vertical common-size balance sheet expresses each category of the balance sheet as a percentage of:
   A. assets.
   B. equity.
   C. revenue.

4. Which of the following ratios are used to measure a firm's liquidity and solvency?

Liquidity	Solvency
A. Current ratio	Quick ratio
B. Debt-to-equity ratio	Financial leverage ratio
C. Cash ratio	Total debt ratio

KEY CONCEPTS

LOS 24.a

Assets are resources controlled as result of past transactions that are expected to provide future economic benefits. Liabilities are obligations as a result of past events that are expected to require an outflow of economic resources. Equity is the owners' residual interest in the assets after deducting the liabilities.

A financial statement item should be recognized if a future economic benefit to or from the firm is probable and the item's value or cost can be measured reliably.

LOS 24.b

The balance sheet can be used to assess a firm's liquidity, solvency, and ability to pay dividends to shareholders.

Balance sheet assets, liabilities, and equity should not be interpreted as market value or intrinsic value. For most firms, the balance sheet consists of a mixture of values including historical cost, amortized cost, and fair value.

Some assets and liabilities are difficult to quantify and are not reported on the balance sheet.

LOS 24.c

A classified balance sheet separately reports current and noncurrent assets and current and noncurrent liabilities. Alternatively, liquidity-based presentations, often used in the banking industry, present assets and liabilities in order of liquidity.

LOS 24.d

Current (noncurrent) assets are those expected to be used up or converted to cash in less than (more than) one year or the firm's operating cycle, whichever is greater.

Current (noncurrent) liabilities are those the firm expects to satisfy in less than (more than) one year or the firm's operating cycle, whichever is greater.

LOS 24.e

Cash equivalents are short-term, highly liquid financial assets that are readily convertible to cash. Their balance sheet values are generally close to identical using either amortized cost or fair value.

Accounts receivable are reported at net realizable value by estimating bad debt expense.

Inventories are reported at the lower of cost or net realizable value (IFRS) or the lower of cost or market (U.S. GAAP). Cost can be measured using standard costing or the retail method. Different cost flow assumptions can affect inventory values.

Property, plant, and equipment (PP&E) can be reported using the cost model or the revaluation model under IFRS. Under U.S. GAAP, only the cost model is allowed. PP&E is impaired if its carrying value exceeds the recoverable amount. Recoveries of impairment losses are allowed under IFRS but not U.S. GAAP.

Intangible assets created internally are expensed as incurred. Purchased intangibles are reported similar to PP&E. Under IFRS, research costs are expensed as incurred and development costs are capitalized. Both research and development costs are expensed under U.S. GAAP.

Goodwill is the excess of purchase price over the fair value of the identifiable net assets (assets minus liabilities) acquired in a business acquisition. Goodwill is not amortized but must be tested for impairment at least annually.

Held-to-maturity securities are reported at amortized cost. Trading securities, available-for-sale securities, and derivatives are reported at fair value. For trading securities and derivatives, unrealized gains and losses are recognized in the income statement. Unrealized gains and losses for available-for-sale securities are reported in equity (other comprehensive income).

Accounts payable are amounts owed to suppliers for goods or services purchased on credit. Accrued liabilities are expenses that have been recognized in the income statement but are not yet contractually due. Unearned revenue is cash collected in advance of providing goods and services.

Financial liabilities not issued at face value, like bonds payable, are reported at amortized cost. Held-for-trading liabilities and derivative liabilities are reported at fair value.

LOS 24.f

Owners' equity includes:

- Contributed capital—the amount paid in by common shareholders.

- Preferred stock—capital stock that has certain rights and privileges not possessed by the common shareholders. Classified as debt if mandatorily redeemable.

- Treasury stock—issued common stock that has been repurchased by the firm.

- Retained earnings—the cumulative undistributed earnings of the firm since inception.

- Noncontrolling (minority) interest—the portion of a subsidiary that is not owned by the parent.

- Accumulated other comprehensive income—includes all changes to equity from sources other than net income and transactions with shareholders.

The statement of changes in stockholders' equity summarizes the transactions during a period that increase or decrease equity, including transactions with shareholders.

LOS 24.g

A vertical common-size balance sheet expresses each item of the balance sheet as a percentage of total assets. The common-size format standardizes the balance sheet by eliminating the effects of size. This allows for comparison over time (time-series analysis) and across firms (cross-sectional analysis).

LOS 24.h

Balance sheet ratios, along with common-size analysis, can be used to evaluate a firm's liquidity and solvency. Liquidity ratios measure the firm's ability to satisfy its short-term obligations as they come due. Liquidity ratios include the current ratio, the quick ratio, and the cash ratio.

Solvency ratios measure the firm's ability to satisfy its long-term obligations. Solvency ratios include the long-term debt-to-equity ratio, the total debt-to-equity ratio, the debt ratio, and the financial leverage ratio.

ANSWER KEY FOR MODULE QUIZZES

Module Quiz 24.1, 24.2

1. **C** An asset is a future economic benefit obtained or controlled as a result of past transactions. Some assets are intangible (e.g., goodwill), and others may be donated. (Module 24.1, LOS 24.a)

2. **C** The balance sheet lists the firm's assets, liabilities, and equity. The capital structure is measured by the mix of debt and equity used to finance the business. (Module 24.2, LOS 24.b)

3. **A** A classified balance sheet groups together similar items (e.g., current and noncurrent assets and liabilities) to arrive at significant subtotals. (Module 24.2, LOS 24.c)

Module Quiz 24.3, 24.4

1. **C** Estimated income taxes for the current year are likely reported as a current liability. To recognize the warranty expense, it must be probable, not just possible. Future operating lease payments are not reported on the balance sheet. (Module 24.3, LOS 24.d)

2. **C** The ticket revenue should not be recognized until it is earned. Even though the tickets are nonrefundable, the seller is still obligated to hold the event. (Module 24.3, LOS 24.e)

3. **A** Inventories are required to be valued at the lower of cost or net realizable value (or "market" under U.S. GAAP). FIFO and average cost are two of the inventory cost flow assumptions among which a firm has a choice. (Module 24.3, LOS 24.e)

4. **C** IFRS permits either the cost model or the revaluation model for property, plant, and equipment. (Module 24.4, LOS 24.d, 24.e)

Module Quiz 24.5, 24.6

1. **B** Goodwill developed internally is expensed as incurred. The purchased patent is reported on the balance sheet. (Module 24.5, LOS 24.e)

2. **B** Purchase price of $7,500,000 [$15 per share × 500,000 shares] – fair value of net assets of $7,000,000 [$6,000,000 book value + $1,000,000 increase in property and equipment] = goodwill of $500,000. (Module 24.5, LOS 24.e)

3. **A** Both trading securities and available-for-sale securities are reported on the balance sheet at their fair values. At year-end, the fair value is $75,000 [$75 per share × 1,000 shares]. (Module 24.6, LOS 24.e)

4. **B** A loss of $1,000 is recognized if the securities are considered trading securities ($4 dividend × $1,000 shares) – ($5 unrealized loss × 1,000 shares). Income is $4,000 if the investment in Company S is considered available-for-sale [$4 dividend × $1,000]. (Module 24.6, LOS 24.e)

Module Quiz 24.7

1. **A** The difference between the issued shares and the outstanding shares is the treasury shares. (LOS 24.f)

2. **B** Total stockholders' equity consists of common stock of $550,000, preferred stock of $175,000, retained earnings of $893,000, and accumulated other comprehensive income of $46,000, for a total of $1,664,000. The $30,000 unrealized gain from the investment in Beta is already included in accumulated other comprehensive income. (LOS 24.f)

3. **A** Each category of the balance sheet is expressed as a percentage of total assets. (LOS 24.g)

4. **C** The current ratio, quick ratio, and cash ratio measure liquidity. Debt-to-equity, the total debt ratio, and the financial leverage ratio measure solvency. (LOS 24.h)

The following is a review of the Financial Reporting and Analysis (2) principles designed to address the learning outcome statements set forth by CFA Institute. Cross-Reference to CFA Institute Assigned Reading #25.

READING
25

Understanding Cash Flow Statements

EXAM FOCUS

This topic review covers the third important required financial statement: the statement of cash flows. Since the income statement is based on the accrual method, net income may not represent cash generated from operations. A company may be generating positive and growing net income but may be headed for insolvency because insufficient cash is being generated from operating activities. Constructing a statement of cash flows, by either the direct or indirect method, is therefore very important in an analysis of a firm's activities and prospects. Make sure you understand the preparation of a statement of cash flows by either method, the classification of various cash flows as operating, financing, or investing cash flows, and the key differences in these classifications between U.S. GAAP and international accounting standards.

MODULE 25.1: CASH FLOW INTRODUCTION

Video covering this content is available online.

The **cash flow statement** provides information beyond that available from the income statement, which is based on accrual, rather than cash, accounting. The cash flow statement provides the following:

- Information about a company's cash receipts and cash payments during an accounting period.

- Information about a company's operating, investing, and financing activities.

- An understanding of the impact of accrual accounting events on cash flows.

The cash flow statement provides information to assess the firm's liquidity, solvency, and financial flexibility. An analyst can use the statement of cash flows to determine whether:

- Regular operations generate enough cash to sustain the business.

- Enough cash is generated to pay off existing debts as they mature.

■ The firm is likely to need additional financing.

■ Unexpected obligations can be met.

■ The firm can take advantage of new business opportunities as they arise.

LOS 25.a: Compare cash flows from operating, investing, and financing activities and classify cash flow items as relating to one of those three categories given a description of the items.

CFA® Program Curriculum, Volume 3, page 219

Items on the cash flow statement come from two sources: (1) income statement items and (2) changes in balance sheet accounts. A firm's cash receipts and payments are classified on the cash flow statement as either operating, investing, or financing activities.

Cash flow from operating activities (CFO), sometimes referred to as "cash flow from operations" or "operating cash flow," consists of the inflows and outflows of cash resulting from transactions that affect a firm's net income.

Cash flow from investing activities (CFI) consists of the inflows and outflows of cash resulting from the acquisition or disposal of long-term assets and certain investments.

Cash flow from financing activities (CFF) consists of the inflows and outflows of cash resulting from transactions affecting a firm's capital structure.

Examples of each cash flow classification, in accordance with U.S. GAAP, are presented in Figure 25.1.

Note that the acquisition of debt and equity investments (other than trading securities) and loans made to others are reported as investing activities; however, the income from these investments (interest and dividends received) is reported as an operating activity. Also, note that principal amounts borrowed from others are reported as financing activities; however, the interest paid is reported as an operating activity. Finally, note that dividends paid to the firm's shareholders are financing activities.

PROFESSOR'S NOTE

Don't confuse dividends received and dividends paid. Under U.S. GAAP, dividends received are operating cash flows and dividends paid are financing cash flows.

Figure 25.1: U.S. GAAP Cash Flow Classifications

Operating Activities	
Inflows	**Outflows**
Cash collected from customers	Cash paid to employees and suppliers
Interest and dividends received	Cash paid for other expenses
Sale proceeds from trading securities	Acquisition of trading securities
	Interest paid on debt or leases
	Taxes paid

Investing Activities	
Inflows	**Outflows**
Sale proceeds from fixed assets	Acquisition of fixed assets
Sale proceeds from debt and equity investments	Acquisition of debt and equity investments
Principal received from loans made to others	Loans made to others

Financing Activities	
Inflows	**Outflows**
Principal amounts of debt issued	Principal paid on debt or leases
Proceeds from issuing stock	Payments to reacquire stock
	Dividends paid to shareholders

LOS 25.b: Describe how non-cash investing and financing activities are reported.

CFA® Program Curriculum, Volume 3, page 221

Noncash investing and financing activities are not reported in the cash flow statement since they do not result in inflows or outflows of cash.

For example, if a firm acquires real estate with financing provided by the seller, the firm has made an investing and financing decision. This transaction is the equivalent of borrowing the purchase price. However, since no cash is involved in the transaction, it is not reported as an investing and financing activity in the cash flow statement.

Another example of a noncash transaction is an exchange of debt for equity. Such an exchange results in a reduction of debt and an increase in equity. However, since no cash is involved in the transaction, it is not reported as a financing activity in the cash flow statement.

Noncash transactions must be disclosed in either a footnote or supplemental schedule to the cash flow statement. Analysts should be aware of the firm's noncash transactions, incorporate them into analysis of past and current performance, and include their effects in estimating future cash flows.

LOS 25.c: Contrast cash flow statements prepared under International Financial Reporting Standards (IFRS) and US generally accepted accounting principles (US GAAP).

CFA® Program Curriculum, Volume 3, page 221

Recall from Figure 25.1 that under U.S. GAAP, dividends paid to the firm's shareholders are reported as financing activities while interest paid is reported in operating activities. Interest received and dividends received from investments are also reported as operating activities.

International Financial Reporting Standards (IFRS) allow more flexibility in the classification of cash flows. Under IFRS, interest and dividends received may be classified as either operating *or* investing activities. Dividends paid to the company's shareholders and interest paid on the company's debt may be classified as either operating *or* financing activities.

Another important difference relates to income taxes paid. Under U.S. GAAP, all taxes paid are reported as operating activities, even taxes related to investing and financing transactions. Under IFRS, income taxes are also reported as operating activities unless the expense is associated with an investing or financing transaction.

For example, consider a company that sells land that was held for investment for $1 million. Income taxes on the sale total $160,000. Under U.S. GAAP, the firm reports an inflow of cash from investing activities of $1 million and an outflow of cash from operating activities of $160,000. Under IFRS, the firm can report a net inflow of $840,000 from investing activities.

LOS 25.d: Distinguish between the direct and indirect methods of presenting cash from operating activities and describe arguments in favor of each method.

CFA® Program Curriculum, Volume 3, page 222

There are two methods of presenting the cash flow statement: the direct method and the indirect method. Both methods are permitted under U.S. GAAP and IFRS. The use of the direct method, however, is encouraged by both standard setters. Regrettably, most firms use the indirect method. The difference between the two methods relates to the presentation of cash flow from operating activities. The presentation of cash flows from investing activities and financing activities is exactly the same under both methods.

Direct Method

Under the **direct method**, each line item of the accrual-based income statement is converted into cash receipts or cash payments. Recall that under the accrual method of accounting, the timing of revenue and expense recognition may differ from the timing of the related cash flows. Under cash-basis accounting, revenue and expense recognition occur when cash is received or paid. Simply stated, the direct method converts an accrual-basis income statement into a cash-basis income statement.

Figure 25.2 contains an example of a presentation of operating cash flow for Seagraves Supply Company using the direct method.

Figure 25.2: Direct Method of Presenting Operating Cash Flow

Seagraves Supply Company Operating Cash Flow – Direct Method For the year ended December 31, 20X7	
Cash collections from customers	$429,980
Cash paid to suppliers	(265,866)
Cash paid for operating expenses	(124,784)
Cash paid for interest	(4,326)
Cash paid for taxes	(14,956)
Operating cash flow	$20,048

Notice the similarities of the direct method cash flow presentation and an income statement. The direct method begins with cash inflows from customers and then deducts cash outflows for purchases, operating expenses, interest, and taxes.

Indirect Method

Under the **indirect method**, net income is converted to operating cash flow by making adjustments for transactions that affect net income but are not cash transactions. These adjustments include eliminating noncash expenses (e.g., depreciation and amortization), nonoperating items (e.g., gains and losses), and changes in balance sheet accounts resulting from accrual accounting events.

Figure 25.3 contains an example of a presentation of operating cash flow for Seagraves Supply Company under the indirect method.

Figure 25.3: Indirect Method of Presenting Operating Cash Flow

Seagraves Supply Company Operating Cash Flow – Indirect Method For the year ended December 31, 20X7	
Net income	$18,788
Adjustments to reconcile net income to cash flow provided by operating activities:	
Depreciation and amortization	7,996
Deferred income taxes	416
Increase in accounts receivable	(1,220)
Increase in inventory	(20,544)
Decrease in prepaid expenses	494
Increase in accounts payable	13,406
Increase in accrued liabilities	712
Operating cash flow	$20,048

Notice that under the indirect method, the starting point is net income, the "bottom line" of the income statement. Under the direct method, the starting point is the top of the income statement, revenues, adjusted to show cash received from customers. Total cash flow from operating activities is exactly the same under both methods, only the presentation methods differ.

Arguments in Favor of Each Method

The primary advantage of the direct method is that it presents the firm's operating cash receipts and payments, while the indirect method only presents the net result of these receipts and payments. Therefore, the direct method provides more information than the indirect method. This knowledge of past receipts and payments is useful in estimating future operating cash flows.

The main advantage of the indirect method is that it focuses on the difference between net income and operating cash flow. This provides a useful link to the income statement when forecasting future operating cash flow. Analysts forecast net income and then derive operating cash flow by adjusting net income for the differences between accrual accounting and the cash basis of accounting.

Disclosure Requirements

Under U.S. GAAP, a direct method presentation must also disclose the adjustments necessary to reconcile net income to cash flow from operating activities. This disclosure is the same information that is presented in an indirect method cash flow statement. This reconciliation is not required under IFRS.

Under IFRS, payments for interest and taxes must be disclosed separately in the cash flow statement under either method (direct or indirect). Under U.S. GAAP, payments for interest and taxes can be reported in the cash flow statement or disclosed in the footnotes.

LOS 25.e: Describe how the cash flow statement is linked to the income statement and the balance sheet.

CFA® Program Curriculum, Volume 3, page 232

The cash flow statement reconciles the beginning and ending balances of cash over an accounting period. The change in cash is a result of the firm's operating, investing, and financing activities as follows:

> Operating cash flow
> + Investing cash flow
> + Financing cash flow
> = Change in cash balance
> + Beginning cash balance
> = Ending cash balance

With a few exceptions, operating activities relate to the firm's current assets and current liabilities. Investing activities typically relate to the firm's noncurrent assets, and financing activities typically relate to the firm's noncurrent liabilities and equity.

Transactions for which the timing of revenue or expense recognition differs from the receipt or payment of cash are reflected in changes in balance sheet accounts. For example, when revenues (sales) exceed cash collections, the firm has sold items on credit and accounts receivable (an asset) increase. The opposite occurs when customers repay more on their outstanding accounts than the firm extends in new credit: cash collections exceed revenues and accounts receivable decrease. When purchases from suppliers exceed cash payments, accounts payable (a liability) increase. When cash payments exceed purchases, payables decrease.

It is helpful to understand how transactions affect each balance sheet account. For example, accounts receivable are increased by sales and decreased by cash collections. We can summarize this relationship as follows:

    Beginning accounts receivable

  + Sales

  – Cash collections

  = Ending accounts receivable

Knowing three of the four variables, we can solve for the fourth. For example, if beginning accounts receivable are €10,000, ending accounts receivable are €15,000, and sales are €68,000, then cash collections must equal €63,000.

Understanding these interrelationships is not only useful in preparing the cash flow statement, but is also helpful in uncovering accounting shenanigans.

MODULE QUIZ 25.1

To best evaluate your performance, enter your quiz answers online.

1. Which of the following items is *least likely* considered a cash flow from financing activity under U.S. GAAP?
   A. Receipt of cash from the sale of bonds.
   B. Payment of cash for dividends.
   C. Payment of interest on debt.

2. Which of the following would be *least likely* to cause a change in investing cash flow?
   A. The sale of a division of the company.
   B. The purchase of new machinery.
   C. An increase in depreciation expense.

3. Which of the following is *least likely* a change in cash flow from operations under U.S. GAAP?
   A. A decrease in notes payable.
   B. An increase in interest expense.
   C. An increase in accounts payable.

4. Sales of inventory would be classified as:
   A. operating cash flow.
   B. investing cash flow.
   C. financing cash flow.

5. Issuing bonds would be classified as:
   A. investing cash flow.
   B. financing cash flow.
   C. no cash flow impact.

6. Sale of land would be classified as:
   A. operating cash flow.
   B. investing cash flow.
   C. financing cash flow.

7. The write-off of obsolete equipment would be classified as:
   A. operating cash flow.
   B. investing cash flow.
   C. no cash flow impact.

8. Under IFRS, interest expense would be classified as:
   A. either operating cash flow or financing cash flow.
   B. operating cash flow only.
   C. financing cash flow only.

9. Under U.S. GAAP, dividends received from investments would be classified as:
   A. operating cash flow.
   B. investing cash flow.
   C. financing cash flow.

10. Torval, Inc. retires debt securities by issuing equity securities. This is considered a:
    A. cash flow from investing.
    B. cash flow from financing.
    C. noncash transaction.

11. Where are dividends paid to shareholders reported in the cash flow statement under U.S. GAAP and IFRS?

U.S. GAAP	IRFS
A. Operating or financing activities	Operating or financing activities
B. Financing activities	Operating or financing activities
C. Operating activities	Financing activities

12. From an analyst's perspective, an advantage of the indirect method for presenting operating cash flow is that the indirect method:
    A. shows operating cash received and paid.
    B. provides more information than the direct method.
    C. shows the difference between net income and operating cash flow.

13. Which balance sheet items are *most likely* to be linked to cash flows from financing?
    A. Long-lived assets.
    B. Current assets and liabilities.
    C. Long-term liabilities and equity.

MODULE 25.2: THE DIRECT AND INDIRECT METHODS

Video covering this content is available online.

LOS 25.f: Describe the steps in the preparation of direct and indirect cash flow statements, including how cash flows can be computed using income statement and balance sheet data.

CFA® Program Curriculum, Volume 3, page 233

PROFESSOR'S NOTE

Throughout the discussion of the direct and indirect methods, remember the following points:

■ CFO is calculated differently, but the result is the same under both methods.

■ The calculation of CFI and CFF is identical under both methods.

■ There is an inverse relationship between changes in assets and changes in cash flows. In other words, an increase in an asset account is a use of cash, and a decrease in an asset account is a source of cash.

■ There is a direct relationship between changes in liabilities and changes in cash flow. In other words, an increase in a liability account is a source of cash, and a decrease in a liability is a use of cash.

■ Sources of cash are positive numbers (cash inflows) and uses of cash are negative numbers (cash outflows).

Direct Method

The direct method of presenting a firm's statement of cash flows shows only cash payments and cash receipts over the period. The sum of these inflows and outflows is the company's CFO. The direct method gives the analyst more information than the indirect method. The analyst can see the actual amounts that went to each use of cash and that were received from each source of cash. This information can help the analyst to better understand the firm's performance over time and to forecast future cash flows.

The following are common components of cash flow that appear on a statement of cash flow presented under the direct method:

■ Cash collected from customers, typically the main component of CFO.

■ Cash used in the production of goods and services (cash inputs).

■ Cash operating expenses.

■ Cash paid for interest.

■ Cash paid for taxes.

PROFESSOR'S NOTE

A common "trick" in direct method questions is to provide information on depreciation expense along with other operating cash flow components. When using the direct method, ignore depreciation expense—it's a noncash charge. We'll see later that we do consider depreciation expense in indirect method computations, but we do this solely because depreciation expense and other noncash expenses have been subtracted in calculating net income (our starting point) and need to be added back to get cash flow.

Investing cash flows (CFI) are calculated by examining the change in the gross asset accounts that result from investing activities, such as property, plant, and equipment, intangible assets, and investment securities. Related accumulated depreciation or amortization accounts are ignored since they do not represent cash expenses.

PROFESSOR'S NOTE

In this context, "gross" simply means an amount that is presented on the balance sheet before deducting any accumulated depreciation or amortization.

When calculating cash paid for a new asset, it is necessary to determine whether old assets were sold. If assets were sold during the period, you must use the following formula:

$$\text{cash paid for new asset} = \text{ending gross assets} + \text{gross cost of old assets sold} - \text{beginning gross assets}$$

PROFESSOR'S NOTE

It may be easier to think in terms of the account reconciliation format discussed earlier. That is, beginning gross assets + cash paid for new assets − gross cost of assets sold = ending gross assets. Given three of the variables, simply solve for the fourth.

When calculating the cash flow from an asset that has been sold, it is necessary to consider any gain or loss from the sale using the following formula:

$$\text{cash from asset sold} = \text{book value of the asset} + \text{gain (or} - \text{loss) on sale}$$

Financing cash flows (CFF) are determined by measuring the cash flows occurring between the firm and its suppliers of capital. Cash flows between the firm and its creditors result from new borrowings (positive CFF) and debt principal repayments (negative CFF). Note that interest paid is technically a cash flow to creditors, but it is included in CFO under U.S. GAAP. Cash flows between the firm and its shareholders occur when equity is issued, shares are repurchased, or dividends are paid. CFF is the sum of these two measures:

$$\text{net cash flows from creditors} = \text{new borrowings} - \text{principal amounts repaid}$$

$$\text{net cash flows from shareholders} = \text{new equity issued} - \text{share repurchases} - \text{cash dividends paid}$$

Cash dividends paid can be calculated from dividends declared and any changes in dividends payable.

Finally, total cash flow is equal to the sum of CFO, CFI, and CFF. If calculated correctly, the total cash flow will equal the change in cash from one balance sheet to the next.

Indirect Method

Cash flow from operations is presented differently under the indirect method, but the amount of CFO is the same under either method. Cash flow from financing and cash flow from investing are presented in the same way on cash flow statements prepared under both the direct and indirect methods of presenting the statement of cash flows.

Under the indirect method of presenting CFO, we begin with net income and adjust it for differences between accounting items and actual cash receipts and cash disbursements. Depreciation, for example, is deducted in calculating net income, but requires no cash outlay in the current period. Therefore, we must add depreciation (and amortization) to net income for the period in calculating CFO.

Another adjustment to net income on an indirect statement of cash flows is to subtract gains on the disposal of assets. Proceeds from the sale of fixed assets are an investing cash flow. Since gains are a portion of such proceeds, we need to subtract them from net income in calculating CFO under the indirect method. Conversely, a loss would be added back to net income in calculating CFO under the indirect method.

Under the indirect method, we also need to adjust net income for change in balance sheet accounts. If, for example, accounts receivable went up during the period, we know that sales during the period were greater than the cash collected from customers. Since sales were used to calculate net income under the accrual method, we need to reduce net income to reflect the fact that credit sales, rather than cash collected were used in calculating net income.

A change in accounts payable indicates a difference between purchases and the amount paid to suppliers. An increase in accounts payable, for example, results when purchases are greater than cash paid to suppliers. Since purchases were subtracted in calculating net income, we need to add any increase in accounts payable to net income so that CFO reflects the actual cash disbursements for purchases (rather than total purchases).

The steps in calculating CFO under the indirect method can be summarized as follows:

Step 1: Begin with net income.

Step 2: Add or subtract changes to balance sheet operating accounts as follows:

- Increases in the operating asset accounts (uses of cash) are subtracted, while decreases (sources of cash) are added.

- Increases in the operating liability accounts (sources of cash) are added, while decreases (uses of cash) are subtracted.

Step 3: Add back all noncash charges to income (such as depreciation and amortization) and subtract all noncash components of revenue.

Step 4: Subtract gains or add losses that resulted from financing or investing cash flows (such as gains from sale of land).

EXAMPLE: Statement of cash flows using the indirect method

Use the following balance sheet and income statement to prepare a statement of cash flows under the indirect method.

Income Statement for 20X7	
Sales	$100,000
Expense	
Cost of goods sold	40,000
Wages	5,000
Depreciation	7,000
Interest	1,000
Total expenses	$53,000
Income from continuing operations	$47,000
Gain from sale of land	10,000
Pretax income	57,000
Provision for taxes	20,000
Net income	$37,000
Common dividends declared	$8,500

Balance Sheets for 20X7 and 20X6		
	20X7	**20X6**
Assets		
Current assets		
Cash	$33,000	$9,500
Accounts receivable	10,000	9,000
Inventory	5,000	7,000
Noncurrent assets		
Land	$35,000	$40,000
Gross plant and equipment	85,000	60,000
Less: Accumulated depreciation	(16,000)	(9,000)
Net plant and equipment	$69,000	$51,500
Goodwill	10,000	10,000
Total assets	$162,000	$126,500

Liabilities

Current liabilities

Accounts payable	$9,000	$5,000
Wages payable	4,500	8,000
Interest payable	3,500	3,000
Taxes payable	5,000	4,000
Dividends payable	6,000	1,000
Total current liabilities	28,000	21,000
Noncurrent liabilities		
Bonds	$15,000	$10,000
Deferred tax liability	20,000	15,000
Total liabilities	$63,000	$46,000
Stockholders' equity		
Common stock	$40,000	$50,000
Retained earnings	59,000	30,500
Total equity	$99,000	$80,000
Total liabilities and stockholders' equity	$162,000	$126,500

Any discrepancies between the changes in accounts reported on the balance sheet and those reported in the statement of cash flows are typically due to business combinations and changes in exchange rates.

Answer:

Operating cash flow:

Step 1: Start with net income of $37,000.

Step 2: Subtract gain from sale of land of $10,000.

Step 3: Add back noncash charges of depreciation of $7,000.

Step 4: Subtract increases in receivables and inventories and add increases of payables and deferred taxes.

Net income	$37,000
Gain from sale of land	(10,000)
Depreciation	7,000
Subtotal	$34,000
Changes in operating accounts	
Increase in receivables	($1,000)
Decrease in inventories	2,000
Increase in accounts payable	4,000
Decrease in wages payable	(3,500)
Increase in interest payable	500
Increase in taxes payable	1,000
Increase in deferred taxes	5,000
Cash flow from operations	$42,000

Investing cash flow:

In this example, we have two components of investing cash flow: the sale of land and the change in gross plant and equipment (P&E).

cash from sale of land = decrease in asset + gain on sale = $5,000 + $10,000 = $15,000 (source)

> beginning land + land purchased − gross cost of land sold = ending land = $40,000 + $0 − $5,000 = $35,000

Note: If the land had been sold at a loss, we would have subtracted the loss amount from the decrease in land.

P&E purchased = ending gross P&E + gross cost of P&E sold − beginning gross P&E = $85,000 + $0 − $60,000 = $25,000 (use)

> beginning gross P&E + P&E purchased − gross cost of P&E sold = ending P&E = $60,000 + $25,000 − $0 = $85,000

Cash from sale of land	$15,000
Purchase of plant and equipment	(25,000)
Cash flow from investments	($10,000)

Financing cash flow:

cash from bond issue = ending bonds payable + bonds repaid − beginning bonds payable = $15,000 + $0 − $10,000 = $5,000 (source)

> beginning bonds payable + bonds issued − bonds repaid = ending bonds payable = $10,000 + $5,000 − $0 = $15,000

cash to reacquire stock = beginning common stock + stock issued − ending common stock = $50,000 + $0 − $40,000 = $10,000 (use, or a net share repurchase of $10,000)

> beginning common stock + stock issued − stock reacquired = ending common stock = $50,000 + $0 − $10,000 = $40,000

cash dividends = −dividend declared + increase in dividends payable = −$8,500* + $5,000 = −$3,500 (use)

> beginning dividends payable + dividends declared − dividends paid = ending dividends payable = $1,000 + $8,500 − $3,500 = $6,000

Note: If the dividend declared amount is not provided, you can calculate the amount as follows: dividends declared = beginning retained earnings + net income − ending retained earnings. Here, $30,500 + $37,000 − $59,000 = $8,500.

Sale of bonds	$5,000
Repurchase of stock	(10,000)
Cash dividends	(3,500)
Cash flow from financing	($8,500)

Total cash flow:

Cash flow from operations	$42,000
Cash flow from investments	(10,000)
Cash flow from financing	(8,500)
Total cash flow	$23,500

The total cash flow of $23,500 is equal to the increase in the cash account. The difference between beginning cash and ending cash should be used as a check figure to ensure that the total cash flow calculation is correct.

Both IFRS and U.S. GAAP encourage the use of a statement of cash flows in the direct format. Under U.S. GAAP, a statement of cash flows under the direct method must include footnote disclosure of the indirect method. Most companies however, report cash flows using the indirect method, which requires no additional disclosure. The next LOS illustrates the method an analyst will use to create a statement of cash flows in the direct method format when the company reports using the indirect method.

MODULE QUIZ 25.2

To best evaluate your performance, enter your quiz answers online.

1. Using the following information, what is the firm's cash flow from operations?

Net income	$120
Decrease in accounts receivable	20
Depreciation	25
Increase in inventory	10
Increase in accounts payable	7
Decrease in wages payable	5
Increase in deferred tax liabilities	15
Profit from the sale of land	2

    A. $158.
    B. $170.
    C. $174.

Assuming U.S. GAAP, use the following data to answer Questions 2 through 4.

Net income	$45
Depreciation	75
Taxes paid	25
Interest paid	5
Dividends paid	10
Cash received from sale of company building	40
Issuance of preferred stock	35
Repurchase of common stock	30
Purchase of machinery	20
Issuance of bonds	50
Debt retired through issuance of common stock	45
Paid off long-term bank borrowings	15
Profit on sale of building	20

2. Cash flow from operations is:
   A. $70.
   B. $100.
   C. $120.

3. Cash flow from investing activities is:
   A. –$30.
   B. $20.
   C. $50.

4. Cash flow from financing activities is:
   A. $30.
   B. $55.
   C. $75.

5. Given the following:

Sales	$1,500
Increase in inventory	100
Depreciation	150
Increase in accounts receivable	50
Decrease in accounts payable	70
After-tax profit margin	25%
Gain on sale of machinery	$30

   Cash flow from operations is:
   A. $115.
   B. $275.
   C. $375.

6. Net income for Monique, Inc. for the year ended December 31, 20X7 was $78,000. Its accounts receivable balance at December 31, 20X7 was $121,000, and this balance was $69,000 at December 31, 20X6. The accounts payable balance at December 31, 20X7 was $72,000 and was $43,000 at December 31, 20X6. Depreciation for 20X7 was $12,000, and there was an unrealized gain of $15,000 included in 20X7 income from the change in value of trading securities. Which of the following amounts represents Monique's cash flow from operations for 20X7?
   A. $52,000.
   B. $67,000.
   C. $82,000.

7. Martin, Inc. had the following transactions during 20X7:
   ■ Purchased new fixed assets for $75,000.

   ■ Converted $70,000 worth of preferred shares to common shares.

   ■ Received cash dividends of $12,000. Paid cash dividends of $21,000.

   ■ Repaid mortgage principal of $17,000.

   Assuming Martin follows U.S. GAAP, which of the following amounts represents Martin's cash flows from investing and cash flows from financing in 20X7, respectively?

	Cash flows from investing	Cash flows from financing
A.	($5,000)	($21,000)
B.	($75,000)	($21,000)
C.	($75,000)	($38,000)

MODULE 25.3: CONVERTING DIRECT TO INDIRECT

LOS 25.g: Convert cash flows from the indirect to direct method.

Video covering this content is available online.

CFA® Program Curriculum, Volume 3, page 245

The only difference between the indirect and direct methods of presentation is in the cash flow from operations (CFO) section. CFO under the direct method can be computed using a combination of the income statement and a statement of cash flows prepared under the indirect method.

There are two major sections in CFO under the direct method: cash inflows (receipts) and cash outflows (payments). We will illustrate the conversion process using some frequently used accounts. Please note that the following list is for illustrative purposes only and is far from all-inclusive of what may be encountered in practice. The general principle here is to adjust each income statement item for its corresponding balance sheet accounts and to eliminate noncash and nonoperating transactions.

Cash collections from customers:

1. Begin with net sales from the income statement.

2. Subtract (add) any increase (decrease) in the accounts receivable balance as reported in the indirect method. If the company has sold more on credit than has been collected from customers, accounts receivable will increase and cash collections will be less than net sales.

3. Add (subtract) an increase (decrease) in unearned revenue. Unearned revenue includes cash advances from customers. Cash received from customers when the goods or services have yet to be delivered is not included in net sales, so the advances must be added to net sales in order to calculate cash collections.

Cash payments to suppliers:

1. Begin with cost of goods sold (COGS) as reported in the income statement.

2. If depreciation and/or amortization have been included in COGS (they increase COGS), these noncash expenses must be added back when computing the cash paid to suppliers.

3. Reduce (increase) COGS by any increase (decrease) in the accounts payable balance as reported in the indirect method. If payables have increased, then more was spent on credit purchases during the period than was paid on existing payables, so cash payments are reduced by the amount of the increase in payables.

4. Add (subtract) any increase (decrease) in the inventory balance as disclosed in the indirect method. Increases in inventory are not included in COGS for the period but still represent the purchase of inputs, so they increase cash paid to suppliers.

5. Subtract an inventory write-off that occurred during the period. An inventory write-off, as a result of applying the lower of cost or market rule, will reduce ending inventory and increase COGS for the period. However, no cash flow is associated with the write-off.

Other items in a direct method cash flow statement follow the same principles. Cash taxes paid, for example, can be derived by starting with income tax expense on the income statement. Adjustment must be made for changes in related balance sheet accounts (deferred tax assets and liabilities, and income taxes payable).

Cash operating expense is equal to selling, general, and administrative expense (SG&A) from the income statement, increased (decreased) for any increase (decrease) in prepaid expenses. Any increase in prepaid expenses is a cash outflow that is not included in SG&A for the current period.

> **EXAMPLE: Direct method for computing CFO**
>
> Prepare a cash flow statement using the direct method, based on the indirect statement of cash flows, balance sheet, and income statement from the previous example.
>
> **Answer:**
>
> **PROFESSOR'S NOTE**
>
> There are many ways to think about these calculations and lots of sources and uses and pluses and minuses to keep track of. It's easier if you use a "+" sign for net sales and a "−" sign for cost of goods sold and other cash expenses used as the starting points. Doing so will

allow you to consistently follow the rule that an increase in assets or decrease in liabilities is a use of cash and a decrease in assets or an increase in liabilities is a source. We'll use this approach in the answer to the example. Remember, sources are always + and uses are always –.

The calculations that follow include a reconciliation of each account, analyzing the transactions that increase and decrease the account for the period. As previously discussed, this reconciliation is useful in understanding the interrelationships between the balance sheet, income statement, and cash flow statement.

Cash from operations:

Keep track of the balance sheet items used to calculate CFO by marking them off the balance sheet. They will not be needed again when determining CFI and CFF.

cash collections = sales – increase in accounts receivable = $100,000 – $1,000 = $99,000

> beginning receivables + sales – cash collections = ending receivables = $9,000 + $100,000 – $99,000 = $10,000

cash paid to suppliers = –COGS + decrease in inventory + increase in accounts payable = –$40,000 + $2,000 + $4,000 = –$34,000

> beginning inventory + purchases – COGS = ending inventory = $7,000 + $38,000 (not provided) – $40,000 = $5,000

> beginning accounts payable + purchases – cash paid to suppliers = ending accounts payable = $5,000 + $38,000 (not provided) – $34,000 = $9,000

cash wages = –wages – decrease in wages payable = –$5,000 – $3,500 = –$8,500

> beginning wages payable + wages expense – wages paid = ending wages payable = $8,000 + $5,000 – $8,500 = $4,500

cash interest = –interest expense + increase in interest payable = –$1,000 + $500 = –$500

> beginning interest payable + interest expense – interest paid = ending interest payable = $3,000 + $1,000 – $500 = $3,500

cash taxes = –tax expense + increase in taxes payable + increase in deferred tax liability = –$20,000 + $1,000 + $5,000 = –$14,000

> beginning taxes payable + beginning deferred tax liability + tax expense – taxes paid = ending taxes payable + ending deferred tax liability = $4,000 + $15,000 + $20,000 – $14,000 = $5,000 + $20,000

Cash collections	$99,000
Cash to suppliers	(34,000)
Cash wages	(8,500)
Cash interest	(500)
Cash taxes	(14,000)
Cash flow from operations	$42,000

LOS 25.h: Analyze and interpret both reported and common-size cash flow statements.

CFA® Program Curriculum, Volume 3, page 246

Major Sources and Uses of Cash

Cash flow analysis begins with an evaluation of the firm's sources and uses of cash from operating, investing, and financing activities. Sources and uses of cash change as the firm moves through its life cycle. For example, when a firm is in the early stages of growth, it may experience negative operating cash flow as it uses cash to finance increases in inventory and receivables. This negative operating cash flow is usually financed externally by issuing debt or equity securities. These sources of financing are not sustainable. Eventually, the firm must begin generating positive operating cash flow or the sources of external capital may no longer be available. Over the long term, successful firms must be able to generate operating cash flows that exceed capital expenditures and provide a return to debt and equity holders.

Operating Cash Flow

An analyst should identify the major determinants of operating cash flow. Positive operating cash flow can be generated by the firm's earnings-related activities. However, positive operating cash flow can also be generated by decreasing noncash working capital, such as liquidating inventory and receivables or increasing payables. Decreasing noncash working capital is not sustainable, since inventories and receivables cannot fall below zero and creditors will not extend credit indefinitely unless payments are made when due.

Operating cash flow also provides a check of the quality of a firm's earnings. A stable relationship of operating cash flow and net income is an indication of quality earnings. (This relationship can also be affected by the business cycle and the firm's life cycle.) Earnings that significantly exceed operating cash flow may be an indication of aggressive (or even improper) accounting choices such as recognizing revenues too soon or delaying the recognition of expenses. The variability of net income and operating cash flow should also be considered.

Investing Cash Flow

The sources and uses of cash from investing activities should be examined. Increasing capital expenditures, a use of cash, is usually an indication of growth. Conversely, a firm may reduce capital expenditures or even sell capital assets in order to save or generate cash. This may result in higher cash outflows in the future as older assets are replaced or growth resumes. As mentioned previously, generating operating cash flow that exceeds capital expenditures is a desirable trait.

Financing Cash Flow

The financing activities section of the cash flow statement reveals information about whether the firm is generating cash flow by issuing debt or equity. It also provides information about whether the firm is using cash to repay debt, reacquire stock, or pay dividends. For example, an analyst would certainly want to know if a firm issued debt and used the proceeds to reacquire stock or pay dividends to shareholders.

Common-Size Cash Flow Statement

Like the income statement and balance sheet, common-size analysis can be used to analyze the cash flow statement.

The cash flow statement can be converted to common-size format by expressing each line item as a percentage of revenue. Alternatively, each inflow of cash can be expressed as a percentage of total cash inflows, and each outflow of cash can be expressed as a percentage of total cash outflows.

A revenue based common-size cash flow statement is useful in identifying trends and forecasting future cash flow. Since each line item of the cash flow statement is stated in terms of revenue, once future revenue is forecast, cash flows can be estimated for those items that are tied to revenue.

> **EXAMPLE:** Common-size cash flow statement analysis
>
> Triple Y Corporation's common-size cash flow statement is shown in the table below. Explain the decrease in Triple Y's total cash flow as a percentage of revenues.
>
> **Triple Y Corporation**
>
> | Cash Flow Statement (Percent of Revenues) | | | |
> |---|---|---|---|
> | Year | 20X9 | 20X8 | 20X7 |
> | Net income | 13.4% | 13.4% | 13.5% |
> | Depreciation | 4.0% | 3.9% | 3.9% |
> | Accounts receivable | –0.6% | –0.6% | –0.5% |
> | Inventory | –10.3% | –9.2% | –8.8% |
> | Prepaid expenses | 0.2% | –0.2% | 0.1% |
> | Accrued liabilities | 5.5% | 5.5% | 5.6% |
> | Operating cash flow | 12.2% | 12.8% | 13.8% |
> | Cash from sale of fixed assets | 0.7% | 0.7% | 0.7% |
> | Purchase of plant and equipment | –12.3% | –12.0% | –11.7% |
> | Investing cash flow | –11.6% | –11.3% | –11.0% |
> | Sale of bonds | 2.6% | 2.5% | 2.6% |
> | Cash dividends | –2.1% | –2.1% | –2.1% |
> | Financing cash flow | 0.5% | 0.4% | 0.5% |
> | Total cash flow | 1.1% | 1.9% | 3.3% |

> **Answer:**
>
> Operating cash flow has decreased as a percentage of revenues. This appears to be due largely to accumulating inventories. Investing activities, specifically purchases of plant and equipment, have also required an increasing percentage of the firm's cash flow.

Video covering this content is available online.

MODULE 25.4: FREE CASH FLOW AND RATIOS

LOS 25.i: Calculate and interpret free cash flow to the firm, free cash flow to equity, and performance and coverage cash flow ratios.

CFA® Program Curriculum, Volume 3, page 254

Free cash flow is a measure of cash that is available for discretionary purposes. This is the cash flow that is available once the firm has covered its capital expenditures. This is a fundamental cash flow measure and is often used for valuation. There are several measures of free cash flow. Two of the more common measures are free cash flow to the firm and free cash flow to equity.

Free Cash Flow to the Firm

Free cash flow to the firm (FCFF) is the cash available to all investors, both equity owners and debt holders. FCFF can be calculated by starting with either net income or operating cash flow.

FCFF is calculated from net income as:

$$FCFF = NI + NCC + [Int \times (1 - \text{tax rate})] - FCInv - WCInv$$

where:
NI = net income
NCC = noncash charges (depreciation and amortization)
Int = cash interest paid
FCInv = fixed capital investment (net capital expenditures)
WCInv = working capital investment

 PROFESSOR'S NOTE

Fixed capital investment is cash spent on fixed assets minus cash received from selling fixed assets. It is not the same as CFI, which includes cash flows from fixed investments, investments in securities, and repaid principal from loans made.

Note that cash interest paid, net of tax, is added back to net income. This is because FCFF is the cash flow available to stockholders and debt holders. Since interest is paid to (and therefore "available to") the debt holders, it must be included in FCFF.

FCFF can also be calculated from operating cash flow as:

FCFF = CFO + [Int × (1 − tax rate)] − FCInv

where:
CFO = cash flow from operations
Int   = cash interest paid
FCInv = fixed capital investment (net capital expenditures)

It is not necessary to adjust for noncash charges and changes in working capital when starting with CFO, since they are already reflected in the calculation of CFO. For firms that follow IFRS, it is not necessary to adjust for interest that is included as a part of financing activities. Additionally, firms that follow IFRS can report dividends paid as operating activities. In this case, the dividends paid would be added back to CFO. Again, the goal is to calculate the cash flow that is available to the shareholders and debt holders. It is not necessary to adjust dividends for taxes since dividends paid are not tax deductible.

Free Cash Flow to Equity

Free cash flow to equity (FCFE) is the cash flow that would be available for distribution to common shareholders. FCFE can be calculated as follows:

FCFE = CFO − FCInv + net borrowing

where:
CFO   = cash flow from operations
FCInv   = fixed capital investment (net capital expenditures)
net borrowing = debt issued − debt repaid

PROFESSOR'S NOTE

If net borrowing is negative (debt repaid exceeds debt issued), we would subtract net borrowing in calculating FCFE.

If firms that follow IFRS have subtracted dividends paid in calculating CFO, dividends must be added back when calculating FCFE.

> **EXAMPLE: Free cash flow**
>
> Using the financial statements from the examples presented earlier, calculate the company's free cash flow to the firm and free cash flow to equity. Assume a tax rate of 40%.
>
> **Answer:**
>
> Free cash flow to the firm = CFO + [interest paid × (1 − tax rate)] − fixed capital investment = $42,000 + $500(1 − 0.4) − $10,000 = $32,300
>
> Free cash flow to equity = CFO − fixed capital investment + net borrowing = $42,000 − $10,000 + $5,000 = $37,000
>
> Alternatively, free cash flow to equity = FCFF − [interest paid × (1 − tax rate)] + net borrowing = $32,300 − $500(1 − 0.4) + $5,000 = $37,000

Other Cash Flow Ratios

Just as with the income statement and balance sheet, the cash flow statement can be analyzed by comparing the cash flows either over time or to those of other firms. Cash flow ratios can be categorized as performance ratios and coverage ratios.

Performance Ratios

The **cash flow-to-revenue ratio** measures the amount of operating cash flow generated for each dollar of revenue.

$$\text{cash flow-to-revenue} = \frac{\text{CFO}}{\text{net revenue}}$$

The **cash return-on-assets ratio** measures the return of operating cash flow attributed to all providers of capital.

$$\text{cash return-on-assets} = \frac{\text{CFO}}{\text{average total assets}}$$

The **cash return-on-equity ratio** measures the return of operating cash flow attributed to shareholders.

$$\text{cash return-on-equity} = \frac{\text{CFO}}{\text{average total equity}}$$

The **cash-to-income ratio** measures the ability to generate cash from firm operations.

$$\text{cash-to-income} = \frac{\text{CFO}}{\text{operating income}}$$

Cash flow per share is a variation of basic earnings per share measured by using CFO instead of net income.

$$\text{cash flow per share} = \frac{\text{CFO} - \text{preferred dividends}}{\text{weighted average number of common shares}}$$

Note: If common dividends were classified as operating activities under IFRS, they should be added back to CFO for purposes of calculating cash flow per share.

Coverage Ratios

The **debt coverage ratio** measures financial risk and leverage.

$$\text{debt coverage} = \frac{\text{CFO}}{\text{total debt}}$$

The **interest coverage ratio** measures the firm's ability to meet its interest obligations.

$$\text{interest coverage} = \frac{\text{CFO} + \text{interest paid} + \text{taxes paid}}{\text{interest paid}}$$

Note: If interest paid was classified as a financing activity under IFRS, no interest adjustment is necessary.

The **reinvestment ratio** measures the firm's ability to acquire long-term assets with operating cash flow.

$$\text{reinvestment} = \frac{\text{CFO}}{\text{cash paid for long-term assets}}$$

The **debt payment ratio** measures the firm's ability to satisfy long-term debt with operating cash flow.

$$\text{debt payment} = \frac{\text{CFO}}{\text{cash long-term debt repayment}}$$

The **dividend payment ratio** measures the firm's ability to make dividend payments from operating cash flow.

$$\text{dividend payment} = \frac{\text{CFO}}{\text{dividends paid}}$$

The **investing and financing ratio** measures the firm's ability to purchase assets, satisfy debts, and pay dividends.

$$\text{investing and financing} = \frac{\text{CFO}}{\text{cash outflows from investing and financing activities}}$$

MODULE QUIZ 25.3, 25.4

To best evaluate your performance, enter your quiz answers online.

1. Continental Corporation reported sales revenue of $150,000 for the current year. If accounts receivable decreased $10,000 during the year and accounts payable increased $4,000 during the year, cash collections were:
   A. $154,000.
   B. $160,000.
   C. $164,000.

2. In preparing a common-size cash flow statement, each cash flow is expressed as a percentage of:
   A. total assets.
   B. total revenues.
   C. the change in cash.

3. To calculate free cash flow to the firm based on operating cash flow, an analyst should add interest expense net of tax and subtract:
   A. noncash charges.
   B. fixed capital investment.
   C. working capital investment.

4. The reinvestment ratio measures a firm's ability to use its operating cash flow to:
   A. pay dividends.
   B. invest in working capital.
   C. acquire long-lived assets.

KEY CONCEPTS

LOS 25.a

Cash flow from operating activities (CFO) consists of the inflows and outflows of cash resulting from transactions that affect a firm's net income.

Cash flow from investing activities (CFI) consists of the inflows and outflows of cash resulting from the acquisition or disposal of long-term assets and certain investments.

Cash flow from financing activities (CFF) consists of the inflows and outflows of cash resulting from transactions affecting a firm's capital structure, such as issuing or repaying debt and issuing or repurchasing stock.

LOS 25.b

Noncash investing and financing activities, such as taking on debt to the seller of a purchased asset, are not reported in the cash flow statement but must be disclosed in the footnotes or a supplemental schedule.

LOS 25.c

Under U.S. GAAP, dividends paid are financing cash flows. Interest paid, interest received, and dividends received are operating cash flows. All taxes paid are operating cash flows.

Under IFRS, dividends paid and interest paid can be reported as either operating or financing cash flows. Interest received and dividends received can be reported as either operating or investing cash flows. Taxes paid are operating cash flows unless they arise from an investing or financing transaction.

LOS 25.d

Under the direct method of presenting CFO, each line item of the accrual-based income statement is adjusted to get cash receipts or cash payments. The main advantage of the direct method is that it presents clearly the firm's operating cash receipts and payments.

Under the indirect method of presenting CFO, net income is adjusted for transactions that affect net income but do not affect operating cash flow, such as depreciation and gains or losses on asset sales, and for changes in balance sheet items. The main advantage of the indirect method is that it focuses on the differences between net income and operating cash flow. This provides a useful link to the income statement when forecasting future operating cash flow.

LOS 25.e

Operating activities typically relate to the firm's current assets and current liabilities. Investing activities typically relate to noncurrent assets. Financing activities typically relate to noncurrent liabilities and equity.

Timing of revenue or expense recognition that differs from the receipt or payment of cash is reflected in changes in balance sheet accounts.

LOS 25.f

The direct method of calculating CFO is to sum cash inflows and cash outflows for operating activities.

- Cash collections from customers—sales adjusted for changes in receivables and unearned revenue.
- Cash paid for inputs—COGS adjusted for changes in inventory and accounts payable.
- Cash operating expenses—SG&A adjusted for changes in related accrued liabilities or prepaid expenses.
- Cash interest paid—interest expense adjusted for the change in interest payable.
- Cash taxes paid—income tax expense adjusted for changes in taxes payable and changes in deferred tax assets and liabilities.

The indirect method of calculating CFO begins with net income and adjusts it for gains or losses related to investing or financing cash flows, noncash charges to income, and changes in balance sheet operating items.

CFI is calculated by determining the changes in asset accounts that result from investing activities. The cash flow from selling an asset is its book value plus any gain on the sale (or minus any loss on the sale).

CFF is the sum of net cash flows from creditors (new borrowings minus principal repaid) and net cash flows from shareholders (new equity issued minus share repurchases minus cash dividends paid).

LOS 25.g

An indirect cash flow statement can be converted to a direct cash flow statement by adjusting each income statement account for changes in associated balance sheet accounts and by eliminating noncash and non-operating items.

LOS 25.h

An analyst should determine whether a company is generating positive operating cash flow over time that is greater than its capital spending needs and whether the company's accounting policies are causing reported earnings to diverge from operating cash flow.

A common-size cash flow statement shows each item as a percentage of revenue or shows each cash inflow as a percentage of total inflows and each outflow as a percentage of total outflows.

LOS 25.i

Free cash flow to the firm (FCFF) is the cash available to all investors, both equity owners and debt holders.

- FCFF = net income + noncash charges + [cash interest paid × (1 − tax rate)] − fixed capital investment − working capital investment.
- FCFF = CFO + [cash interest paid × (1 − tax rate)] − fixed capital investment.

Free cash flow to equity (FCFE) is the cash flow that is available for distribution to the common shareholders after all obligations have been paid.

FCFE = CFO − fixed capital investment + net borrowing

Cash flow performance ratios, such as cash return on equity or on assets, and cash coverage ratios, such as debt coverage or cash interest coverage, provide information about the firm's operating performance and financial strength.

©2018 Kaplan, Inc.

ANSWER KEY FOR MODULE QUIZZES

Module Quiz 25.1

1. **C** The payment of interest on debt is an *operating* cash flow under U.S. GAAP. (LOS 25.a)

2. **C** Depreciation does not represent a cash flow. To the extent that it affects the firm's taxes, an increase in depreciation changes operating cash flows, but not investing cash flows. (LOS 25.a)

3. **A** A change in notes payable is a financing cash flow. (LOS 25.a)

4. **A** Sales of inventory would be classified as operating cash flow. (LOS 25.a)

5. **B** Issuing bonds would be classified as financing cash flow. (LOS 25.a)

6. **B** Sale of land would be classified as investing cash flow. (LOS 25.a)

7. **C** Write-off of obsolete equipment has no cash flow impact. (LOS 25.a)

8. **A** Under IFRS, interest expense can be classified as either an operating cash flow or financing cash flow. (LOS 25.a)

9. **A** Dividends received from investments would be classified as operating cash flow under U.S. GAAP. (LOS 25.a)

10. **C** The exchange of debt securities for equity securities is a noncash transaction. (LOS 25.b)

11. **B** Under U.S. GAAP, dividends paid are reported as financing activities. Under IFRS, dividends paid can be reported as either operating or financing activities. (LOS 25.c)

12. **C** The indirect method reconciles the difference between net income and CFO. The direct method shows operating cash received and paid and, therefore, provides more information on its face than the indirect method. (LOS 25.d)

13. **C** Financing cash flows are linked primarily to changes in long-term liabilities and equity. Changes in current assets and liabilities tend to be linked to operating cash flows. Changes in long-lived assets are typically linked to investing cash flows. (LOS 25.e)

Module Quiz 25.2

1. **B** Net income – profits from sale of land + depreciation + decrease in receivables – increase in inventories + increase in accounts payable – decrease in wages payable + increase in deferred tax liabilities = 120 – 2 + 25 + 20 – 10 + 7 – 5 + 15 = $170. Note that the profit on the sale of land should be subtracted from net income because this transaction is classified as investing, not operating. (LOS 25.a, 25.f)

2. **B** Net income – profit on sale of building + depreciation = 45 – 20 + 75 = $100. Note that taxes and interest are already deducted in calculating net income, and that the profit on the sale of the building should be subtracted from net income. (LOS 25.a, 25.f)

3. **B** Cash from sale of building – purchase of machinery = 40 – 20 = $20. (LOS 25.a, 25.f)

4. **A** Sale of preferred stock + issuance of bonds – principal payments on bank borrowings – repurchase of common stock – dividends paid = 35 + 50 – 15 – 30 – 10 = $30. Note that we did not include $45 of debt retired through issuance of common stock since this was a noncash transaction. Knowing how to handle noncash transactions is important. (LOS 25.a, 25.f)

5. **B** Net income = $1,500 × 0.25 = $375, and cash flow from operations = net income – gain on sale of machinery + depreciation – increase in accounts receivable – increase in inventory – decrease in accounts payable = 375 – 30 + 150 – 50 – 100 – 70 = $275. (LOS 25.a, 25.f)

6. **A**

Net income	$78,000
Depreciation	12,000
Unrealized gain	(15,000)
Increase in accounts receivable	(52,000)
Increase in accounts payable	29,000
Cash flow from operations	$52,000

(LOS 25.f)

7. **C** Purchased new fixed assets for $75,000 – cash <u>outflow</u> from investing

Converted $70,000 of preferred shares to common shares – noncash transaction

Received dividends of $12,000 – cash <u>inflow</u> from operations

Paid dividends of $21,000 – cash <u>outflow</u> from financing

Mortgage repayment of $17,000 – cash <u>outflow</u> from financing

CFI = –75,000

CFF = –21,000 – 17,000 = –$38,000

(LOS 25.a, 25.f)

Module Quiz 25.3, 25.4

1. **B** $150,000 sales + $10,000 decrease in accounts receivable = $160,000 cash collections. The change in accounts payable does not affect cash collections. Accounts payable result from a firm's purchases from its suppliers. (Module 25.3, LOS 25.f, 25.g)

2. **B** The cash flow statement can be converted to common-size format by expressing each line item as a percentage of revenue. (Module 25.3, LOS 25.h)

3. **B** FCFF can be calculated from CFO by adding interest expense net of tax and subtracting fixed capital investment. (Module 25.4, LOS 25.i)

4. **C** The reinvestment ratio is CFO / cash paid for long-term assets. (Module 25.4, LOS 25.i)

READING
26

Financial Analysis Techniques

EXAM FOCUS

This topic review presents a "tool box" for an analyst. It would be nice if you could calculate all these ratios, but it is imperative that you understand what firm characteristic each one is measuring, and even more important, that you know whether a higher or lower ratio is better in each instance. Different analysts calculate some ratios differently. It would be helpful if analysts were always careful to distinguish between total liabilities, total interest-bearing debt, long-term debt, and creditor and trade debt, but they do not. Some analysts routinely add deferred tax liabilities to debt or exclude goodwill when calculating assets and equity; others do not. Statistical reporting services almost always disclose how each of the ratios they present was calculated. So do not get too tied up in the details of each ratio, but understand what each one represents and what factors would likely lead to significant changes in a particular ratio. The DuPont formulas have been with us a long time and were in the curriculum when I took the exams back in the 1980s. Decomposing ROE into its components is an important analytic technique and it should definitely be in your tool box.

MODULE 26.1: INTRODUCTION TO FINANCIAL RATIOS

Video covering this content is available online.

LOS 26.a: Describe tools and techniques used in financial analysis, including their uses and limitations.

CFA® Program Curriculum, Volume 3, page 274

Various tools and techniques are used to convert financial statement data into formats that facilitate analysis. These include ratio analysis, common-size analysis, graphical analysis, and regression analysis.

Ratio Analysis

Ratios are useful tools for expressing relationships among data that can be used for internal comparisons and comparisons across firms. They are often most useful in identifying questions that need to be answered, rather than answering questions directly. Specifically, ratios can be used to do the following:

■ Project future earnings and cash flow.

■ Evaluate a firm's flexibility (the ability to grow and meet obligations even when unexpected circumstances arise).

■ Assess management's performance.

■ Evaluate changes in the firm and industry over time.

■ Compare the firm with industry competitors.

Analysts must also be aware of the limitations of ratios, including the following:

■ Financial ratios are not useful when viewed in isolation. They are only informative when compared to those of other firms or to the company's historical performance.

■ Comparisons with other companies are made more difficult by different accounting treatments. This is particularly important when comparing U.S. firms to non-U.S. firms.

■ It is difficult to find comparable industry ratios when analyzing companies that operate in multiple industries.

■ Conclusions cannot be made by calculating a single ratio. All ratios must be viewed relative to one another.

■ Determining the target or comparison value for a ratio is difficult, requiring some range of acceptable values.

It is important to understand that the definitions of ratios can vary widely among the analytical community. For example, some analysts use all liabilities when measuring leverage, while other analysts only use interest-bearing obligations. Consistency is paramount. Analysts must also understand that reasonable values of ratios can differ among industries.

Common-Size Analysis

Common-size statements normalize balance sheets and income statements and allow the analyst to more easily compare performance across firms and for a single firm over time.

■ A vertical common-size balance sheet expresses all balance sheet accounts as a percentage of total assets.

■ A vertical common-size income statement expresses all income statement items as a percentage of sales.

In addition to comparisons of financial data across firms and time, common-size analysis is appropriate for quickly viewing certain financial ratios. For example, the gross profit margin, operating profit margin, and net profit margin are all clearly indicated within a common-size income statement. Vertical common-size income statement ratios are especially useful for studying trends in costs and profit margins.

$$\text{vertical common-size income statement ratios} = \frac{\text{income statement account}}{\text{sales}}$$

Balance sheet accounts can also be converted to common-size ratios by dividing each balance sheet item by total assets.

$$\text{vertical common-size balance-sheet ratios} = \frac{\text{balance sheet account}}{\text{total assets}}$$

> **EXAMPLE: Constructing common-size statements**
>
> The common-size statements in Figure 26.1 show balance sheet items as percentages of assets, and income statement items as percentages of sales.
>
> - You can convert all asset and liability amounts to their actual values by multiplying the percentages listed below by their total assets of $57,100; $55,798; and $52,071, respectively for 20X6, 20X5, and 20X4 (data is USD millions).
>
> - Also, all income statement items can be converted to their actual values by multiplying the given percentages by total sales, which were $29,723; $29,234; and $22,922, respectively, for 20X6, 20X5, and 20X4.

Figure 26.1: Vertical Common-Size Balance Sheet and Income Statement

Balance Sheet, fiscal year-end	20X6	20X5	20X4
Assets			
Cash & cash equivalents	0.38%	0.29%	0.37%
Accounts receivable	5.46%	5.61%	6.20%
Inventories	5.92%	5.42%	5.84%
Deferred income taxes	0.89%	0.84%	0.97%
Other current assets	0.41%	0.40%	0.36%
Total current assets	13.06%	12.56%	13.74%
Gross fixed assets	25.31%	23.79%	25.05%
Accumulated depreciation	8.57%	7.46%	6.98%
Net gross fixed assets	16.74%	16.32%	18.06%
Other long-term assets	70.20%	71.12%	68.20%
Total assets	100.00%	100.00%	100.00%
Liabilities			
Accounts payable	3.40%	3.40%	3.79%
Short-term debt	1.00%	2.19%	1.65%
Other current liabilities	8.16%	10.32%	9.14%
Total current liabilities	12.56%	15.91%	14.58%
Long-term debt	18.24%	14.58%	5.18%
Other long-term liabilities	23.96%	27.44%	53.27%
Total liabilities	54.76%	57.92%	73.02%
Preferred equity	0.00%	0.00%	0.00%
Common equity	45.24%	42.08%	26.98%
Total liabilities & equity	100.00%	100.00%	100.00%

Figure 26.1: **Vertical Common-Size Balance Sheet and Income Statement (continued)**

Income Statement, fiscal year	20X6	20X5	20X4
Revenues	**100.00%**	100.00%	100.00%
Cost of goods sold	**59.62%**	60.09%	60.90%
Gross profit	**40.38%**	39.91%	39.10%
Selling, general & administrative	**16.82%**	17.34%	17.84%
Depreciation	**2.39%**	2.33%	2.18%
Amortization	**0.02%**	3.29%	2.33%
Other operating expenses	**0.58%**	0.25%	–0.75%
Operating income	**20.57%**	16.71%	17.50%
Interest and other debt expense	**2.85%**	4.92%	2.60%
Income before taxes	**17.72%**	11.79%	14.90%
Provision for income taxes	**6.30%**	5.35%	6.17%
Net income	**11.42%**	6.44%	8.73%

Even a cursory inspection of the income statement in Figure 26.1 can be quite instructive. Beginning at the bottom, we can see that the profitability of the company has increased nicely in 20X6 after falling slightly in 20X5. We can examine the 20X6 income statement values to find the source of this greatly improved profitability. Cost of goods sold seems to be stable, with an improvement (decrease) in 20X6 of only 0.48%. SG&A was down approximately one-half percent as well.

These improvements from (relative) cost reduction, however, only begin to explain the 5% increase in the net profit margin for 20X6. Improvements in two items, "amortization" and "interest and other debt expense," appear to be the most significant factors in the firm's improved profitability in 20X6. Clearly the analyst must investigate further in both areas to learn whether these improvements represent permanent improvements or whether these items can be expected to return to previous percentage-of-sales levels in the future.

We can also note that interest expense as a percentage of sales was approximately the same in 20X4 and 20X6. We must investigate the reasons for the higher interest costs in 20X5 to determine whether the current level of 2.85% can be expected to continue into the next period. In addition, more than 3% of the 5% increase in net profit margin in 20X6 is due to a decrease in amortization expense. Since this is a noncash expense, the decrease may have no implications for cash flows looking forward.

This discussion should make clear that common-size analysis doesn't tell an analyst the whole story about this company, but can certainly point the analyst in the right direction to find out the circumstances that led to the increase in the net profit margin and to determine the effects, if any, on firm cash flow going forward.

Another way to present financial statement data that is quite useful when analyzing trends over time is a **horizontal common-size balance sheet or income statement**.

The divisor here is the first-year values, so they are all standardized to 1.0 by construction. Figure 26.2 illustrates this approach.

Figure 26.2: Horizontal Common-Size Balance Sheet Data

	20X4	20X5	20X6
Inventory	1.0	1.1	1.4
Cash and marketable securities	1.0	1.3	1.2
Long-term debt	1.0	1.6	1.8
PP&E (net of depreciation)	1.0	0.9	0.8

Trends in the values of these items, as well as the relative growth in these items, are readily apparent from a horizontal common-size balance sheet.

PROFESSOR'S NOTE

We have presented data in Figure 26.1 with information for the most recent period on the left, and in Figure 26.2 we have presented the historical values from left to right. Both presentation methods are common, and on the exam you should pay special attention to which method is used in the data presented for any question.

We can view the values in the common-size financial statements as ratios. Net income is shown on the common-size income statement as net income/revenues, which is the net profit margin, and tells the analyst the percentage of each dollar of sales that remains for shareholders after all expenses related to the generation of those sales are deducted. One measure of financial leverage, long-term debt to total assets, can be read directly from the vertical common-size financial statements. Specific ratios commonly used in financial analysis and interpretation of their values are covered in detail in this review.

Graphical Analysis

Graphs can be used to visually present performance comparisons and composition of financial statement elements over time.

A **stacked column graph** (also called a *stacked bar graph*) shows the changes in items from year to year in graphical form. Figure 26.3 presents such data for a hypothetical corporation.

Another alternative for graphic presentation of data is a **line graph**. Figure 26.4 presents the same data as Figure 26.3, but as a line graph. The increase in trade payables and the decrease in cash are evident in either format and would alert the analyst to potential liquidity problems that require further investigation and analysis.

Regression Analysis

Regression analysis can be used to identify relationships between variables. The results are often used for forecasting. For example, an analyst might use the relationship between GDP and sales to prepare a sales forecast.

Figure 26.3: Stacked Column (Stacked Bar) Graph

Figure 26.4: Line Graph

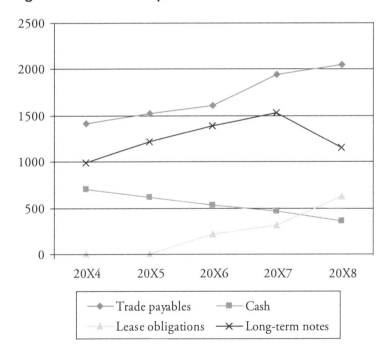

MODULE 26.2: FINANCIAL RATIOS, PART 1

Video covering this content is available online.

LOS 26.b: Classify, calculate, and interpret activity, liquidity, solvency, profitability, and valuation ratios.

CFA® Program Curriculum, Volume 3, page 291

Financial ratios can be segregated into different classifications by the type of information about the company they provide. One such classification scheme is:

■ **Activity ratios.** This category includes several ratios also referred to asset utilization or turnover ratios (e.g., inventory turnover, receivables turnover, and total assets turnover). They often give indications of how well a firm utilizes various assets such as inventory and fixed assets.

■ **Liquidity ratios.** Liquidity here refers to the ability to pay short-term obligations as they come due.

■ **Solvency ratios.** Solvency ratios give the analyst information on the firm's financial leverage and ability to meet its longer-term obligations.

■ **Profitability ratios.** Profitability ratios provide information on how well the company generates operating profits and net profits from its sales.

■ **Valuation ratios.** Sales per share, earnings per share, and price to cash flow per share are examples of ratios used in comparing the relative valuation of companies.

> **PROFESSOR'S NOTE**
>
> We examine valuation ratios in another LOS concerning equity analysis later in this review, and in the Equity Investments topic area.

It should be noted that these categories are not mutually exclusive. An activity ratio such as payables turnover may also provide information about the liquidity of a company, for example. There is no one standard set of ratios for financial analysis. Different analysts use different ratios and different calculation methods for similar ratios. Some ratios are so commonly used that there is very little variation in how they are defined and calculated. We will note some alternative treatments and alternative terms for single ratios as we detail the commonly used ratios in each category.

Activity Ratios

Activity ratios (also known as asset utilization ratios or operating efficiency ratios) measure how efficiently the firm is managing its assets.

■ A measure of accounts receivable turnover is *receivables turnover:*

$$\text{receivables turnover} = \frac{\text{annual sales}}{\text{average receivables}}$$

PROFESSOR'S NOTE

In most cases when a ratio compares a balance sheet account (such as receivables) with an income or cash flow item (such as sales), the balance sheet item will be the average of the account instead of simply the end-of-year balance. Averages are calculated by adding the beginning-of-year account value to the end-of-year account value, then dividing the sum by two.

It is considered desirable to have a receivables turnover figure close to the industry norm.

■ The inverse of the receivables turnover times 365 is the *average collection period*, or *days of sales outstanding*, which is the average number of days it takes for the company's customers to pay their bills:

$$\text{days of sales outstanding} = \frac{365}{\text{receivables turnover}}$$

It is considered desirable to have a collection period (and receivables turnover) close to the industry norm. The firm's credit terms are another important benchmark used to interpret this ratio. A collection period that is too high might mean that customers are too slow in paying their bills, which means too much capital is tied up in assets. A collection period that is too low might indicate that the firm's credit policy is too rigorous, which might be hampering sales.

■ A measure of a firm's efficiency with respect to its processing and inventory management is *inventory turnover*:

$$\text{inventory turnover} = \frac{\text{cost of goods sold}}{\text{average inventory}}$$

PROFESSOR'S NOTE

Pay careful attention to the numerator in the turnover ratios. For inventory turnover, be sure to use cost of goods sold, not sales.

■ The inverse of the inventory turnover times 365 is the *average inventory processing period*, *number of days of inventory*, or *days of inventory on hand*:

$$\text{days of inventory on hand} = \frac{365}{\text{inventory turnover}}$$

As is the case with accounts receivable, it is considered desirable to have days of inventory on hand (and inventory turnover) close to the industry norm. A processing period that is too high might mean that too much capital is tied up in inventory and could mean that the inventory is obsolete. A processing period that is too low might indicate that the firm has inadequate stock on hand, which could hurt sales.

■ A measure of the use of trade credit by the firm is the *payables turnover* ratio:

$$\text{payables turnover} = \frac{\text{purchases}}{\text{average trade payables}}$$

PROFESSOR'S NOTE

You can use the inventory equation to calculate purchases from the financial statements. Purchases = ending inventory – beginning inventory + cost of goods sold.

■ The inverse of the payables turnover ratio multiplied by 365 is the *payables payment period* or *number of days of payables*, which is the average amount of time it takes the company to pay its bills:

$$\text{number of days of payables} = \frac{365}{\text{payables turnover ratio}}$$

> **PROFESSOR'S NOTE**
>
> We have shown days calculations for payables, receivables, and inventory based on annual turnover and a 365-day year. If turnover ratios are for a quarter rather than a year, the number of days in the quarter should be divided by the quarterly turnover ratios in order to get the "days" form of these ratios.

■ The effectiveness of the firm's use of its total assets to create revenue is measured by its *total asset turnover:*

$$\text{total asset turnover} = \frac{\text{revenue}}{\text{average total assets}}$$

Different types of industries might have considerably different turnover ratios. Manufacturing businesses that are capital-intensive might have asset turnover ratios near one, while retail businesses might have turnover ratios near 10. As was the case with the current asset turnover ratios discussed previously, it is desirable for the total asset turnover ratio to be close to the industry norm. Low asset turnover ratios might mean that the company has too much capital tied up in its asset base. A turnover ratio that is too high might imply that the firm has too few assets for potential sales, or that the asset base is outdated.

■ The utilization of fixed assets is measured by the *fixed asset turnover* ratio:

$$\text{fixed asset turnover} = \frac{\text{revenue}}{\text{average net fixed assets}}$$

As was the case with the total asset turnover ratio, it is desirable to have a fixed asset turnover ratio close to the industry norm. Low fixed asset turnover might mean that the company has too much capital tied up in its asset base or is using the assets it has inefficiently. A turnover ratio that is too high might imply that the firm has obsolete equipment, or at a minimum, that the firm will probably have to incur capital expenditures in the near future to increase capacity to support growing revenues. Since "net" here refers to net of accumulated depreciation, firms with more recently acquired assets will typically have lower fixed asset turnover ratios.

■ How effectively a company is using its working capital is measured by the *working capital turnover* ratio:

$$\text{working capital turnover} = \frac{\text{revenue}}{\text{average working capital}}$$

Working capital (sometimes called *net* working capital) is current assets minus current liabilities. The working capital turnover ratio gives us information about the utilization of working capital in terms of dollars of sales per dollar of working capital. Some firms may have very low working capital if outstanding payables equal or exceed inventory and receivables. In this case the working capital turnover ratio will be very large, may vary significantly from period to period, and is less informative about changes in the firm's operating efficiency.

Liquidity Ratios

Liquidity ratios are employed by analysts to determine the firm's ability to pay its short-term liabilities.

■ The *current ratio* is the best-known measure of liquidity:

$$\text{current ratio} = \frac{\text{current assets}}{\text{current liabilities}}$$

The higher the current ratio, the more likely it is that the company will be able to pay its short-term bills. A current ratio of less than one means that the company has negative working capital and is probably facing a liquidity crisis. Working capital equals current assets minus current liabilities.

■ The *quick ratio* is a more stringent measure of liquidity because it does not include inventories and other assets that might not be very liquid:

$$\text{quick ratio} = \frac{\text{cash} + \text{marketable securities} + \text{receivables}}{\text{current liabilities}}$$

The higher the quick ratio, the more likely it is that the company will be able to pay its short-term bills. Marketable securities are short-term debt instruments, typically liquid and of good credit quality.

■ The most conservative liquidity measure is the *cash ratio:*

$$\text{cash ratio} = \frac{\text{cash} + \text{marketable securities}}{\text{current liabilities}}$$

The higher the cash ratio, the more likely it is that the company will be able to pay its short-term bills.

The current, quick, and cash ratios differ only in the assumed liquidity of the current assets that the analyst projects will be used to pay off current liabilities.

■ The *defensive interval ratio* is another measure of liquidity that indicates the number of days of average cash expenditures the firm could pay with its current liquid assets:

$$\text{defensive interval} = \frac{\text{cash} + \text{marketable securities} + \text{receivables}}{\text{average daily expenditures}}$$

Expenditures here include cash expenses for costs of goods, SG&A, and research and development. If these items are taken from the income statement, noncash charges such as depreciation should be added back just as in the preparation of a statement of cash flows by the indirect method.

■ The *cash conversion cycle* is the length of time it takes to turn the firm's cash investment in inventory back into cash, in the form of collections from the sales of that inventory. The cash conversion cycle is computed from days sales outstanding, days of inventory on hand, and number of days of payables:

$$\text{cash conversion cycle} = \begin{pmatrix} \text{days} \\ \text{sales} \\ \text{outstanding} \end{pmatrix} + \begin{pmatrix} \text{days of} \\ \text{inventory} \\ \text{on hand} \end{pmatrix} - \begin{pmatrix} \text{number of} \\ \text{days of} \\ \text{payables} \end{pmatrix}$$

High cash conversion cycles are considered undesirable. A conversion cycle that is too high implies that the company has an excessive amount of capital investment in the sales process.

MODULE 26.3: FINANCIAL RATIOS, PART 2

Solvency Ratios

Video covering this content is available online.

Solvency ratios measure a firm's financial leverage and ability to meet its long-term obligations. Solvency ratios include various **debt ratios** that are based on the balance sheet and **coverage ratios** that are based on the income statement.

- A measure of the firm's use of fixed-cost financing sources is the *debt-to-equity* ratio:

$$\text{debt-to-equity} = \frac{\text{total debt}}{\text{total shareholders' equity}}$$

Increases and decreases in this ratio suggest a greater or lesser reliance on debt as a source of financing.

Total debt is calculated differently by different analysts and different providers of financial information. Here, we will define it as long-term debt plus interest-bearing short-term debt.

Some analysts include the present value of lease obligations and/or non-interest-bearing current liabilities, such as trade payables.

- Another way of looking at the usage of debt is the *debt-to-capital* ratio:

$$\text{debt-to-capital} = \frac{\text{total debt}}{\text{total debt + total shareholders' equity}}$$

Capital equals all short-term and long-term debt plus preferred stock and equity. Increases and decreases in this ratio suggest a greater or lesser reliance on debt as a source of financing.

- A slightly different way of analyzing debt utilization is the *debt-to-assets* ratio:

$$\text{debt-to-assets} = \frac{\text{total debt}}{\text{total assets}}$$

Increases and decreases in this ratio suggest a greater or lesser reliance on debt as a source of financing.

- Another measure that is used as an indicator of a company's use of debt financing is the *financial leverage* ratio (or leverage ratio):

$$\text{financial leverage} = \frac{\text{average total assets}}{\text{average total equity}}$$

Average here means the average of the values at the beginning and at the end of the period. Greater use of debt financing increases financial leverage and, typically, risk to equity holders and bondholders alike.

■ The remaining risk ratios help determine the firm's ability to repay its debt obligations. The first of these is the *interest coverage ratio:*

$$\text{interest coverage} = \frac{\text{earnings before interest and taxes}}{\text{interest payments}}$$

The lower this ratio, the more likely it is that the firm will have difficulty meeting its debt payments.

■ A second ratio that is an indicator of a company's ability to meet its obligations is the *fixed charge coverage* ratio:

$$\text{fixed charge coverage} = \frac{\text{earnings before interest and taxes} + \text{lease payments}}{\text{interest payments} + \text{lease payments}}$$

Here, lease payments are added back to operating earnings in the numerator and also added to interest payments in the denominator. Significant lease obligations will reduce this ratio significantly compared to the interest coverage ratio. Fixed charge coverage is the more meaningful measure for companies that lease a large portion of their assets, such as some airlines.

PROFESSOR'S NOTE

With all solvency ratios, the analyst must consider the variability of a firm's cash flows when determining the reasonableness of the ratios. Firms with stable cash flows are usually able to carry more debt.

Profitability Ratios

Profitability ratios measure the overall performance of the firm relative to revenues, assets, equity, and capital.

■ The *net profit margin* is the ratio of net income to revenue:

$$\text{net profit margin} = \frac{\text{net income}}{\text{revenue}}$$

Analysts should be concerned if this ratio is too low. The net profit margin should be based on net income from continuing operations, because analysts should be primarily concerned about future expectations, and below-the-line items such as discontinued operations will not affect the company in the future.

Operating profitability ratios look at how good management is at turning their efforts into profits. Operating ratios compare the top of the income statement (sales) to profits. The different ratios are designed to isolate specific costs.

Know these terms:

gross profits	= net sales – COGS
operating profits	= earnings before interest and taxes = EBIT
net income	= earnings after taxes but before dividends
total capital	= long-term debt + short-term debt + common and preferred equity
total capital	= total assets

PROFESSOR'S NOTE

The difference between these two definitions of total capital is working capital liabilities, such as accounts payable. Some analysts consider these liabilities a source of financing for a firm and include them in total capital. Other analysts view total capital as the sum of a firm's debt and equity.

How they relate in the income statement:

Net sales
− Cost of goods sold

Gross profit
− Operating expenses

Operating profit (EBIT)
− Interest

Earnings before taxes (EBT)
− Taxes

Earnings after taxes (EAT)
+/− Below the line items adjusted for tax

Net income
− Preferred dividends

Income available to common

■ The *gross profit margin* is the ratio of gross profit (sales less cost of goods sold) to sales:

$$\text{gross profit margin} = \frac{\text{gross profit}}{\text{revenue}}$$

An analyst should be concerned if this ratio is too low. Gross profit can be increased by raising prices or reducing costs. However, the ability to raise prices may be limited by competition.

■ The *operating profit margin* is the ratio of operating profit (gross profit less selling, general, and administrative expenses) to sales. Operating profit is also referred to as earnings before interest and taxes (EBIT):

$$\text{operating profit margin} = \frac{\text{operating income}}{\text{revenue}} \text{ or } \frac{\text{EBIT}}{\text{revenue}}$$

Strictly speaking, EBIT includes some nonoperating items, such as gains on investment. The analyst, as with other ratios with various formulations, must be consistent in his calculation method and know how published ratios are calculated. Analysts should be concerned if this ratio is too low. Some analysts prefer to calculate the operating profit margin by adding back depreciation and any amortization expense to arrive at earnings before interest, taxes, depreciation, and amortization (EBITDA).

■ Sometimes profitability is measured using earnings before tax (EBT), which can be calculated by subtracting interest from EBIT or from operating earnings. The *pretax margin* is calculated as:

$$\text{pretax margin} = \frac{\text{EBT}}{\text{revenue}}$$

■ Another set of profitability ratios measure profitability relative to funds invested in the company by common stockholders, preferred stockholders, and suppliers of debt financing. The first of these measures is the *return on assets* (ROA). Typically, ROA is calculated using net income:

$$\text{return on assets (ROA)} = \frac{\text{net income}}{\text{average total assets}}$$

This measure is a bit misleading, however, because interest is excluded from net income but total assets include debt as well as equity. Adding interest adjusted for tax back to net income puts the returns to both equity and debt holders in the numerator. The interest expense that should be added back is gross interest expense, not net interest expense (which is gross interest expense less interest income). This results in an alternative calculation for ROA:

$$\text{return on assets (ROA)} = \frac{\text{net income} + \text{interest expense} (1 - \text{tax rate})}{\text{average total assets}}$$

■ A measure of return on assets that includes both taxes and interest in the numerator is the *operating return on assets*:

$$\text{operating return on assets} = \frac{\text{operating income}}{\text{average total assets}} \text{ or } \frac{\text{EBIT}}{\text{average total assets}}$$

■ The *return on total capital* (ROTC) is the ratio of net income before interest and taxes to total capital:

$$\text{return on total capital} = \frac{\text{EBIT}}{\text{average total capital}}$$

Total capital includes short- and long-term debt, preferred equity, and common equity. Analysts should be concerned if this ratio is too low.

An alternative method for computing ROTC is to include the present value of operating leases on the balance sheet as a fixed asset and as a long-term liability. This adjustment is especially important for firms that are dependent on operating leases as a major form of financing. Calculations related to leasing will be discussed in the next Study Session.

■ The *return on equity* (ROE) is the ratio of net income to average total equity (including preferred stock):

$$\text{return on equity} = \frac{\text{net income}}{\text{average total equity}}$$

Analysts should be concerned if this ratio is too low. It is sometimes called return on total equity.

■ A similar ratio to the return on equity is the *return on common equity:*

$$\text{return on common equity} = \frac{\text{net income} - \text{preferred dividends}}{\text{average common equity}}$$

$$= \frac{\text{net income available to common}}{\text{average common equity}}$$

This ratio differs from the return on total equity in that it only measures the accounting profits available to, and the capital invested by, common stockholders, instead of common and preferred stockholders. That is why preferred dividends are deducted from net income in the numerator. Analysts should be concerned if this ratio is too low.

The return on common equity is often more thoroughly analyzed using the DuPont decomposition, which is described later in this topic review.

> **EXAMPLE: Calculating ratios**
>
> A balance sheet and income statement for Sedgwick Company are shown in the following tables for this year and the previous year.
>
> Using the company information provided, calculate the following ratios for the current year: current ratio, total asset turnover, net profit margin, return on common equity, and total debt to equity.
>
> | Sedgwick Company Balance Sheet | | |
> |---|---|---|
> | Year | Current Year | Previous Year |
> | **Assets** | | |
> | Cash and marketable securities | $105 | $95 |
> | Receivables | 205 | 195 |
> | Inventories | 310 | 290 |
> | **Total current assets** | 620 | 580 |
> | Gross property, plant, and equipment | 1,800 | $1,700 |
> | Accumulated depreciation | 360 | 340 |
> | Net property, plant, and equipment | 1,440 | 1,360 |
> | **Total assets** | $2,060 | $1,940 |
> | **Liabilities** | | |
> | Payables | $110 | $90 |
> | Short-term debt | 160 | 140 |
> | Current portion of long-term debt | 55 | 45 |
> | **Current liabilities** | 325 | $275 |
> | Long-term debt | 610 | $690 |
> | Deferred taxes | 105 | 95 |
> | Common stock at par | 300 | 300 |
> | Additional paid in capital | 400 | 400 |
> | Retained earnings | 320 | 180 |
> | Common shareholders equity | 1,020 | 880 |
> | **Total liabilities and equity** | $2,060 | $1,940 |

Sedgwick Company Income Statement	
Year	**Current Year**
Sales	$4,000
Cost of goods sold	3,000
Gross profit	1,000
Operating expenses	650
Operating profit	350
Interest expense	50
Earnings before taxes	300
Taxes	100
Net income	200
Common dividends	60

Answer:

- current ratio $= \dfrac{\text{current assets}}{\text{current liabilities}}$

  current ratio $= \dfrac{620}{325} = 1.9$

- total asset turnover $= \dfrac{\text{revenue}}{\text{average assets}}$

  total asset turnover $= \dfrac{4{,}000}{(2{,}060 + 1{,}940) / 2} = 2.0$

- net profit margin $= \dfrac{\text{net income}}{\text{revenue}}$

  net profit margin $= \dfrac{200}{4{,}000} = 5.0\%$

- return on common equity $= \dfrac{\text{net income} - \text{preferred dividends}}{\text{average common equity}}$

  return on common equity $= \dfrac{200}{(1{,}020 + 880) / 2} = 21.1\%$

- debt-to-equity ratio $= \dfrac{\text{total debt}}{\text{total equity}}$

  debt-to-equity ratio $= \dfrac{610 + 160 + 55}{1{,}020} = 80.9\%$

  Note that preferred equity would be included in the denominator if there were any, and that we have included short-term debt and the current portion of long-term debt in calculating total (interest-bearing) debt.

LOS 26.c: Describe relationships among ratios and evaluate a company using ratio analysis.

CFA® Program Curriculum, Volume 3, page 311

EXAMPLE: Relationships among ratios

An analyst calculates the following activity and liquidity ratios for a company over the last three years:

	20X8	20X7	20X6
Current ratio	2.0	1.5	1.2
Quick ratio	0.5	0.8	1.0
Days of inventory	60	50	30
Days' sales outstanding	20	30	40

Determine what the analyst should infer from these ratios taken together.

Answer:

The current ratio has increased over this period, while the quick ratio has decreased. This could result from inventories increasing or from current assets other than inventories decreasing. The increase in days of inventory on hand suggests increasing inventories explain the opposing trends in the current and quick ratios.

The decrease in days' sales outstanding indicates that the company has been collecting cash from customers sooner than it had been in the past. Taken together, these ratios suggest the company may be accelerating its collections to make up for a drain on cash from poor inventory management.

EXAMPLE: Using ratios to evaluate a company

An analyst is comparing the values of several ratios for the current year to their prior-year values, the current industry average values, and industry average ratios for Sedgwick Company. These selected ratio values are shown in the following table.

	Current Year	Previous Year	Industry Average
Current ratio	1.9	2.1	1.5
Total asset turnover	2.0	2.3	2.4
Net profit margin	5.0%	5.8%	6.5%
Return on common equity	21.1%	24.1%	19.8%
Debt-to-equity	80.9%	99.4%	35.7%

Discuss how these ratios compare with the company's performance last year and with the industry performance.

Answer:

Although the firm's liquidity, as measured by the current ratio, has decreased over the past year, it remains above the industry average.

Total asset turnover has declined over the past year and now appears to be significantly lower than the industry average.

Net profit margin is lower than last year and much lower than the industry average.

Return on equity is lower than last year but still higher than the industry average. Given the decline in net profit margin and total asset turnover, it is likely that higher-than-average financial leverage is the reason for this ROE outperformance.

Our supposition about the firm's financial leverage is confirmed by its debt-to-equity ratios. While the current year's ratio is lower than last year's, it is still more than twice the industry-average ratio. The significant decrease in the company's debt-to-equity ratio over the past year suggests the company is trying to get its debt level more in line with the industry average.

MODULE QUIZ 26.1, 26.2, 26.3

To best evaluate your performance, enter your quiz answers online.

1. To study trends in a firm's cost of goods sold (COGS), the analyst should standardize the cost of goods sold numbers to a common-sized basis by dividing COGS by:
   A. assets.
   B. sales.
   C. net income.

2. Which of the following is *least likely* a limitation of financial ratios?
   A. Data on comparable firms are difficult to acquire.
   B. Determining the target or comparison value for a ratio requires judgment.
   C. Different accounting treatments require the analyst to adjust the data before comparing ratios.

3. RGB, Inc.'s purchases during the year were $100,000. The balance sheet shows an average accounts payable balance of $12,000. RGB's payables payment period is *closest* to:
   A. 37 days.
   B. 44 days.
   C. 52 days.

4. RGB, Inc. has a gross profit of $45,000 on sales of $150,000. The balance sheet shows average total assets of $75,000 with an average inventory balance of $15,000. RGB's total asset turnover and inventory turnover are *closest* to:

	Asset turnover	Inventory turnover
A.	7.00 times	2.00 times
B.	2.00 times	7.00 times
C.	0.50 times	0.33 times

5. If RGB, Inc. has annual sales of $100,000, average accounts payable of $30,000, and average accounts receivable of $25,000, RGB's receivables turnover and average collection period are *closest* to:

Receivables turnover	Average collection period
A. 2.1 times	174 days
B. 3.3 times	111 days
C. 4.0 times	91 days

6. A company's current ratio is 1.9. If some of the accounts payable are paid off from the cash account, the:
   A. numerator would decrease by a greater percentage than the denominator, resulting in a lower current ratio.
   B. denominator would decrease by a greater percentage than the numerator, resulting in a higher current ratio.
   C. numerator and denominator would decrease proportionally, leaving the current ratio unchanged.

7. A company's quick ratio is 1.2. If inventory were purchased for cash, the:
   A. numerator would decrease more than the denominator, resulting in a lower quick ratio.
   B. denominator would decrease more than the numerator, resulting in a higher current ratio.
   C. numerator and denominator would decrease proportionally, leaving the current ratio unchanged.

8. All other things held constant, which of the following transactions will increase a firm's current ratio if the ratio is greater than one?
   A. Accounts receivable are collected and the funds received are deposited in the firm's cash account.
   B. Fixed assets are purchased from the cash account.
   C. Accounts payable are paid with funds from the cash account.

9. RGB, Inc.'s receivable turnover is ten times, the inventory turnover is five times, and the payables turnover is nine times. RGB's cash conversion cycle is *closest* to:
   A. 69 days.
   B. 104 days.
   C. 150 days.

10. An analyst who is interested in a company's long-term solvency would *most likely* examine the:
    A. return on total capital.
    B. defensive interval ratio.
    C. fixed charge coverage ratio.

11. RGB, Inc.'s income statement shows sales of $1,000, cost of goods sold of $400, pre-interest operating expense of $300, and interest expense of $100. RGB's interest coverage ratio is *closest* to:
    A. 2 times.
    B. 3 times.
    C. 4 times.

Video covering this content is available online.

MODULE 26.4: DUPONT ANALYSIS

LOS 26.d: Demonstrate the application of DuPont analysis of return on equity and calculate and interpret effects of changes in its components.

CFA® Program Curriculum, Volume 3, page 313

The **DuPont system of analysis** is an approach that can be used to analyze return on equity (ROE). It uses basic algebra to break down ROE into a function of different ratios, so an analyst can see the impact of leverage, profit margins, and turnover on shareholder returns. There are two variants of the DuPont system: The original three-part approach and the extended five-part system.

For the **original approach**, start with ROE defined as:

$$\text{return on equity} = \left(\frac{\text{net income}}{\text{average equity}} \right)$$

Average or year-end values for equity can be used. Multiplying ROE by (revenue/revenue) and rearranging terms produces:

$$\text{return on equity} = \left(\frac{\text{net income}}{\text{revenue}} \right) \left(\frac{\text{revenue}}{\text{average equity}} \right)$$

The first term is the profit margin, and the second term is the equity turnover:

$$\text{return on equity} = \left(\frac{\text{net profit}}{\text{margin}} \right) \left(\frac{\text{equity}}{\text{turnover}} \right)$$

We can expand this further by multiplying these terms by (assets/assets), and rearranging terms:

$$\text{return on equity} = \left(\frac{\text{net income}}{\text{revenue}} \right) \left(\frac{\text{revenue}}{\text{average total assets}} \right) \left(\frac{\text{average total assets}}{\text{equity}} \right)$$

The first term is still the profit margin, the second term is now asset turnover, and the third term is a financial leverage ratio that will increase as the use of debt financing increases:

$$\text{return on equity} = \left(\frac{\text{net profit}}{\text{margin}} \right) \left(\frac{\text{asset}}{\text{turnover}} \right) \left(\frac{\text{leverage}}{\text{ratio}} \right)$$

PROFESSOR'S NOTE

The leverage ratio is sometimes called the "equity multiplier."

This is the original DuPont equation. It is arguably the most important equation in ratio analysis, since it breaks down a very important ratio (ROE) into three key components. If ROE is relatively low, it must be that at least one of the following is true: The company has a poor profit margin, the company has poor asset turnover, or the firm has too little leverage.

PROFESSOR'S NOTE

Often candidates get confused and think the DuPont method is a way to calculate ROE. While you can calculate ROE given the components of either the original or extended DuPont equations, this isn't necessary if you have the financial statements. If you have net income and equity, you can calculate ROE. The DuPont method is a way to decompose ROE, to better see what changes are driving the changes in ROE.

EXAMPLE: Decomposition of ROE with original DuPont

Staret, Inc. has maintained a stable and relatively high ROE of approximately 18% over the last three years. Use traditional DuPont analysis to decompose this ROE into its three components and comment on trends in company performance.

Staret, Inc. Selected Balance Sheet and Income Statement Items (Millions)			
Year	20X3	20X4	20X5
Net income	21.5	22.3	21.9
Revenue	305	350	410
Average equity	119	124	126
Average assets	230	290	350

Answer:

ROE

   20X3: 21.5 / 119 = 18.1%

   20X4: 22.3 / 124 = 18.0%

   20X5: 21.9 / 126 = 17.4%

DuPont

   20X3: 7.0% × 1.33 × 1.93

   20X4: 6.4% × 1.21 × 2.34

   20X5: 5.3% × 1.17 × 2.78

(some rounding in values)

While ROE has dropped only slightly, both total asset turnover and net profit margin have declined. The effects of declining net margins and turnover on ROE have been offset by a significant increase in leverage. The analyst should be concerned about the decrease in net margin and determine the combination of pricing pressure and/or increasing expenses that caused this. Note that the company has become more risky due to increased debt financing.

> **EXAMPLE: Computing ROE using original DuPont**
>
> A company has a net profit margin of 4%, asset turnover of 2.0, and a debt-to-assets ratio of 60%. What is the ROE?
>
> **Answer:**
>
> Debt-to-assets = 60%, which means equity to assets is 40%; this implies assets to equity (the leverage ratio) is 1 / 0.4 = 2.5
>
> $$\text{ROE} = \left(\begin{array}{c}\text{net profit}\\\text{margin}\end{array}\right)\left(\begin{array}{c}\text{total asset}\\\text{turnover}\end{array}\right)\left(\frac{\text{average assets}}{\text{average equity}}\right)$$
>
> $$= (0.04)(2.00)(2.50) = 0.20, \text{ or } 20\%$$

The **extended (5-way) DuPont equation** takes the net profit margin and breaks it down further.

$$\text{ROE} = \left(\frac{\text{net income}}{\text{EBT}}\right)\left(\frac{\text{EBT}}{\text{EBIT}}\right)\left(\frac{\text{EBIT}}{\text{revenue}}\right)\left(\frac{\text{revenue}}{\text{average assets}}\right)\left(\frac{\text{average assets}}{\text{average equity}}\right)$$

Note that the first term in the 3-part DuPont equation, net profit margin, has been decomposed into three terms:

$\dfrac{\text{net income}}{\text{EBT}}$ is called the *tax burden* and is equal to (1 – tax rate).

$\dfrac{\text{EBT}}{\text{EBIT}}$ is called the *interest burden*.

$\dfrac{\text{EBIT}}{\text{revenue}}$ is called the *EBIT margin*.

We then have:

$$\text{ROE} = \left(\begin{array}{c}\text{tax}\\\text{burden}\end{array}\right)\left(\begin{array}{c}\text{interest}\\\text{burden}\end{array}\right)\left(\begin{array}{c}\text{EBIT}\\\text{margin}\end{array}\right)\left(\begin{array}{c}\text{asset}\\\text{turnover}\end{array}\right)\left(\begin{array}{c}\text{financial}\\\text{leverage}\end{array}\right)$$

An increase in interest expense as proportion of EBIT will increase the interest burden (i.e., decrease the interest burden ratio). Increases in either the tax burden or the interest burden (i.e., decreases in the ratios) will tend to decrease ROE.

EBIT in the second two expressions can be replaced by operating earnings. In this case, we have the operating margin rather than the EBIT margin. The interest burden term would then show the effects of nonoperating income as well as the effect of interest expense.

Note that in general, high profit margins, leverage, and asset turnover will lead to high levels of ROE. However, this version of the formula shows that more leverage *does not always* lead to higher ROE. As leverage rises, so does the interest burden. Hence, the positive effects of leverage can be offset by the higher interest payments that accompany more debt. Note that higher taxes will always lead to lower levels of ROE.

EXAMPLE: Extended DuPont analysis

An analyst has gathered data from two companies in the same industry. Calculate the ROE for both companies and use the extended DuPont analysis to explain the critical factors that account for the differences in the two companies' ROEs.

Selected Income and Balance Sheet Data		
	Company A	**Company B**
Revenues	$500	$900
EBIT	35	100
Interest expense	5	0
EBT	30	100
Taxes	10	40
Net income	20	60
Average assets	250	300
Total debt	100	50
Average equity	$150	$250

Answer:

EBIT margin = EBIT / revenue

    Company A: EBIT margin = 35 / 500 = 7.0%
    Company B: EBIT margin = 100 / 900 = 11.1%

asset turnover = revenue / average assets

    Company A: asset turnover = 500 / 250 = 2.0
    Company B: asset turnover = 900 / 300 = 3.0

interest burden = EBT / EBIT

    Company A: interest burden = 30 / 35 = 85.7%
    Company B: interest burden = 100 / 100 = 1

financial leverage = average assets / average equity

    Company A: financial leverage = 250 / 150 = 1.67
    Company B: financial leverage = 300 / 250 = 1.2

tax burden = net income / EBT

    Company A: tax burden = 20 / 30 = 66.7%
    Company B: tax burden = 60 / 100 = 60.0%

Company A: ROE = 0.667 × 0.857 × 0.07 × 2.0 × 1.67 = 13.4%

Company B: ROE = 0.608 × 1.0 × 0.111 × 3.0 × 1.2 = 24%

Company B has a higher tax burden but a lower interest burden (a lower ratio indicates a higher burden). Company B has better EBIT margins and better asset utilization (perhaps management of inventory, receivables, or payables, or a lower cost basis in its fixed assets due to their age), and less leverage. Its higher EBIT margins and asset turnover are the main factors leading to its significantly higher ROE, which it achieves with less leverage than Company A.

MODULE QUIZ 26.4

To best evaluate your performance, enter your quiz answers online.

1. Return on equity using the traditional DuPont formula equals:
    A. (net profit margin) (interest component) (solvency ratio).
    B. (net profit margin) (total asset turnover) (tax retention rate).
    C. (net profit margin) (total asset turnover) (financial leverage multiplier).

2. RGB, Inc. has a net profit margin of 12%, a total asset turnover of 1.2 times, and a financial leverage multiplier of 1.2 times. RGB's return on equity is *closest* to:
    A. 12.0%.
    B. 14.2%.
    C. 17.3%.

3. Use the following information for RGB, Inc.:

    ■ EBIT / revenue = 10%

    ■ Tax retention rate = 60%

    ■ Revenue / assets = 1.8 times

    ■ Current ratio = 2 times

    ■ EBT / EBIT = 0.9 times

    ■ Assets / equity = 1.9 times

    RGB, Inc.'s return on equity is *closest* to:
    A. 10.5%.
    B. 14.0%.
    C. 18.5%.

4. Which of the following equations *least accurately* represents return on equity?
    A. (net profit margin)(equity turnover).
    B. (net profit margin)(total asset turnover)(assets / equity).
    C. (ROA)(interest burden)(tax retention rate).

5. Paragon Co. has an operating profit margin (EBIT / revenue) of 11%; an asset turnover ratio of 1.2; a financial leverage multiplier of 1.5 times; an average tax rate of 35%; and an interest burden of 0.7. Paragon's return on equity is *closest* to:
    A. 9%.
    B. 10%.
    C. 11%.

Video covering this content is available online.

MODULE 26.5: MORE FINANCIAL RATIOS

LOS 26.e: Calculate and interpret ratios used in equity analysis and credit analysis.

CFA® Program Curriculum, Volume 3, page 319

Valuation ratios are used in analysis for investment in common equity. The most widely used valuation ratio is the *price-to-earnings* (P/E) ratio, the ratio of the current market price of a share of stock divided by the company's earnings per share. Related measures based on price per share are the *price-to-cash flow*, the *price-to-sales*, and the *price-to-book value* ratios.

PROFESSOR'S NOTE

The use of the above valuation ratios is covered in Equity Investments.

Per-share valuation measures include *earnings per share* (EPS). *Basic EPS* is net income available to common divided by the weighted average number of common shares outstanding.

Diluted EPS is a "what if" value. It is calculated to be the lowest possible EPS that could have been reported if all firm securities that can be converted into common stock, and that would decrease basic EPS if they had been, were converted. That is, if all dilutive securities had been converted. Potentially dilutive securities include convertible debt and convertible preferred stock, as well as options and warrants issued by the company. The numerator of diluted EPS is increased by the after-tax interest savings on any dilutive debt securities and by the dividends on any dilutive convertible preferred stock. The denominator is increased by the common shares that would result from conversion or exchange of dilutive securities into common shares.

PROFESSOR'S NOTE

Refer back to our topic review of Understanding Income Statements for details and examples of how to calculate basic and diluted EPS.

Other per-share measures include *cash flow per share, EBIT per share*, and *EBITDA per share*. Per share measures are not comparable because the number of outstanding shares differ among firms. For example, assume Firm A and Firm B both report net income of $100. If Firm A has 100 shares outstanding, its EPS is $1 per share. If Firm B has 20 shares outstanding, its EPS is $5 per share.

Dividends

Dividends are declared on a per-common-share basis. Total dividends on a firm-wide basis are referred to as *dividends declared*. Neither EPS nor net income is reduced by the payment of common stock dividends. Net income minus dividends declared is retained earnings, the earnings that are used to grow the corporation rather than being distributed to equity holders. The proportion of a firm's net income that is retained to fund growth is an important determinant of the firm's *sustainable growth rate*.

To estimate the sustainable growth rate for a firm, the rate of return on resources is measured as the return on equity capital, or the ROE. The proportion of earnings reinvested is known as the *retention rate* (RR).

- The formula for the sustainable growth rate, which is how fast the firm can grow without additional external equity issues while holding leverage constant, is:

$$g = RR \times ROE$$

■ The calculation of the retention rate is:

$$\text{retention rate} = \frac{\text{net income available to common} - \text{dividends declared}}{\text{net income available to common}}$$

$$= 1 - \text{dividend payout ratio}$$

where:

$$\text{dividend payout ratio} = \frac{\text{dividends declared}}{\text{net income available to common}}$$

> **EXAMPLE: Calculating sustainable growth**
>
> The following figure provides data for three companies.
>
> | Growth Analysis Data | | | |
> |---|---|---|---|
> | **Company** | **A** | **B** | **C** |
> | Earnings per share | $3.00 | $4.00 | $5.00 |
> | Dividends per share | 1.50 | 1.00 | 2.00 |
> | Return on equity | 14% | 12% | 10% |
>
> Calculate the sustainable growth rate for each company.
>
> **Answer:**
>
> RR = 1 – (dividends / earnings)
>
> > Company A: RR = 1 – (1.50 / 3.00) = 0.500
> > Company B: RR = 1 – (1.00 / 4.00) = 0.750
> > Company C: RR = 1 – (2.00 / 5.00) = 0.600
>
> g = RR × ROE
>
> > Company A: g = 0.500 × 14% = 7.0%
> > Company B: g = 0.750 × 12% = 9.0%
> > Company C: g = 0.600 × 10% = 6.0%

Some ratios have specific applications in certain industries.

Net income per employee and *sales per employee* are used in the analysis and valuation of service and consulting companies.

Growth in same-store sales is used in the restaurant and retail industries to indicate growth without the effects of new locations that have been opened. It is a measure of how well the firm is doing at attracting and keeping existing customers and, in the case of locations with overlapping markets, may indicate that new locations are taking customers from existing ones.

Sales per square foot is another metric commonly used in the retail industry.

Business Risk

The standard deviation of revenue, standard deviation of operating income, and the standard deviation of net income are all indicators of the variation in and the uncertainty about a firm's performance. Since they all depend on the size of the firm to a great extent, analysts employ a size-adjusted measure of variation. The **coefficient of variation** for a variable is its standard deviation divided by its expected value.

PROFESSOR'S NOTE

We saw this before as a measure of portfolio risk in Quantitative Methods.

Certainly, different industries have different levels of uncertainty about revenues, expenses, taxes, and nonoperating items. Comparing coefficients of variation for a firm across time, or among a firm and its peers, can aid the analyst in assessing both the relative and absolute degree of risk a firm faces in generating income for its investors.

$$\text{CV sales} = \frac{\text{standard deviation of sales}}{\text{mean sales}}$$

$$\text{CV operating income} = \frac{\text{standard deviation of operating income}}{\text{mean operating income}}$$

$$\text{CV net income} = \frac{\text{standard deviation of net income}}{\text{mean net income}}$$

Banks, insurance companies, and other financial firms carry their own challenges for analysts. Part of the challenge is to understand the commonly used terms and the ratios they represent.

Capital adequacy typically refers to the ratio of some dollar measure of the risk, both operational and financial, of the firm to its equity capital. Other measures of capital are also used. A common measure of capital risk is *value-at-risk*, which is an estimate of the dollar size of the loss that a firm will exceed only some specific percent of the time, over a specific period of time.

Banks are subject to minimum *reserve requirements*. Their ratios of various liabilities to their central bank reserves must be above the minimums. The ratio of a bank's liquid assets to certain liabilities is called the *liquid asset requirement*.

The performance of financial companies that lend funds is often summarized as the *net interest margin*, which is simply interest income divided by the firm's interest-earning assets.

Credit Analysis

Credit analysis is based on many of the ratios that we have already covered in this review. In assessing a company's ability to service and repay its debt, analysts use interest coverage ratios (calculated with EBIT or EBITDA), return on capital, and debt-to-assets ratios. Other ratios focus on various measures of cash flow to total debt.

Ratios have been used to analyze and predict firm bankruptcies. Altman (2000)[1] developed a Z-score that is useful in predicting firm bankruptcies (a low score indicates high probability of failure). The predictive model was based on a firm's working capital to assets, retained earnings to assets, EBIT to assets, market to book value of a share of stock, and revenues to assets.

> **PROFESSOR'S NOTE**
>
> Credit analysis is covered in more detail in Fixed Income.

LOS 26.f: Explain the requirements for segment reporting and calculate and interpret segment ratios.

CFA® Program Curriculum, Volume 3, page 327

A **business segment** is a portion of a larger company that accounts for more than 10% of the company's revenues or assets, and is distinguishable from the company's other lines of business in terms of the risk and return characteristics of the segment. **Geographic segments** are also identified when they meet the size criterion above and the geographic unit has a business environment that is different from that of other segments or the remainder of the company's business.

For example, in its 2016 annual report, Boeing described its business segments as follows (see Boeing.com):

> We are organized based on the products and services we offer. We operate in five principal segments:
>
> - Commercial Airplanes;
> - Our Defense, Space & Security (BDS) business comprises three segments:
>   - Boeing Military Aircraft (BMA)
>   - Network & Space Systems (N&SS)
>   - Global Services & Support (GS&S)
> - Boeing Capital (BCC).

Both U.S. GAAP and IFRS require companies to report segment data, but the required disclosure items are only a subset of the required disclosures for the company as a whole. Nonetheless, an analyst can prepare a more detailed analysis and forecast by examining the performance of business or geographic segments separately. Segment profit margins, asset utilization (turnover), and return on assets can be very useful in gaining a clear picture of a firm's overall operations. For forecasting, growth rates of segment revenues and profits can be used to estimate future sales and profits and to determine the changes in company characteristics over time.

---

1. Edward I. Altman, "Predicting Financial Distress of Companies: Revisiting the Z-Score and Zeta® Models," July 2000.

LOS 26.g: Describe how ratio analysis and other techniques can be used to model and forecast earnings.

CFA® Program Curriculum, Volume 3, page 330

Ratio analysis can be used in preparing pro forma financial statements that provide estimates of financial statement items for one or more future periods. The preparation of pro forma financial statements and related forecasts is covered in some detail in the Study Session on corporate finance. Here, some examples will suffice.

A forecast of financial results that begins with an estimate of a firm's next-period revenues might use the most recent COGS, or an average of COGS, from a common-size income statement. On a common-size income statement, COGS is calculated as a percentage of revenue. If the analyst has no reason to believe that COGS in relation to sales will change for the next period, the COGS percentage from a common-size income statement can be used in constructing a pro forma income statement for the next period based on the estimate of sales.

Similarly, the analyst may believe that certain ratios will remain the same or change in one direction or the other for the next period. In the absence of any information indicating a change, an analyst may choose to incorporate the operating profit margin from the prior period into a pro forma income statement for the next period. Beginning with an estimate of next-period sales, the estimated operating profit margin can be used to forecast operating profits for the next period.

Rather than point estimates of sales and net and operating margins, the analyst may examine possible changes in order to create a range of possible values for key financial variables.

Three methods of examining the variability of financial outcomes around point estimates are: *sensitivity analysis*, *scenario analysis*, and *simulation*. Sensitivity analysis is based on "what if" questions such as: What will be the effect on net income if sales increase by 3% rather than the estimated 5%? Scenario analysis is based on specific scenarios (a specific set of outcomes for key variables) and will also yield a range of values for financial statement items. Simulation is a technique in which probability distributions for key variables are selected and a computer is used to generate a distribution of values for outcomes based on repeated random selection of values for the key variables.

MODULE QUIZ 26.5

To best evaluate your performance, enter your quiz answers online.

1. A firm has a dividend payout ratio of 40%, a net profit margin of 10%, an asset turnover of 0.9 times, and a financial leverage multiplier of 1.2 times. The firm's sustainable growth rate is *closest* to:
    A. 4.3%.
    B. 6.5%.
    C. 8.0%.

2. Accounting standards require segment reporting for a distinguishable part of a firm that comprises at least:
   A. 10% of assets.
   B. 5% of revenues.
   C. 10% of earnings.

3. An analyst who needs to model and forecast a company's earnings for the next three years would be *least likely* to:
   A. assume that key financial ratios will remain unchanged for the forecast period.
   B. use common-size financial statements to estimate expenses as a percentage of net income.
   C. examine the variability of the predicted outcomes by performing a sensitivity or scenario analysis.

KEY CONCEPTS

LOS 26.a

Ratios can be used to project earnings and future cash flow, evaluate a firm's flexibility, assess management's performance, evaluate changes in the firm and industry over time, and compare the firm with industry competitors.

Vertical common-size data are stated as a percentage of sales for income statements or as a percentage of total assets for balance sheets. Horizontal common-size data present each item as a percentage of its value in a base year.

Ratio analysis has limitations. Ratios are not useful when viewed in isolation and require adjustments when different companies use different accounting treatments. Comparable ratios may be hard to find for companies that operate in multiple industries. Ratios must be analyzed relative to one another, and determining the range of acceptable values for a ratio can be difficult.

LOS 26.b

Activity ratios indicate how well a firm uses its assets. They include receivables turnover, days of sales outstanding, inventory turnover, days of inventory on hand, payables turnover, payables payment period, and turnover ratios for total assets, fixed assets, and working capital.

Liquidity ratios indicate a firm's ability to meet its short-term obligations. They include the current, quick, and cash ratios, the defensive interval, and the cash conversion cycle.

Solvency ratios indicate a firm's ability to meet its long-term obligations. They include the debt-to-equity, debt-to-capital, debt-to-assets, financial leverage, interest coverage, and fixed charge coverage ratios.

Profitability ratios indicate how well a firm generates operating income and net income. They include net, gross, and operating profit margins, pretax margin, return on assets, operating return on assets, return on total capital, return on total equity, and return on common equity.

Valuation ratios are used to compare the relative values of stocks. They include earnings per share and price-to-earnings, price-to-sales, price-to-book value, and price-to-cash-flow ratios.

LOS 26.c

An analyst should use an appropriate combination of different ratios to evaluate a company over time and relative to comparable companies. The interpretation of an increase in ROE, for example, may be quite different for a firm that has significantly increased its financial leverage compared to one that has maintained or decreased its financial leverage.

LOS 26.d

Basic DuPont equation:

$$\text{ROE} = \left(\frac{\text{net income}}{\text{sales}}\right)\left(\frac{\text{sales}}{\text{assets}}\right)\left(\frac{\text{assets}}{\text{equity}}\right)$$

Extended DuPont equation:

$$\text{ROE} = \left(\frac{\text{net income}}{\text{EBT}}\right)\left(\frac{\text{EBT}}{\text{EBIT}}\right)\left(\frac{\text{EBIT}}{\text{revenue}}\right)\left(\frac{\text{revenue}}{\text{total assets}}\right)\left(\frac{\text{total assets}}{\text{total equity}}\right)$$

LOS 26.e

Ratios used in equity analysis include price-to-earnings, price-to-cash flow, price-to-sales, and price-to-book value ratios, and basic and diluted earnings per share. Other ratios are relevant to specific industries such as retail and financial services.

Credit analysis emphasizes interest coverage ratios, return on capital, debt-to-assets ratios, and cash flow to total debt.

LOS 26.f

A business or geographic segment is a portion of a firm that has risk and return characteristics distinguishable from the rest of the firm and accounts for more than 10% of the firm's sales or assets.

Firms are required to report some items for significant business and geographic segments. Profitability, leverage, and turnover ratios by segment can give the analyst a better understanding of the performance of the overall business.

LOS 26.g

Ratio analysis in conjunction with other techniques can be used to construct pro forma financial statements based on a forecast of sales growth and assumptions about the relation of changes in key income statement and balance sheet items to growth of sales.

ANSWER KEY FOR MODULE QUIZZES

Module Quiz 26.1, 26.2, 26.3

1. **B** With a vertical common-size income statement, all income statement accounts are divided by sales. (Module 26.1, LOS 26.a)

2. **A** Company and industry data are widely available from numerous private and public sources. The other statements describe limitations of financial ratios. (Module 26.1, LOS 26.a)

3. **B** payables turnover = (purchases / avg. AP) = 100 / 12 = 8.33

    payables payment period = 365 / 8.33 = 43.8 days

    (Module 26.2, LOS 26.b)

4. **B** total asset turnover = (sales / total assets) = 150 / 75 = 2 times

    inventory turnover = (COGS / avg. inventory) = (150 – 45) / 15 = 7 times

    (Module 26.2, LOS 26.b)

5. **C** receivables turnover = (S / avg. AR) = 100 / 25 = 4

    average collection period = 365 / 4 = 91.25 days

    (Module 26.2, LOS 26.b)

6. **B** Current ratio = current assets / current liabilities. If cash (a current asset) and AP (a current liability) decrease by the same amount and the current ratio is greater than 1, then the numerator decreases less in percentage terms than the denominator, and the current ratio increases. (Module 26.2, LOS 26.b)

7. **A** Quick ratio = (cash + marketable securities + AR) / current liabilities. If cash decreases, the quick ratio will also decrease. The denominator is unchanged. (Module 26.2, LOS 26.b)

8. **C** Current ratio = current assets / current liabilities. If CR is > 1, then if CA and CL both fall, the overall ratio will increase. (Module 26.2, LOS 26.b)

9. **A** (365 / 10 + 365 / 5 – 365 / 9) = 69 days

    (Module 26.2, LOS 26.b)

10. **C** Fixed charge coverage is a solvency ratio. Return on total capital is a measure of profitability and the defensive interval ratio is a liquidity measure. (Module 26.3, LOS 26.b)

11. **B** Interest coverage ratio = EBIT / I = (1,000 – 400 – 300) / 100 = 3 times

    (Module 26.3, LOS 26.b)

Module Quiz 26.4

1. **C** This is the correct formula for the three-ratio DuPont model for ROE. (LOS 26.d)

2. **C** return on equity $= \left(\dfrac{\text{net income}}{\text{sales}}\right)\left(\dfrac{\text{sales}}{\text{assets}}\right)\left(\dfrac{\text{assets}}{\text{equity}}\right) = (0.12)(1.2)(1.2) =$
    $0.1728 = 17.28\%$

    (LOS 26.d)

3. **C** Tax burden $= (1 - \text{tax rate}) = \text{tax retention rate} = 0.6$.

    ROE $= 0.6 \times 0.9 \times 0.1 \times 1.8 \times 1.9 = 0.1847 = 18.47\%$.

    (LOS 26.d)

4. **C** (ROA)(interest burden)(tax retention rate) is not one of the DuPont models for calculating ROE. (LOS 26.d)

5. **A** Tax burden $= 1 - 0.35 = 0.65$.

    ROE $= 0.65 \times 0.7 \times 0.11 \times 1.2 \times 1.5 = 0.0901$.

    (LOS 26.d)

Module Quiz 26.5

1. **B** g = (retention rate)(ROE)

    ROE = net profit margin × asset turnover × equity multiplier = $(0.1)(0.9)(1.2) = 0.108$

    g = $(1 - 0.4)(0.108) = 6.5\%$

    (LOS 26.e)

2. **A** For segment reporting, a business segment is a distinguishable portion of the overall company that produces more than 10% of its revenues or accounts for more than 10% of its assets. (LOS 26.f)

3. **B** An earnings forecast model would typically estimate expenses as a percentage of sales. (LOS 26.g)

READING 27

Inventories

EXAM FOCUS

This topic review discusses the different inventory cost flow methods: FIFO, LIFO, and weighted average cost. You must understand how to calculate COGS, ending inventory, and gross profit under each of these methods. Also, you must understand the effects of each method on a firm's liquidity, profitability, activity, and solvency ratios. Be able to apply the appropriate inventory valuation method under IFRS (lower of cost or net realizable value) and U.S. GAAP (lower of cost or market), and calculate inventory losses and loss reversals, if allowed. Finally, be able to evaluate a firm's effectiveness in managing its inventory.

MODULE 27.1: COST FLOW METHODS

Video covering this content is available online.

Merchandising firms, such as wholesalers and retailers, purchase inventory that is ready for sale. In this case, inventory is reported in one account on the balance sheet. Manufacturing firms normally report inventory using three separate accounts: raw materials, work-in-process, and finished goods.

Cost of goods sold (COGS), also referred to as cost of sales (COS) under IFRS, is related to the beginning balance of inventory, purchases, and the ending balance of inventory. The relationship is summarized in the following equation:

COGS = beginning inventory + purchases − ending inventory

This equation can be rearranged to solve for any of the four variables:

purchases = ending inventory − beginning inventory + COGS

beginning inventory = COGS − purchases + ending inventory

ending inventory = beginning inventory + purchases − COGS

PROFESSOR'S NOTE

Many candidates find the inventory equation easiest to remember in this last form. If you start with beginning inventory, add the goods that came in (purchases), and subtract the goods that went out (COGS), the result must be ending inventory.

LOS 27.a: Distinguish between costs included in inventories and costs recognised as expenses in the period in which they are incurred.

CFA® Program Curriculum, Volume 3, page 347

Cost is the basis for most inventory valuation. The main issue involves determining the amounts that should be included in cost.

The costs included in inventory are similar under IFRS and U.S. GAAP. These costs, known as **product costs**, are capitalized in the Inventories account on the balance sheet and include:

- Purchase cost less trade discounts and rebates.

- Conversion (manufacturing) costs including labor and overhead.

- Other costs necessary to bring the inventory to its present location and condition.

By capitalizing inventory cost as an asset, expense recognition is delayed until the inventory is sold and revenue is recognized.

Not all inventory costs are capitalized; some costs are expensed in the period incurred. These costs, known as **period costs**, include:

- Abnormal waste of materials, labor, or overhead.

- Storage costs (unless required as part of production).

- Administrative overhead.

- Selling costs.

EXAMPLE: Costs included in inventory

Vindaloo Company manufactures a single product. The following information was taken from the company's production and cost records last year:

Units produced	5,000
Raw materials	$15,000
Conversion cost for finished goods	$20,000
Freight-in to plant	$800
Storage cost for finished goods	$500
Abnormal waste	$100
Freight-out customers	$1,100

Assuming no abnormal waste is included in conversion cost, calculate the capitalized cost of one unit.

©2018 Kaplan, Inc.

Answer:

Capitalized inventory cost includes the raw materials cost, conversion cost, and freight-in to plant, as follows:

Raw materials	$15,000	
Conversion cost	$20,000	
Freight-in to plant	$800	
Total capitalized cost	$35,800	
Units produced	5,000	
Capitalized cost per unit	$7.16	($35,800 / 5,000 units)

The storage cost, abnormal waste, and the freight-out to customers are expensed as incurred.

LOS 27.b: Describe different inventory valuation methods (cost formulas).

CFA® Program Curriculum, Volume 3, page 348

If the cost of inventory remains constant over time, determining the firm's COGS and ending inventory is simple. To compute COGS, simply multiply the number of units sold by the cost per unit. Similarly, to compute ending inventory, multiply the number of units remaining by the cost per unit.

However, it is likely that the cost of purchasing or producing inventory will change over time. As a result, firms must select a cost flow method (known as the *cost flow assumption* under U.S. GAAP and *cost flow formula* under IFRS) to allocate the inventory cost to the income statement (COGS) and the balance sheet (ending inventory).

Under IFRS, the permissible methods are:

- Specific identification.
- First-in, first-out.
- Weighted average cost.

U.S. GAAP permits these same cost flow methods, as well as the last-in, first-out (LIFO) method. LIFO is not allowed under IFRS.

A firm can use one or more of the inventory cost flow methods. However, the firm must employ the same cost flow method for inventories of similar nature and use.

Under the **specific identification** method, each unit sold is matched with the unit's actual cost. Specific identification is appropriate when inventory items are not interchangeable and is commonly used by firms with a small number of costly and easily distinguishable items such as jewelry. Specific identification is also appropriate for special orders or projects outside a firm's normal course of business.

Under the **first-in, first-out** (FIFO) method, the first item purchased is assumed to be the first item sold. The advantage of FIFO is that ending inventory is valued based on the most recent purchases, arguably the best approximation of current cost. Conversely, FIFO COGS is based on the earliest purchase costs. In an inflationary environment, COGS will be understated compared to current cost. As a result, earnings will be overstated.

Under the **last-in, first-out** (LIFO) method, the item purchased most recently is assumed to be the first item sold. In an inflationary environment, LIFO COGS will be higher than FIFO COGS, and earnings will be lower. Lower earnings translate into lower income taxes, which increase cash flow. Under LIFO, ending inventory on the balance sheet is valued using the earliest costs. Therefore, in an inflationary environment, LIFO ending inventory is less than current cost.

 PROFESSOR'S NOTE

The income tax advantages of using LIFO explain its popularity among U.S. firms. The tax savings result in the peculiar situation where lower reported earnings are associated with higher cash flow from operations.

Weighted average cost is a simple and objective method. The average cost per unit of inventory is computed by dividing the total cost of goods available for sale (beginning inventory + purchases) by the total quantity available for sale. To compute COGS, the average cost per unit is multiplied by the number of units sold. Similarly, to compute ending inventory, the average cost per unit is multiplied by the number of units that remain.

During inflationary or deflationary periods, the weighted average cost method will produce an inventory value between those produced by FIFO and LIFO.

Figure 27.1: Inventory Cost Flow Comparison

Method	Assumption	Cost of Goods Sold Consists of...	Ending Inventory Consists of...
FIFO (U.S. and IFRS)	The items first purchased are the first to be sold.	first purchased	most recent purchases
LIFO (U.S. only)	The items last purchased are the first to be sold.	last purchased	earliest purchases
Weighted average cost (U.S. and IFRS)	Items sold are a mix of purchases.	average cost of all items	average cost of all items

LOS 27.c: Calculate and compare cost of sales, gross profit, and ending inventory using different inventory valuation methods and using perpetual and periodic inventory systems.

CFA® Program Curriculum, Volume 3, page 350

The following example demonstrates how to calculate COGS and ending inventory using the FIFO, LIFO, and weighted average cost flow methods.

EXAMPLE: Inventory cost flow methods

Use the inventory data in the following figure to calculate the cost of goods sold and ending inventory under the FIFO, LIFO, and weighted average cost methods.

Inventory Data

January 1 (beginning inventory)	2 units @ $2 per unit =	$4
January 7 purchase	3 units @ $3 per unit =	$9
January 19 purchase	5 units @ $5 per unit =	$25
Cost of goods available	10 units	$38
Units sold during January	7 units	

Answer:

FIFO cost of goods sold. Value the seven units sold at the unit cost of the first units purchased. Start with the earliest units purchased and work down, as illustrated in the following figure.

FIFO COGS Calculation

From beginning inventory	2 units @ $2 per unit =	$4
From first purchase	3 units @ $3 per unit =	$9
From second purchase	2 units @ $5 per unit =	$10
FIFO cost of goods sold	7 units	$23
Ending inventory	3 units @ $5 =	$15

LIFO cost of goods sold. Value the seven units sold at the unit cost of the last units purchased. Start with the most recently purchased units and work up, as illustrated in the following figure.

LIFO COGS Calculation

From second purchase	5 units @ $5 per unit =	$25
From first purchase	2 units @ $3 per unit =	$6
LIFO cost of goods sold	7 units	$31
Ending inventory	2 units @ $2 + 1 unit @ $3 =	$7

Average cost of goods sold. Value the seven units sold at the average unit cost of goods available.

Weighted Average COGS Calculation

Average unit cost	$38 / 10 =	$3.80 per unit
Weighted average cost of goods sold	7 units @ $3.80 per unit =	$26.60
Ending inventory	3 units @ $3.80 per unit =	$11.40

	Summary	
Inventory system	**COGS**	**Ending Inventory**
FIFO	$23.00	$15.00
LIFO	$31.00	$7.00
Average cost	$26.60	$11.40

Note that prices and inventory levels were rising over the period and that purchases during the period were the same for all cost flow methods.

MODULE QUIZ 27.1

To best evaluate your performance, enter your quiz answers online.

1. Which of the following is *most likely* included in a firm's ending inventory?
   A. Storage costs of finished goods.
   B. Variable production overhead.
   C. Selling and administrative costs.

2. Under which inventory cost flow assumption does inventory on the balance sheet *best* approximate its current cost?
   A. First-in, first-out.
   B. Weighted average cost.
   C. Last-in, first-out.

3. During the year, a firm's inventory purchases were as follows:

Quarter	Units Purchased	Cost per Unit	Total
1	400	$3.30	$1,320
2	100	3.60	360
3	200	3.90	780
4	50	4.20	210
	750		$2,670

   ■ The firm uses a periodic inventory system and calculates inventory and COGS at the end of the year.

   ■ Beginning inventory was 200 units at $3 per unit = $600.

   ■ Sales for the year were 600 units.

   Compute COGS for the year under FIFO and LIFO.

FIFO	LIFO
A. $1,920	$2,175
B. $1,920	$1,850
C. $2,070	$2,175

4. During May, a firm's inventory account included the following transactions:

May 1	Inventory	25 units @ $4.00
May 12	Purchased	60 units @ $4.20
May 16	Sold	40 units @ $6.00
May 27	Purchased	30 units @ $4.25
May 29	Sold	40 units @ $6.10

Assuming periodic FIFO inventory costing, gross profit for May was:
A. $132.
B. $147.
C. $153.

5. In periods of rising prices and stable inventory quantities, which of the following *best* describes the effect on gross profit of using LIFO as compared to using FIFO?
A. Lower.
B. Higher.
C. The same.

MODULE 27.2: INVENTORY SYSTEMS

Video covering this content is available online.

Firms account for changes in inventory using either a periodic or perpetual system. In a **periodic inventory system**, inventory values and COGS are determined at the end of the accounting period. No detailed records of inventory are maintained; rather, inventory acquired during the period is reported in a Purchases account. At the end of the period, purchases are added to beginning inventory to arrive at cost of goods available for sale. To calculate COGS, ending inventory is subtracted from goods available for sale.

In a **perpetual inventory system**, inventory values and COGS are updated continuously. Inventory purchased and sold is recorded directly in inventory when the transactions occur. Thus, a Purchases account is not necessary.

For the FIFO and specific identification methods, ending inventory values and COGS are the same whether a periodic or perpetual system is used. However, periodic and perpetual inventory systems can produce different values for inventory and COGS under the LIFO and weighted average cost methods.

The following example illustrates the differences.

EXAMPLE: Periodic vs. perpetual inventory system

Our earlier cost flow illustration was actually an example of a periodic system. Accordingly, we waited until the end of January to calculate COGS and ending inventory. Now assume the purchases and sales occurred as follows:

January 1 (beginning inventory)	2 units @ $2 per unit
January 7 purchase	3 units @ $3 per unit
January 12 sale	4 units
January 19 purchase	5 units @ $5 per unit
January 29 sale	3 units

Recalculate COGS and ending inventory under the FIFO and LIFO cost flow methods using a perpetual inventory system.

Answer:

In the case of FIFO, ending inventory and COGS will be the same as with the periodic system illustrated in the earlier example.

FIFO Perpetual System

The January 12 sale of 4 units consists of:

Units	From		Cost
2	Jan 1 beginning inventory	2 units × $2 =	$4
2	Jan 7 purchase	2 units × $3 =	$6
			$10

The January 29 sale of 3 units consists of:

Units	From		Cost
1	Jan 7 purchase	1 unit × $3 =	$3
2	Jan 19 purchase	2 units × $5 =	$10
			$13

Total FIFO COGS for January		$23

January ending inventory consists of:

Units	From		Cost
3	Jan 19 purchase	3 units × $5 =	$15

FIFO COGS and ending inventory are the same whether a perpetual or periodic system is used because the first-in (and therefore the first-out) values are the same regardless of subsequent purchases.

In the case of LIFO, COGS and ending inventory under a periodic system will be different from those calculated under a perpetual system. In our earlier example, LIFO COGS and ending inventory for January were $31 and $7, respectively, using a periodic system. Using a perpetual system, LIFO COGS and ending inventory are $26 and $12.

LIFO Perpetual System

The January 12 sale of 4 units consists of:

Units	From		Cost
3	Jan 7 purchase	3 units × $3 =	$9
1	Jan 1 purchase	1 units × $2 =	$2
			$11

The January 29 sale of 3 units consists of:

Units	From		Cost
3	Jan 19 purchase	3 units × $5 =	$15

Total LIFO COGS for January		$26

January ending inventory consists of:

Units	From		Cost
1	Jan 1 beginning inventory	1 units × $2 =	$2
2	Jan 19 purchase	2 units × $5 =	$10
LIFO ending inventory for January			$12

A periodic system matches the total purchases for the month with the total withdrawals of inventory units for the month. Conversely, a perpetual system matches each unit withdrawn with the immediately preceding purchases.

Summary

Inventory System	FIFO COGS	LIFO COGS	FIFO Inventory	LIFO Inventory
Periodic	$23	$31	$15	$7
Perpetual	$23	$26	$15	$12

Notice the relationship of higher COGS under LIFO and lower ending inventory under LIFO (assuming inflation) still holds whether the firm uses a periodic or perpetual inventory system. The point of this example is that under a perpetual system, LIFO COGS and ending inventory will differ from those calculated under a periodic system.

LOS 27.d: Calculate and explain how inflation and deflation of inventory costs affect the financial statements and ratios of companies that use different inventory valuation methods.

CFA® Program Curriculum, Volume 3, page 354

During inflationary periods and with stable or increasing inventory quantities, LIFO COGS is higher than FIFO COGS. This is because the last units purchased have a higher cost than the first units purchased. Under LIFO, the more costly last units purchased are assumed to be the first units sold (to COGS). Of course, higher COGS under LIFO will result in lower gross profit and net income compared to FIFO.

Using similar logic, we can see that LIFO ending inventory is lower than FIFO ending inventory because under LIFO, ending inventory is valued using older, lower costs.

During deflationary periods and stable or increasing inventory quantities, the cost flow effects of using LIFO and FIFO will be reversed; that is, LIFO COGS will be lower and LIFO ending inventory will be higher. This makes sense because the most recent lower-cost purchases are assumed to be sold first under LIFO, and the units in ending inventory are assumed to be the earliest purchases with higher costs.

Consider the diagram in Figure 27.2 to help visualize the FIFO-LIFO difference during periods of rising prices and growing inventory levels.

Figure 27.2:   LIFO and FIFO Diagram—Rising Prices and Growing Inventory Balances

INVENTORY IN

INVENTORY OUT

FIFO Inventory

FIFO = Big Inventory
CR = CA/CL = Big
WC = CA – CL = Big

LIFO COGS

FIFO COGS

LIFO = Small Inventory
CR = CA/CL = Small
WC = CA – CL = Small

LIFO Inv

INVENTORY OUT

INVENTORY IN

FIFO Income Stmt
SALES – COGS (Small)
Net Income (Big)

Higher Taxes
Lower Cash Flows

LIFO Income Stmt
SALES – COGS (Big)
Net Income (Small)

Lower Taxes
Higher Cash Flows

Remember, it's not the older or newer physical inventory units that are reported in the income statement and balance sheet; rather, it is the *costs* that are assigned to the units sold and to the units remaining in inventory.

PROFESSOR'S NOTE

Be able to describe the effects of LIFO and FIFO, assuming inflation, in your sleep. When prices are falling, the effects are simply reversed. When you are finished with this review, take the time to look at these graphs and relationships again to solidify the concepts in your mind.

During periods of stable prices, all three cost flow methods will yield the same results for inventory, COGS, and gross profit. During periods of trending prices (up or down), different cost flow methods may result in significant differences in these items.

 PROFESSOR'S NOTE

The presumption in this section is that inventory quantities are stable or increasing.

Ending inventory. When prices are rising or falling, FIFO provides the most useful measure of ending inventory. This is a critical point. Recall that FIFO inventory is made up of the most recent purchases. These purchase costs can be viewed as a better approximation of current cost, and thus a better approximation of economic value. LIFO inventory, by contrast, is based on older costs that may differ significantly from current economic value.

Cost of goods sold. Changing prices can also produce significant differences between COGS under LIFO and FIFO. Recall that LIFO COGS is based on the most recent purchases. As a result, when prices are rising, LIFO COGS will be higher than FIFO COGS. When prices are falling, LIFO COGS will be lower than FIFO COGS. Because LIFO COGS is based on the most recent purchases, LIFO produces a better approximation of current cost in the income statement.

When prices are changing, the weighted average cost method will produce values of COGS and ending inventory between those of FIFO and LIFO.

Gross profit. Because COGS is subtracted from revenue in calculating gross profit, gross profit is also affected by the choice of cost flow method. Assuming inflation, higher COGS under LIFO will result in lower gross profit. In fact, all profitability measures (gross profit, operating profit, income before taxes, and net income) will be affected by the choice of cost flow method.

Figure 27.3: **Effects of Inventory Valuation Methods**

	FIFO	**LIFO**
Cost of sales	Lower	Higher
Ending inventory	Higher	Lower
Gross profit	Higher	Lower

Note: Assumes increasing prices and stable or increasing inventory levels.

MODULE QUIZ 27.2

To best evaluate your performance, enter your quiz answers online.

1. A firm's purchases and sales during a period occur in the following order:

Beginning inventory	3 units @ $390 per unit
Purchase	7 units @ $385 per unit
Sale	5 units
Purchase	4 units @ $380 per unit
Sale	8 units
Purchase	5 units @ $370 per unit

    Using LIFO and a perpetual inventory system, the firm's cost of sales for the period is:
    A. $4,605.
    B. $4,995.
    C. $5,145.

2. In a period of falling prices, a firm reporting under LIFO, compared to reporting under FIFO, will have a higher:
    A. cost of sales.
    B. gross profit margin.
    C. inventory turnover ratio.

3. Compared to reporting under FIFO for both tax and financial statements, a firm that chooses to report under LIFO during a period of falling prices would be *most likely* to report a lower:
    A. inventory.
    B. gross profit.
    C. cash balance.

MODULE 27.3: CONVERTING LIFO TO FIFO

Video covering this content is available online.

LOS 27.e: **Explain LIFO reserve and LIFO liquidation and their effects on financial statements and ratios.**

LOS 27.f: **Convert a company's reported financial statements from LIFO to FIFO for purposes of comparison.**

CFA® Program Curriculum, Volume 3, page 357

When prices are rising, firms that report inventory under LIFO will report lower inventory values and higher cost of goods sold than firms that report under FIFO. Because these differences affect key ratios used to evaluate and compare companies, analysts may adjust the financial statements of LIFO firms so they can be compared to those of FIFO firms.

These four relations hold when prices have been rising over the relevant period:

1. LIFO inventory < FIFO inventory.

2. LIFO COGS > FIFO COGS.

3. LIFO net income < FIFO net income.

4. LIFO tax < FIFO tax.

Firms that report under LIFO must also report a **LIFO reserve**, the amount by which LIFO inventory is less than FIFO inventory. To make financial statements prepared under LIFO comparable to those of FIFO firms, an analyst must:

1. add the LIFO reserve to LIFO inventory on the balance sheet.

2. increase the retained earnings component of shareholders' equity by the LIFO reserve.

When prices are increasing, a LIFO firm will pay less in taxes than it would pay under FIFO. For this reason, analysts often decrease a LIFO firm's cash by the tax rate times the LIFO reserve and increase its retained earnings by the LIFO reserve times (1 – tax rate) instead of the full LIFO reserve.

For example, consider a firm with a LIFO reserve of $150 that faces a tax rate of 40%. To convert the balance sheet to FIFO, increase inventory by $150, decrease cash by $60 ($150 × 40%), and increase stockholders' equity (retained earnings) by $90 [$150 × (1 – 40%)]. This will bring the accounting equation back into balance. The net effect of the adjustments is an increase in assets and shareholders' equity of $90, which is equal to the LIFO reserve net of tax.

For comparison purposes, it is also necessary to convert the LIFO firm's COGS to FIFO COGS. The difference between LIFO COGS and FIFO COGS is equal to the *change* in the LIFO reserve for the period. To convert COGS from LIFO to FIFO, simply subtract the change in the LIFO reserve:

FIFO COGS = LIFO COGS – (ending LIFO reserve – beginning LIFO reserve)

Assuming inflation, FIFO COGS is lower than LIFO COGS, so subtracting the change in the LIFO reserve from LIFO COGS makes intuitive sense. When prices are falling, we still subtract the change in the LIFO reserve to convert from LIFO COGS to FIFO COGS. In this case, however, the change in the LIFO reserve is negative and subtracting it will result in higher COGS. This again makes sense. When prices are falling, FIFO COGS is greater than LIFO COGS.

> **EXAMPLE:** Converting financial statements from LIFO to FIFO
>
> Witz Company reported that at the end of last year, LIFO inventory was $14,000, cost of goods sold was $40,000, and net income was $2,400. Witz's LIFO reserve was $8,000 at the beginning of the year and $10,000 at year-end. The company's tax rate was 40%. Determine the effects on the balance sheet and income statement had the FIFO inventory costing method been used, including an adjustment for taxes.
>
> **Answer:**
>
> *Adjustments to the balance sheet*
>
> Ending inventory under FIFO would be higher by the amount of the LIFO reserve.
>
> FIFO ending inventory = LIFO ending inventory + LIFO reserve = $14,000 + $10,000 = $24,000

If FIFO had been used, cash would be lower (because taxes would have been cumulatively higher) by the LIFO reserve times the tax rate, or $10,000 × 40% = $4,000.

With inventories $10,000 higher and cash $4,000 lower, total assets would be $6,000 higher if FIFO had been used. This would be balanced by a $6,000 increase in shareholders' equity. This adjustment is equal to the LIFO reserve times (1 – tax rate).

Adjustments to the income statement

Cost of goods sold under FIFO would have been lower by the change in the LIFO reserve.

FIFO cost of sales = LIFO cost of sales – (ending LIFO reserve – beginning LIFO reserve) = $40,000 – ($10,000 – $8,000) = $38,000

Had COGS been $2,000 less, pretax income would have been higher by $2,000, so taxes would have been higher by $2,000 × 40% = $800.

As a result, net income would have been higher by the change in the LIFO reserve net of tax.

FIFO net income = LIFO net income + (1 – tax rate)(ending LIFO reserve – beginning LIFO reserve) = $2,400 + ($2,000)(1 – 0.40) = $3,600

PROFESSOR'S NOTE

Later in this topic review, we present a more comprehensive example of converting financial statements from LIFO to FIFO for comparison with other companies.

Effects on Ratios

Again assuming increasing prices, we can trace the ratio effects of the adjustments of LIFO values to FIFO values.

Profitability. As compared to FIFO, LIFO produces higher COGS in the income statement and results in lower earnings. Any profitability measure that includes COGS will be higher under FIFO. For example, reducing COGS will result in higher gross, operating, and net profit margins as compared to LIFO.

Liquidity. Compared to FIFO, LIFO results in a lower inventory value on the balance sheet. Because inventory (a current asset) is higher under FIFO, the current ratio, a popular measure of liquidity, is also higher under FIFO. Working capital is higher under FIFO as well, because current assets are higher.

Activity. Inventory turnover (COGS / average inventory) is higher for firms that use LIFO compared to firms that use FIFO. Under LIFO, COGS is valued at more recent, higher costs (higher numerator), while inventory is valued at older, lower costs (lower denominator). Adjusting to FIFO values will result in lower turnover and higher days of inventory on hand (365 / inventory turnover).

Solvency. Adjusting to FIFO results in higher total assets because inventory is higher. Higher total assets under FIFO result in higher stockholders' equity (assets − liabilities). Because total assets and stockholders' equity are higher under FIFO, the debt ratio and the debt-to-equity ratio are lower under FIFO compared to LIFO.

LIFO Liquidation

Recall that the LIFO reserve is equal to the difference between LIFO inventory and FIFO inventory. The LIFO reserve will increase when prices are rising and inventory quantities are stable or increasing. If a firm is liquidating its inventory, or if prices are falling, the LIFO reserve will decline.

A **LIFO liquidation** occurs when a LIFO firm's inventory quantities decline. Older, lower costs are included in COGS compared to a situation in which inventory quantities are not declining. LIFO liquidation results in higher profit margins and higher income taxes compared to what they would be if inventory quantities were not declining. The extra profit reported with a LIFO liquidation inflates operating margins by recognizing historical inflationary gains from increasing inventory prices as income in the current period. Increases in profit margins from LIFO liquidation are not sustainable, however, because a firm cannot continue forever to sell existing inventory without replenishment.

Management could use a LIFO liquidation (draw down inventory) to artificially inflate current period earnings. Inventory declines can also be caused by events outside management's control, such as strikes or materials shortages at a key supplier that make inventory reduction involuntary, or a decline in expected customer orders that results in a voluntary reduction in inventory to suit market conditions.

Analysts must look to the LIFO reserve disclosures in the footnotes to see if the LIFO reserve has decreased over the period, which would indicate the possibility of a LIFO liquidation that requires adjustment of profit margins if its impact has been significant.

Regardless of the underlying reason for a LIFO liquidation, the resulting decrease in COGS will increase gross profits, pretax income, and net income. Decreased cash expenses (from not producing inventory) will increase operating cash flow, although higher income taxes on higher earnings will partially offset this increase in cash flows.

The following example illustrates the calculation of the extra profits earned as a result of inventory liquidation for a firm that uses LIFO for inventory valuation.

> **EXAMPLE: LIFO liquidation**
>
> At the beginning of 20X7, Big 4 Manufacturing Company had 400 units of inventory as follows:
>
> | Year Purchased | Number of Units | Cost Per Unit | Total Cost |
> |:---:|:---:|:---:|:---:|
> | 20X4 | 120 | $10 | $1,200 |
> | 20X5 | 140 | 11 | 1,540 |
> | 20X6 | 140 | 12 | 1,680 |
> | | 400 | | $4,420 |

Big 4 reports inventory under LIFO. Due to a strike, no units were produced during 20X7. During 20X7, Big 4 sold 280 units. In the absence of the strike, Big 4 would have had a cost of $14 for each unit produced. Compute the extra profit that resulted from the inventory liquidation.

Answer:

Because of the LIFO liquidation, actual COGS was $3,220 as follows:

	Units	Cost	
Beginning inventory	400	$4,420	
+ Purchases	-0-	-0-	
– Ending inventory	120	1,200	($10 × 120 units)
= COGS (actual)	280	$3,220	

Had Big 4 produced 280 units during 20X7, COGS would have been 280 × $14 = $3,920.

Due to the LIFO liquidation, COGS was lower by $700 ($3,920 – $3,220); thus, pretax profit was higher by $700. The higher profit is unsustainable because Big 4 will need to produce units at the new higher cost in future periods.

MODULE QUIZ 27.3

To best evaluate your performance, enter your quiz answers online.

1. In an inflationary environment, a LIFO liquidation will *most likely* result in an increase in:
   A. inventory.
   B. accounts payable.
   C. operating profit margin.

2. Bangor Company discloses that its LIFO reserve was $625,000 at the end of the previous year and $675,000 at the end of the current year. For the current year, beginning inventory was $2,350,000 and ending inventory was $2,525,000. The firm's tax rate is 30%. What would Bangor's ending inventory have been using FIFO?
   A. $2,575,000.
   B. $2,997,500.
   C. $3,200,000.

3. A firm that uses LIFO for inventory accounting reported COGS of $300,000 and ending inventory of $200,000 for the current period, and a LIFO reserve that decreased from $40,000 to $35,000 over the period. If the firm had reported using FIFO, its gross profit would have been:
   A. the same.
   B. $5,000 higher.
   C. $5,000 lower.

MODULE 27.4: INVENTORY VALUATION

LOS 27.g: Describe the measurement of inventory at the lower of cost and net realisable value.

Video covering this content is available online.

CFA® Program Curriculum, Volume 3, page 368

Under IFRS, inventory is reported on the balance sheet at the lower of cost or net realizable value. **Net realizable value** (NRV) is equal to the expected sales price less the estimated selling costs and completion costs. If net realizable value is less than the balance sheet value of inventory, the inventory is "written down" to net realizable value and the loss is recognized in the income statement. If there is a subsequent recovery in value, the inventory can be "written up" and the gain is recognized in the income statement by reducing COGS by the amount of the recovery. Because inventory is valued at the lower of cost or net realizable value, inventory cannot be written up by more than it was previously written down.

PROFESSOR'S NOTE

The write-down, or subsequent write-up, of inventory is usually accomplished through the use of a valuation allowance account. A valuation allowance account is a contra-asset account, similar to accumulated depreciation. By using a valuation allowance account, the firm is able to separate the original cost of inventory from the carrying value of the inventory.

Under U.S. GAAP, companies that use inventory cost methods other than LIFO or the retail method report inventories at the lower of cost or NRV. For companies using LIFO or the retail method, inventory is reported on the balance sheet at the **lower of cost or market**. Market is usually equal to replacement cost, but cannot be greater than NRV or less than NRV minus a normal profit margin. If replacement cost exceeds NRV, then market is NRV. If replacement cost is less than NRV minus a normal profit margin, then market is NRV minus a normal profit margin.

PROFESSOR'S NOTE

Think of lower of cost or market, where "market" cannot be outside a range of values. The range is from net realizable value minus a normal profit margin, to net realizable value. So the size of the range is the normal profit margin. "Net" means sales price less selling and completion costs.

If cost exceeds market, the inventory is written down to market on the balance sheet. The decrease in value is recognized in the income statement by increasing COGS for relatively small changes in value or by recording the loss from the inventory write-down separately for a relatively large change in value. The market value becomes the new cost basis.

If there is a subsequent recovery in value, no write-up is allowed under U.S. GAAP. This applies to companies using lower of cost or NRV as well as those using lower of cost or market.

EXAMPLE: Inventory write-down

Zoom, Inc. sells digital cameras. Per-unit cost information pertaining to Zoom's inventory is as follows:

Original cost	$210
Estimated selling price	$225
Estimated selling costs	$22
Net realizable value	$203
Replacement cost	$197
Normal profit margin	$12

What are the per-unit carrying values of Zoom's inventory using *lower of cost or NRV* and *lower of cost or market*?

Answer:

Using the lower of cost or net realizable value, because original cost of $210 exceeds net realizable value ($225 – $22 = $203), the inventory is written down to the net realizable value of $203 and the $7 decrease in value ($203 net realizable value – $210 original cost) is reported in the income statement.

Using the lower of cost or market, market is equal to replacement cost of $197, since net realizable value of $203 is greater than replacement cost, and net realizable value minus a normal profit margin ($203 – $12 = $191) is less than replacement cost. Since original cost exceeds market (replacement cost), the inventory is written down to $197 and a $13 loss ($197 replacement cost – $210 original cost) is reported in the income statement.

EXAMPLE: Inventory write-up

Assume that in the year after the write-down in the previous example, net realizable value and replacement cost both increase by $10. What is the impact of the recovery under IFRS, and under U.S. GAAP if lower of cost or market is used?

Answer:

Under IFRS, Zoom will write up inventory to $210 per unit and recognize a $7 gain in its income statement. The write-up (gain) is limited to the original write-down of $7. The carrying value cannot exceed original cost.

Under U.S. GAAP, no write-up is allowed. The per-unit carrying value will remain at $197. Zoom will simply recognize higher profit when the inventory is sold.

Recall that LIFO ending inventory is based on older, lower costs (assuming inflation) than under FIFO. Because cost is the basis for determining whether an impairment has occurred, LIFO firms are less likely to recognize inventory write-downs than firms using FIFO or weighted average cost.

Analysts must understand how an inventory write-down or write-up affects a firm's ratios. For example, a write-down may significantly affect inventory turnover in current and future periods. Thus, comparability of ratios across periods may be an issue.

In certain industries, reporting inventory above historical cost is permitted under IFRS and U.S. GAAP. This exception applies primarily to producers and dealers of commodity-like products, such as agricultural and forest products, mineral ores, and precious metals. Under this exception, inventory is reported at net realizable value and any unrealized gains and losses from changing market prices are recognized in the income statement. If an active market exists for the commodity, the quoted market price is used to value the inventory. Otherwise, recent market transactions are used.

LOS 27.h: Describe implications of valuing inventory at net realisable value for financial statements and ratios.

CFA® Program Curriculum, Volume 3, page 370

A write-down of inventory to net realizable value affects the financial statements and ratios in several ways. Assuming the write-down is reported as part of the cost of sales, these effects in the period of the write-down include:

- As inventory is part of current assets, an inventory write-down decreases both current and total assets.

- Current ratio (CA/CL) decreases. However, the quick ratio is unaffected because inventories are not included in the numerator of the quick ratio.

- Inventory turnover (COGS/average inventory) is increased, which decreases days' inventory on hand and the cash conversion cycle.

- The decrease in total assets increases total asset turnover and increases the debt-to-assets ratio.

- Equity is decreased, increasing the debt-to-equity ratio.

- The increase in COGS reduces gross margin, operating margin, and net margin.

- The percentage decrease in net income can be expected to be greater than the percentage decrease assets or equity. As a result, both ROA and ROE are decreased.

For periods subsequent to a write-down of inventory to net realizable value, COGS may be decreased by lower inventory carrying values, which will increase profitability. Together with the decreases in assets and equity from the prior-period write-down, an increase in net income from decreased COGS will increase reported ROA and ROE in subsequent periods.

LOS 27.i: Describe the financial statement presentation of and disclosures relating to inventories.

CFA® Program Curriculum, Volume 3, page 375

Inventory disclosures, usually found in the financial statement footnotes, are useful in evaluating the firm's inventory management. The disclosures are also useful in making adjustments to facilitate comparisons with other firms in the industry.

Required inventory disclosures are similar under U.S. GAAP and IFRS and include:
- The cost flow method (LIFO, FIFO, etc.) used.

- Total carrying value of inventory, with carrying value by classification (raw materials, work-in-process, and finished goods) if appropriate.

- Carrying value of inventories reported at fair value less selling costs.

- The cost of inventory recognized as an expense (COGS) during the period.

- Amount of inventory write-downs during the period.

- Reversals of inventory write-downs during the period, including a discussion of the circumstances of reversal (IFRS only because U.S. GAAP does not allow reversals).

- Carrying value of inventories pledged as collateral.

Inventory Changes

Although rare, a firm can change inventory cost flow methods. In most cases, the change is made retrospectively; that is, the prior years' financial statements are recast based on the new cost flow method. The cumulative effect of the change is reported as an adjustment to the beginning retained earnings of the earliest year presented.

Under IFRS, the firm must demonstrate that the change will provide reliable and more relevant information. Under U.S. GAAP, the firm must explain why the change in cost flow method is preferable.

An exception to retrospective application applies when a firm changes *to LIFO* from another cost flow method. In this case, the change is applied prospectively; no adjustments are made to the prior periods. With prospective application, the carrying value of inventory under the old method simply becomes the first layer of inventory under LIFO in the period of the change.

LOS 27.j: Explain issues that analysts should consider when examining a company's inventory disclosures and other sources of information.

CFA® Program Curriculum, Volume 3, page 375

Merchandising firms, such as wholesalers and retailers, purchase inventory that is ready for sale. In this case, inventory is reported in one account on the balance sheet. On the other hand, manufacturing firms normally report inventory using three separate accounts: raw materials, work-in-process, and finished goods. Analysts can use these disclosures, along with other sources of information such as Management's Discussion and Analysis, economic data specific to the industry, industry trade publications, and other sections of the firm's financial reports, as a signal of a firm's future revenues and earnings.

For example, an increase in raw materials and/or work-in-process inventory may be an indication of an expected increase in demand. Higher demand should result in higher revenues and earnings. Conversely, an increase in finished goods inventory, while raw materials and work-in-process are decreasing, may be an indication of decreasing demand and potential inventory write-downs in the future.

Analysts should also examine the relationship between sales and finished goods. Finished goods inventory growing faster than sales may indicate declining demand and excessive or potentially obsolete inventory. Obsolete inventory will result in lower earnings in the future when the inventory is written down. In addition, too much inventory is costly as the firm may incur storage costs, insurance premiums, and inventory taxes. Too much inventory uses cash that might be more efficiently used somewhere else.

The inventory turnover ratio measures how quickly a firm is selling its inventory. Generally, high inventory turnover (low days of inventory on hand) is desirable. However, inventory turnover can be too high. A firm with an inventory turnover ratio that is too high may not be carrying enough inventory to satisfy customers' needs, which can cause the firm to lose sales. High inventory turnover may also indicate that inventory write-downs have occurred. Write-downs are usually the result of poor inventory management.

To further assess the explanation for high inventory turnover, we can look at inventory turnover relative to sales growth within the firm and industry. High turnover with slower growth may be an indication of inadequate inventory quantities. Alternatively, sales growth at or above the industry average supports the conclusion that high inventory turnover reflects greater efficiency.

MODULE 27.5: INVENTORY ANALYSIS

Video covering this content is available online.

LOS 27.k: Calculate and compare ratios of companies, including companies that use different inventory methods.

LOS 27.l: Analyze and compare the financial statements of companies, including companies that use different inventory methods.

CFA® Program Curriculum, Volume 3, page 377

In the following example, we calculate key ratios for a corporation that reports under LIFO and compare them to those that would be reported if the firm had used the FIFO cost flow method.

> **EXAMPLE: Comparing financial ratios under LIFO and FIFO**
>
> Viper Corp. is a high-performance bicycle manufacturer. Viper's balance sheets for 20X5 and 20X6 and an income statement for 20X6 are as shown. The balance sheets and income statement were prepared using LIFO. Calculate the current ratio, inventory turnover, long-term debt-to-equity ratio, gross profit margin, net profit margin, and return on assets ratio for 20X6 for both LIFO and FIFO inventory cost flow methods.

Viper Balance Sheet

(Prepared using LIFO)	20X6	20X5
Assets		
Cash	$115	$95
Receivables	205	195
Inventories	310	290
Total current assets	$630	$580
Gross plant and equipment	$1,800	$1,700
Accumulated depreciation	360	340
Net plant and equipment	$1,440	$1,360
Total assets	$2,070	$1,940
Liabilities and equity		
Payables	$110	$90
Short-term debt	215	185
Current liabilities	$325	$275
Long-term debt	715	785
Common stock	300	300
Additional paid-in-capital	400	400
Retained earnings	330	180
Total liabilities and equity	$2,070	$1,940

Viper Income Statement

(Prepared using LIFO)	20X6
Revenue	$4,000
Cost of goods sold	3,000
Gross profit	$1,000
Operating expenses	650
Operating profit	350
Interest expense	50
Earnings before tax	300
Taxes	60
Net income	240
Common dividends	$90

Inventory footnote: The company uses the LIFO inventory cost flow method. Had FIFO been used, inventories would have been $100 higher in 20X6 and $90 higher in 20X5.

Income tax footnote: The tax rate for 20X5 and 20X6 was 20%.

Answer:

The analyst would recast the financial statements assuming FIFO for comparison purposes as follows:

Viper Balance Sheet

(Adjusted from LIFO to FIFO)	20X6	20X5
Assets		
Cash[1]	$95	$77
Receivables	205	195
Inventories[2]	410	380
Total current assets	$710	$652
Gross plant and equipment	$1,800	$1,700
Accumulated depreciation	360	340
Net plant and equipment	$1,440	$1,360
Total assets	$2,150	$2,012
Liabilities and equity		
Payables	$110	$90
Short-term debt	215	185
Current liabilities	$325	$275
Long-term debt	715	785
Common stock	300	300
Additional paid-in-capital	400	400
Retained earnings[3]	410	252
Total liabilities and equity	$2,150	$2,012

[1] Subtract taxes on LIFO reserve of $20 and $18 for 20X6 and 20X5, respectively.
[2] Add LIFO reserve of $100 and $90 for 20X6 and 20X5, respectively.
[3] Add LIFO reserve (net of tax) of $80 and $72 for 20X6 and 20X5, respectively.

Viper Income Statement

(Adjusted from LIFO to FIFO)	20X6
Revenue	$4,000
Cost of goods sold[4]	2,990
Gross profit	$1,010
Operating expenses	650
Operating profit	360
Interest expense	50
Earnings before tax	310
Taxes[5]	62
Net income	248
Common dividends	$90

[4] Subtract $10 change in reserve for 20X6.
[5] Add $2 taxes on change in the reserve for 20X6.

Current ratio

The current ratio (current assets / current liabilities) under LIFO is $630 / $325 = 1.9.

To convert to FIFO, the 20X6 LIFO reserve of $100 is added to current assets (inventory) and income taxes on the LIFO reserve of $20 are subtracted from cash.

Thus, under FIFO, the current ratio is ($630 + $100 LIFO reserve – $20 taxes) / $325 = 2.2. The current ratio is higher under FIFO as ending inventory now approximates current cost.

Inventory turnover

The inventory turnover ratio (COGS / average inventory) under LIFO is $3,000 / $300 = 10.0.

To convert to FIFO COGS, it is necessary to subtract the change in the LIFO reserve from LIFO COGS. The change in the LIFO reserve is $100 ending reserve – $90 beginning reserve = $10.

To convert LIFO average inventory to FIFO, the average LIFO reserve is added to average LIFO inventory: ($90 beginning reserve + $100 ending reserve) / 2 = $95. Alternatively, we can calculate average FIFO inventory by averaging the beginning and ending FIFO inventory: ($290 beginning LIFO inventory + $90 beginning LIFO reserve + $310 ending LIFO inventory + $100 ending LIFO reserve) / 2 = $395.

Thus, under FIFO, inventory turnover is ($3,000 – 10 change in LIFO reserve) / ($300 + $95 average LIFO reserve) = 7.6. Inventory turnover is lower under FIFO due to higher average inventory in the denominator and lower COGS in the numerator (assuming inflation).

Long-term debt-to-equity ratio

The long-term debt-to-equity ratio (long-term debt / stockholders' equity) under LIFO is $715 / $1,030 = 0.6942.

To convert to FIFO, the 20X6 LIFO reserve, net of tax, is added to stockholders' equity. The adjustment to stockholders' equity is necessary to make the accounting equation balance. The 20X6 LIFO reserve of $100 was added to inventory and $20 of income taxes was subtracted from cash, so the difference of $80 is added to stockholders' equity.

Thus, under FIFO, long-term debt-to-equity is $715 / ($1,030 + $80 ending LIFO reserve, net of tax) = 0.6441. Long-term debt-to-equity is lower under FIFO (assuming inflation) because stockholders' equity is higher, since it reflects the effects of bringing the LIFO reserve onto the balance sheet.

Gross profit margin

The gross profit margin (gross profit / revenue) under LIFO is $1,000 / $4,000 = 25.0%.

To convert to FIFO gross profit margin, the $10 change in the LIFO reserve is subtracted from LIFO COGS. Thus, under FIFO, gross profit margin is

($1,000 + $10 change in LIFO reserve) / $4,000 = 25.3%. Gross profit margin is higher under FIFO because COGS is lower under FIFO.

Net profit margin

The net profit margin (net income / revenue) under LIFO is $240 / $4,000 = 6.0%.

To convert to FIFO net profit margin, subtract the $10 change in the LIFO reserve from LIFO COGS to get FIFO COGS and increase income taxes $2 ($10 increase in reserve × 20% tax rate). The increase in income taxes is the result of applying the 20X6 tax rate to the increase in taxable profit (lower COGS).

Thus, under FIFO, net profit margin is ($240 + $10 change in LIFO reserve – $2 taxes) / $4,000 = 6.2%. The net profit margin is greater under FIFO because COGS is less under FIFO (assuming inflation).

 PROFESSOR'S NOTE

We did not recognize the entire tax effect of the 20X6 LIFO reserve in the 20X6 income statement. The change from LIFO to FIFO is handled retrospectively. In other words, had we been using FIFO all along, the resulting higher taxes would have already been recognized in the previous years' income statements.

Return on assets

Return on assets (net income/average assets) under LIFO is $240 / $2,005 = 11.97%.

To convert to FIFO return on assets, LIFO net income is increased by the change in the LIFO reserve, net of tax. Thus, FIFO net income is equal to $240 + $10 change in reserve – $2 taxes = $248.

To convert LIFO average assets, add the beginning and ending LIFO reserves, net of tax, to total assets. Thus, FIFO average assets is equal to ($2,070 20X6 assets + $80 20X6 reserve, net of tax + $1,940 20X5 assets + $72 20X5 reserve, net of tax) / 2 = $2,081.

Thus, the FIFO return on assets is $248 / $2,081 = 11.92%. In this example, the increase in FIFO net income is roughly proportionate to the increase in FIFO average assets. This is not always the case.

For comparison purposes, the following table summarizes our findings. The results of Viper's peer group have been included for analytical purposes.

Figure 27.4: Ratio Comparison

Year Ended 20X6	Viper		Peer Group
	LIFO	FIFO	FIFO
Current ratio	1.9	2.2	1.7
Inventory turnover	10.0	7.6	9.8
Long-term debt-to-equity	0.7	0.6	0.6
Gross profit margin	25.0%	25.3%	32.1%
Net profit margin	6.0%	6.2%	6.8%
Return on assets	11.97%	11.92%	12.5%

Analysis of Viper's ratios relative to a group of industry peers

Liquidity: The after-tax LIFO adjustment resulted in an increase in Viper's current ratio. The adjusted ratio exceeds the peer group, indicating greater liquidity. Because inventory is the largest component of Viper's current assets, additional analysis is needed.

Activity: Viper's adjusted inventory turnover declined as expected due to the decrease in COGS and the increase in average inventory. Adjusted inventory turnover is less than the peer group, which indicates that it takes Viper longer to sell its goods. In terms of inventory days (365 / inventory turnover), Viper has 48.0 days of inventory on hand while the peer group has 37.2 days on hand. Too much inventory is costly and can also be an indication of obsolescence.

Solvency: Viper's adjusted long-term debt-to-equity ratio of 0.6 is in line with the peer group.

Profitability: As expected, Viper's adjusted gross profit and net profit margin ratios increased because COGS is lower under FIFO. However, the adjusted margin ratios are significantly less than the peer group's ratios. Coupled with lower adjusted inventory turnover, Viper's lower gross profit margin may be an indication that Viper is reducing sales prices to move its inventory. This is another indication that some of Viper's inventory may be obsolete. As previously discussed, obsolete (impaired) inventory must be written down.

MODULE QUIZ 27.4, 27.5

To best evaluate your performance, enter your quiz answers online.

1. Kamp, Inc., sells specialized bicycle shoes. At year-end, due to a sudden increase in manufacturing costs, the replacement cost per pair of shoes is $55. The original cost is $43, and the current selling price is $50. The normal profit margin is 10% of the selling price, and the selling costs are $3 per pair. Using the lower of cost or market method under U.S. GAAP, which of the following amounts should each pair of shoes be reported on Kamp's year-end balance sheet?
    A. $42.
    B. $43.
    C. $47.

2. Poulter Products reports under IFRS and wrote its inventory value down from cost of $400,000 to net realizable value of $380,000. The *most likely* financial statement effect of this change is:
    A. an increase in cost of sales.
    B. a decrease in depreciation charges.
    C. a loss reported as other comprehensive income.

3. Which of the following inventory disclosures would *least likely* be found in the footnotes of a firm following IFRS?
    A. The amount of loss reversals, from previously written-down inventory, recognized during the period.
    B. The carrying value of inventories that collateralize a short-term loan.
    C. The separate carrying values of raw materials, work-in-process, and finished goods computed under the LIFO cost flow method.

4. Paul Neimer calculates the following horizontal common-size inventory data for Redpine Manufacturing, Inc.:

	Year 1	Year 2	Year 3	Year 4
Sales	1.00	1.10	1.18	1.25
Inventories:				
Raw materials	1.00	1.09	1.07	1.04
Work in process	1.00	1.11	1.15	1.17
Finished goods	1.00	1.10	1.21	1.33

Based on these data, Neimer should *most likely* conclude that Redpine:
A. has an increasing inventory turnover ratio.
B. anticipates declining demand for its products.
C. might be losing sales due to inadequate inventory.

5. Which of the following is *most likely* for a firm with high inventory turnover and lower sales growth than the industry average? The firm:
A. is managing its inventory effectively.
B. may have obsolete inventory that requires a write-down.
C. may be losing sales by not carrying enough inventory.

6. During a period of increasing prices, compared to reporting under LIFO, a firm that reports using average cost for inventory will have a:
A. lower gross margin.
B. higher current ratio.
C. higher asset turnover.

KEY CONCEPTS

LOS 27.a

Costs included in inventory on the balance sheet include purchase cost, conversion costs, and other costs necessary to bring the inventory to its present location and condition. All of these costs for inventory acquired or produced in the current period are added to beginning inventory value and then allocated either to cost of goods sold for the period or to ending inventory.

Period costs, such as abnormal waste, most storage costs, administrative costs, and selling costs, are expensed as incurred.

LOS 27.b

Inventory cost flow methods:

- FIFO: The cost of the first item purchased is the cost of the first item sold. Ending inventory is based on the cost of the most recent purchases, thereby approximating current cost.

- LIFO: The cost of the last item purchased is the cost of the first item sold. Ending inventory is based on the cost of the earliest items purchased. LIFO is prohibited under IFRS.

- Weighted average cost: COGS and inventory values are between their FIFO and LIFO values.

- Specific identification: Each unit sold is matched with the unit's actual cost.

LOS 27.c

Under LIFO, cost of sales reflects the most recent purchase or production costs, and balance sheet inventory values reflect older outdated costs.

Under FIFO, cost of sales reflects the oldest purchase or production costs for inventory, and balance sheet inventory values reflect the most recent costs.

Under the weighted average cost method, cost of sales and balance sheet inventory values are between those of LIFO and FIFO.

When purchase or production costs are rising, LIFO cost of sales is higher than FIFO cost of sales, and LIFO gross profit is lower than FIFO gross profit as a result. LIFO inventory is lower than FIFO inventory.

When purchase or production costs are falling, LIFO cost of sales is lower than FIFO cost of sales, and LIFO gross profit is higher than FIFO gross profit as a result. LIFO inventory is higher than FIFO inventory.

In either case, LIFO cost of sales and FIFO inventory values better represent economic reality (replacement costs).

In a periodic system, inventory values and COGS are determined at the end of the accounting period. In a perpetual system, inventory values and COGS are updated continuously.

In the case of FIFO and specific identification, ending inventory values and COGS are the same whether a periodic or perpetual system is used. LIFO and weighted average cost, however, can produce different inventory values and COGS depending on whether a periodic or perpetual system is used.

LOS 27.d

When prices are *increasing* and inventory quantities are stable or increasing:

LIFO results in:	**FIFO results in:**
higher COGS	lower COGS
lower gross profit	higher gross profit
lower inventory balances	higher inventory balances
higher inventory turnover	lower inventory turnover

When prices are *decreasing* and inventory quantities are stable or increasing:

LIFO results in:	**FIFO results in:**
lower COGS	higher COGS
higher gross profit	lower gross profit
higher inventory balances	lower inventory balances
lower inventory turnover	higher inventory turnover

The weighted average cost method results in values between those of LIFO and FIFO if prices are increasing or decreasing.

LOS 27.e

A firm that reports under LIFO must disclose a LIFO reserve, which is the difference between LIFO inventory reported and inventory had the firm used the FIFO method. LIFO reserve will be positive during periods of rising inventory costs and negative during periods of falling inventory costs.

A LIFO liquidation occurs when a firm using LIFO sells more inventory during a period than it produces. During periods of rising prices, this drawdown in inventory reduces cost of goods sold because the lower cost of previously produced inventory is used, resulting in an unsustainable increase in gross profit margin.

LOS 27.f

To convert a firm's financial statements from LIFO to what they would have been under FIFO:

1. Add the LIFO reserve to LIFO inventory.

2. Subtract the change in the LIFO reserve for the period from COGS.

3. Decrease cash by LIFO reserve × tax rate.

4. Increase retained earnings (equity) by LIFO reserve × (1 − tax rate).

LOS 27.g

Under IFRS, inventories are valued at the lower of cost or net realizable value. Inventory write-ups are allowed, but only to the extent that a previous write-down to net realizable value was recorded.

Under U.S. GAAP, inventories are valued at the lower of cost or net realizable value for companies using cost methods other than LIFO or the retail method. For companies using LIFO or the retail method, inventories are valued at the lower of cost or market. Market is usually equal to replacement cost but cannot exceed net realizable value or be less than net realizable value minus a normal profit margin. No subsequent write-up is allowed for any company reporting under U.S. GAAP.

LOS 27.h

A write-down of inventory value from cost to net realizable value will:

- Decrease inventory, assets, and equity.

- Increase asset turnover, the debt to equity ratio and the debt to assets ratio.

- Result in a loss on the income statement, which will decrease net income and the net profit margin, as well as ROA and ROE for a typical firm.

LOS 27.i

Required inventory disclosures:

- The cost flow method (LIFO, FIFO, etc.) used.

- Total carrying value of inventory and carrying value by classification (raw materials, work-in-process, and finished goods) if appropriate.

- Carrying value of inventories reported at fair value less selling costs.

- The cost of inventory recognized as an expense (COGS) during the period.

- Amount of inventory write-downs during the period.

- Reversals of inventory write-downs during the period (IFRS only because U.S. GAAP does not allow reversals).

- Carrying value of inventories pledged as collateral.

LOS 27.j

An analyst should examine inventory disclosures to determine whether:

- The finished goods category is growing while raw materials and goods in process are declining, which may indicate decreasing demand and potential future inventory write-downs.

- Raw materials and goods in process are increasing, which may indicate increasing future demand and higher earnings.

- Increases in finished goods are greater than increases in sales, which may indicate decreasing demand or inventory obsolescence and potential future inventory write-downs.

LOS 27.k

Inventory turnover, days of inventory on hand, and gross profit margin can be used to evaluate the quality of a firm's inventory management.

- Inventory turnover that is too low (high days of inventory on hand) may be an indication of slow-moving or obsolete inventory.

- High inventory turnover together with low sales growth relative to the industry may indicate inadequate inventory levels and lost sales because customer orders could not be fulfilled.

- High inventory turnover together with high sales growth relative to the industry average suggests that high inventory turnover reflects greater efficiency rather than inadequate inventory.

LOS 27.l

Comparison of company financial statements may require statements to be adjusted to reflect the same inventory costing methods for both firms, or for the subject firm and any industry or peer group of firms used for comparison.

ANSWER KEY FOR MODULE QUIZZES

Module Quiz 27.1

1. **B** Variable production overhead is capitalized as a part of inventory. Storage costs not related to the production process, and selling and administrative costs are expensed as incurred. (LOS 27.a)

2. **A** Under FIFO, ending inventory is made up of the most recent purchases, thereby providing a closer approximation of current cost. (LOS 27.b)

3. **A** FIFO COGS

200 units from beginning inventory × \$3.00 =	\$600
400 units from 1st quarter × \$3.30 =	1,320
	\$1,920

    LIFO COGS

50 units from 4th quarter × \$4.20 =	\$210
200 units from 3rd quarter × \$3.90 =	780
100 units from 2nd quarter × \$3.60 =	360
250 units from 1st quarter × \$3.30 =	825
	\$2,175

    Note the shortcut. Once FIFO COGS of \$1,920 is calculated, look at the LIFO column. We know that during inflation and stable or increasing inventory quantities, LIFO COGS is higher than FIFO. Only LIFO COGS of \$2,175 meets this condition. (LOS 27.c)

4. **C** Under FIFO, the first units purchased are the first units sold. FIFO COGS is the same under a periodic system and a perpetual system.

Revenue	\$484	(40 units × \$6.00) + (40 units × \$6.10)
COGS	\$331	(25 units × \$4.00) + (55 units × \$4.20)
Gross profit	\$153	

    (LOS 27.c)

5. **A** Compared to FIFO, COGS calculated under LIFO will be higher because the most recent, higher cost units are assumed to be the first units sold. Higher COGS under LIFO will result in lower gross profit (revenue – COGS). (LOS 27.c)

Module Quiz 27.2

1. **B** The cost of the first five units sold is $385 per unit. Of the next eight units sold, the cost of four of them is $380 per unit, two have a cost of $385 per unit, and two have a cost of $390 per unit. Cost of sales = 5 × $385 + 4 × $380 + 2 × $385 + 2 × $390 = $4,995. (LOS 27.c)

2. **B** With falling prices, LIFO COGS will include the cost of lower priced inventory and COGS will be less when compared to FIFO COGS. Because of this, the firm would report a higher gross profit margin under LIFO than under FIFO, while LIFO inventory will be higher and inventory turnover lower. (LOS 27.d)

3. **C** When prices are falling, LIFO would result in lower COGS (higher gross profit) and higher ending inventory than FIFO. Higher gross profit with LIFO would result in higher taxes payable which would reduce cash balances (as long they pay their taxes). (LOS 27.d)

Module Quiz 27.3

1. **C** In a LIFO liquidation, older and lower costs are included in cost of sales. Thus, cost of sales per unit decreases and profit margins increase. (LOS 27.e)

2. **C** FIFO inventory = LIFO inventory + LIFO reserve = $2,525,000 + $675,000 = $3,200,000. (LOS 27.f)

3. **C** FIFO COGS = LIFO COGS – (ending LIFO reserve – beginning LIFO reserve)

    Ending LIFO reserve – beginning LIFO reserve = $35,000 – $ 40,000 = –$5,000

    With FIFO COGS $5,000 greater than LIFO COGS, gross profit under FIFO would be $5,000 lower than under LIFO. (LOS 27.f)

Module Quiz 27.4, 27.5

1. **B** Market is equal to the replacement cost as long as replacement cost is within a specific range. The upper bound is net realizable value (NRV) which is equal to the selling price ($50) less selling costs ($3) for a NRV of $47. The lower bound is NRV ($47) less normal profit margin (10% of selling price = $5) for a net amount of $42. Because replacement cost is greater than NRV ($47), market equals NRV ($47). Additionally, we have to use the lower of cost ($43) or market ($47) principle, so the shoes should be recorded at a cost of $43. (Module 27.4, LOS 27.g)

2. **A** The write-down in inventory value from cost to net realizable value is reported on the income statement either as an addition to cost of sales or as a separate line item, not as other comprehensive income. Depreciation will not be affected as inventory is not depreciated. (Module 27.4, LOS 27.h)

3. **C** While the separate carrying values of raw materials, work-in-process, and finished goods are required disclosure for some firms, LIFO is not permitted under IFRS. (Module 27.4, LOS 27.i)

4. **B** Redpine's finished goods inventory is growing faster than sales, while work-in-process inventory is growing more slowly than sales and raw materials inventory is decreasing. These data are consistent with Redpine reducing production in response to decreasing demand. Inventory turnover ratios cannot be calculated directly from the common-size data given, but finished goods inventory increasing faster than sales suggests inventory turnover is likely decreasing. (Module 27.4, LOS 27.j)

5. **C** High inventory turnover coupled with low sales growth relative to the industry may be an indication of inadequate inventory levels. In this case, the firm may be losing sales by not carrying enough inventory. (Module 27.5, LOS 27.k)

6. **B** Compared to using LIFO, using average cost would produce lower COGS, higher gross operating income, and higher ending inventory, so current assets and the current ratio would be higher. Consequently, gross margin would be higher and asset turnover would be lower under the average cost inventory method. (Module 27.5, LOS 27.k, 27.l)

The following is a review of the Financial Reporting and Analysis (3) principles designed to address the learning outcome statements set forth by CFA Institute. Cross-Reference to CFA Institute Assigned Reading #28.

READING
28

Long-Lived Assets

EXAM FOCUS

Long-lived assets include tangible assets, intangible assets, and financial assets. Firms make many estimates and choices in accounting for long-lived assets that affect the firms' profits, ratios, and cash flow classifications. You must understand the effects of and issues concerning capitalization versus immediate expensing of various costs, including construction interest, research and development, and software costs. For capitalized costs, you must be familiar with the effects of the different depreciation and amortization methods and be able to dctcrmine if an asset is impaired. Finally, you must be familiar with the revaluation (fair value) model under IFRS and the disclosure requirements for financial reporting.

MODULE 28.1: CAPITALIZATION VS. EXPENSING

Video covering this content is available online.

LOS 28.a: Distinguish between costs that are capitalised and costs that are expensed in the period in which they are incurred.

CFA® Program Curriculum, Volume 3, page 417

When a firm makes an expenditure, it can either **capitalize** the cost as an asset on the balance sheet or **expense** the cost in the income statement in the period incurred. As a general rule, an expenditure that is expected to provide a future economic benefit over multiple accounting periods is capitalized; however, if the future economic benefit is unlikely or highly uncertain, the expenditure is expensed in the period incurred.

An expenditure that is capitalized is initially recorded as an asset on the balance sheet at cost, typically its fair value at acquisition plus any costs necessary to prepare the asset for use. Except for land and intangible assets with indefinite lives (such as acquisition goodwill), the cost is then allocated to the income statement over the life of the asset as **depreciation** expense (for tangible assets) or **amortization** expense (for intangible assets with finite lives).

Alternatively, if an expenditure is immediately expensed, current period pretax income is reduced by the amount of the expenditure.

Once an asset is capitalized, subsequent related expenditures that provide more future economic benefits (e.g., rebuilding the asset) are also capitalized. Subsequent expenditures that merely sustain the usefulness of the asset (e.g., regular maintenance) are expensed when incurred.

> **EXAMPLE:** Capitalizing versus expensing
>
> Northwood Corp. purchased new equipment to be used in its manufacturing plant. The cost of the equipment was $250,000 including $5,000 freight and $12,000 of taxes. In addition to the equipment cost, Northwood paid $10,000 to install the equipment and $7,500 to train its employees to use the equipment. Over the asset's life, Northwood paid $35,000 for repair and maintenance. At the end of five years, Northwood extended the life of the asset by rebuilding the equipment's motors at a cost of $85,000.
>
> What amounts should be capitalized on Northwood's balance sheet and what amounts should be expensed in the period incurred?
>
> **Answer:**
>
> Northwood should capitalize all costs that provide future economic benefits, including the costs that are necessary to get the asset ready for use. Rebuilding the equipment's motors extended its life and thus increased its future benefits.
>
> **Capitalized Costs**
>
> | | | |
> |---|---|---|
> | Purchase price | $250,000 | (including freight & taxes) |
> | Installation costs | 10,000 | |
> | Rebuilt motors | 85,000 | |
> | | $345,000 | |
>
> Costs that do not provide future economic benefits are expensed in the period incurred. The initial training costs are not necessary to get the asset ready for use. Rather, the training costs are necessary to get the employees ready to use the asset. Thus, the training costs are immediately expensed. Repair and maintenance costs are operating expenditures that do not extend the life of the equipment.
>
> **Costs Expensed When Incurred**
>
> | | |
> |---|---|
> | Initial training costs | $7,500 |
> | Repair and maintenance | 35,000 |
> | | $42,500 |

Capitalized Interest

When a firm constructs an asset for its own use or, in limited circumstances, for resale, the interest that accrues during the construction period is capitalized as a part of the asset's cost. The reasons for capitalizing interest are to accurately measure the cost of the asset and to better match the cost with the revenues generated by the constructed asset. The treatment of construction interest is similar under U.S. GAAP and IFRS.

Capitalized interest is not reported in the income statement as interest expense. Once construction interest is capitalized, the interest cost is allocated to the income statement through depreciation expense (if the asset is held for use), or COGS (if the asset is held for sale).

Generally, capitalized interest is reported in the cash flow statement as an outflow from investing activities, while interest expense is reported as an outflow from operating activities.

PROFESSOR'S NOTE

Interest expense can be reported on the cash flow statement as either an operating activity or financing activity under IFRS.

LOS 28.b: Compare the financial reporting of the following types of intangible assets: purchased, internally developed, acquired in a business combination.

CFA® Program Curriculum, Volume 3, page 420

Intangible assets are long-term assets that lack physical substance, such as patents, brand names, copyrights, and franchises. Some intangible assets have finite lives while others have indefinite lives.

The cost of a finite-lived intangible asset is amortized over its useful life. Indefinite-lived intangible assets are not amortized, but are tested for impairment at least annually. If impaired, the reduction in value is recognized in the income statement as a loss in the period in which the impairment is recognized.

Intangible assets are also considered either identifiable or unidentifiable. Under IFRS, an **identifiable intangible asset** must be:

- Capable of being separated from the firm or arise from a contractual or legal right.
- Controlled by the firm.
- Expected to provide future economic benefits.

In addition, the future economic benefits must be probable and the asset's cost must be reliably measurable.

An **unidentifiable intangible asset** is one that cannot be purchased separately and may have an indefinite life. The most common example of an unidentifiable intangible asset is goodwill. Goodwill is the excess of purchase price over the fair value of the identifiable assets (net of liabilities) acquired in a business combination.

Not all intangible assets are reported on the balance sheet. Accounting for an intangible asset depends on whether the asset was created internally, purchased externally, or obtained as part of a business combination.

Intangible Assets Created Internally

With some exceptions, costs to create intangible assets are expensed as incurred. Important exceptions are research and development costs (under IFRS) and software development costs.

Research and development costs. Under IFRS, **research costs**, which are costs aimed at the discovery of new scientific or technical knowledge and understanding, are expensed as incurred. However, **development costs** may be capitalized. Development costs are incurred to translate research findings into a plan or design of a new product or process. To recognize an intangible asset in development, a firm must show that it can complete the asset and intends to use or sell the completed asset, among other criteria.

Under U.S. GAAP, both research and development costs are generally expensed as incurred. However, the costs of creating software for sale to others are treated in a manner similar to the treatment of research and development costs under IFRS. Costs incurred to develop software for sale to others are expensed as incurred until the product's technological feasibility has been established, after which the costs of developing a salable product are capitalized.

Purchased Intangible Assets

Like tangible assets, an intangible asset purchased from another party is initially recorded on the balance sheet at cost, typically its fair value at acquisition.

If the intangible asset is purchased as part of a group, the total purchase price is allocated to each asset on the basis of its fair value. For analytical purposes, an analyst is usually more interested in the type of asset acquired rather than the value assigned on the balance sheet. For example, recently acquired franchise rights may provide insight into the firm's future operating performance. In this case, the allocation of cost is not as important.

The financial statement effects of capitalizing intangible assets are the same as the effects of capitalizing other expenditures. Capitalizing results in higher net income in the first year and lower net income in the subsequent years. Similarly, assets, equity, and operating cash flow are all higher when expenditures are capitalized.

Intangible Assets Obtained in a Business Combination

The **acquisition method** is used to account for business combinations. Under the acquisition method, the purchase price is allocated to the identifiable assets and liabilities of the acquired firm on the basis of fair value. Any remaining amount of the purchase price is recorded as **goodwill**. Goodwill is said to be an unidentifiable asset that cannot be separated from the business itself.

Only goodwill created in a business combination is capitalized on the balance sheet. The costs of any internally generated "goodwill" are expensed in the period incurred.

LOS 28.c: Explain and evaluate how capitalising versus expensing costs in the period in which they are incurred affects financial statements and ratios.

CFA® Program Curriculum, Volume 3, page 423

Although it may make no operational difference, the choice between capitalizing costs and expensing them will affect net income, shareholders' equity, total assets, cash flow from operations, cash flow from investing, and numerous financial ratios.

Net Income

Capitalizing an expenditure delays the recognition of an expense in the income statement. Thus, in the period that an expenditure is capitalized, the firm will report higher net income compared to immediately expensing. In subsequent periods, the firm will report lower net income compared to expensing, as the capitalized expenditure is allocated to the income statement through depreciation expense. This allocation process reduces the variability of net income by spreading the expense over multiple periods.

PROFESSOR'S NOTE

For growing firms, capitalizing expenditures may result in earnings that are higher over many periods compared to an otherwise identical expensing firm. This is because the amount of depreciation from previously capitalized expenditures is less than the amount of additional costs that are being newly capitalized each period.

Conversely, if a firm expenses an expenditure in the current period, net income is reduced by the after-tax amount of the expenditure. In subsequent periods, no allocation of cost is necessary. Thus, net income in future periods is higher than if the expenditure had been capitalized.

Over the life of an asset, *total* net income is identical whether the asset's cost is capitalized or expensed. Timing of the expense recognition in the income statement is the only difference.

Shareholders' Equity

Because capitalization results in higher net income in the period of the expenditure compared to expensing, it also results in higher shareholders' equity because retained earnings are greater. Total assets are greater with capitalization and liabilities are unaffected, so the accounting equation (A = L + E) remains balanced. As the cost is allocated to the income statement in subsequent periods, net income, retained earnings, and shareholders' equity will be reduced.

If the expenditure is immediately expensed, retained earnings and shareholders' equity will reflect the entire reduction in net income in the period of the expenditure.

Cash Flow From Operations

A capitalized expenditure is usually reported in the cash flow statement as an outflow from investing activities. If immediately expensed, the expenditure is reported as an outflow from operating activities. Thus, capitalizing an expenditure will result in higher operating cash flow and lower investing cash flow compared to expensing. Assuming no differences in tax treatment, *total* cash flow will be the same. The classification of the cash flow is the only difference.

Recall that when an expenditure is capitalized, depreciation expense is recognized in subsequent periods. Depreciation is a noncash expense and, aside from any tax effects, does not affect operating cash flow.

PROFESSOR'S NOTE

If the tax treatment is changed to match the financial reporting treatment of the expenditure, expensing will result in higher operating cash flow in the first year because of the tax savings. However, if the tax treatment is independent of the financial reporting treatment, taxes, and therefore cash flows, are unaffected by the choice.

Financial Ratios

Capitalizing an expenditure initially results in higher assets and higher equity compared to expensing. Thus, both the debt-to-assets ratio and the debt-to-equity ratio are lower (they have larger denominators) with capitalization.

Capitalizing an expenditure will *initially* result in higher return on assets (ROA) and higher return on equity (ROE). This is the result of higher net income in the first year. In subsequent years, ROA and ROE will be lower for a capitalizing firm because net income is reduced by the depreciation expense.

Because an expensing firm recognizes the entire expense in the first year, ROA and ROE will be lower in the first year and higher in the subsequent years. After the first year, net income (numerator) is higher, and assets and equity (denominators) are lower, than they would be if the firm had capitalized the expenditure. Analysts must be careful when comparing firms because immediately expensing an expenditure gives the appearance of growth after the first year.

The interest coverage ratio (EBIT / interest expense) measures a firm's ability to make required interest payments on its debt. In the year of the expenditure, capitalizing interest results in lower interest expense compared to expensing. The result is a higher interest coverage ratio (smaller denominator) when interest is capitalized.

Many analysts calculate the interest coverage ratio based on total interest expense, including capitalized interest. Because the interest is a required payment, this may be a better measure of the firm's solvency. Treating the capitalized interest as interest expense for analytical purposes reduces the interest coverage ratio. Bond rating agencies often make this adjustment.

The financial effects of capitalizing versus expensing are summarized in Figure 28.1.

Figure 28.1: Financial Statement Effects of Capitalizing vs. Expensing

	Capitalizing	Expensing
Total assets	Higher	Lower
Shareholders' equity	Higher	Lower
Income variability	Lower	Higher
Net income (first year)	Higher	Lower
Net income (subsequent years)	Lower	Higher
Cash flow from operations	Higher	Lower
Cash flow from investing	Lower	Higher
Debt ratio & debt-to-equity	Lower	Higher
Interest coverage (first year)	Higher	Lower
Interest coverage (subsequent years)	Lower	Higher

MODULE QUIZ 28.1

To best evaluate your performance, enter your quiz answers online.

1. If a company purchases an asset with future economic benefits that are highly uncertain, the company should:
   A. expense the purchase.
   B. use straight-line depreciation.
   C. use an accelerated depreciation method.

2. The cost of an intangible asset is *most likely* to be amortized if the asset has:
   A. a finite life and was purchased.
   B. a finite life and was created internally.
   C. an indefinite life and was acquired in a business combination.

3. Red Company immediately expenses its development costs while Black Company capitalizes its development costs. All else equal, Red Company will:
   A. show smoother reported earnings than Black Company.
   B. report higher operating cash flow than Black Company.
   C. report higher asset turnover than Black Company.

Video covering this content is available online.

MODULE 28.2: DEPRECIATION

LOS 28.d: Describe the different depreciation methods for property, plant, and equipment and calculate depreciation expense.

CFA® Program Curriculum, Volume 3, page 435

Depreciation is the systematic allocation of an asset's cost over time. Two important terms are:

- **Carrying (book) value.** The net value of an asset or liability on the balance sheet. For property, plant, and equipment, carrying value equals historical cost minus accumulated depreciation.

- **Historical cost.** The original purchase price of the asset including installation and transportation costs. Historical cost is also known as *gross investment in the asset*.

Depreciation is a real and significant operating expense. Even though depreciation doesn't require current cash expenditures (the cash outflow was made in the past when the asset was purchased), it is an expense nonetheless and cannot be ignored.

The analyst must decide whether the reported depreciation expense is more or less than *economic depreciation*, which is the actual decline in the value of the asset over the period. One chain of video rental stores was found to be overstating income by depreciating its stock of movies by equal amounts each year. In fact, a greater portion of the decrease in the value of newly released movies occurs in the first year. Depreciating the rental assets by a greater amount during the first year would have better approximated economic depreciation and reduced reported income.

Depreciation Methods

Depreciation of a capitalized cost (asset) may be reported using straight-line, accelerated, or units-of-production methods.

Straight-line depreciation is the predominant method of computing depreciation for financial reporting. Depreciation is the same amount each year over the asset's estimated life:

$$\text{depreciation expense} = \frac{\text{original cost} - \text{salvage value}}{\text{depreciable life}}$$

> **EXAMPLE: Calculating straight-line depreciation expense**
>
> Littlefield Company recently purchased a machine at a cost of $12,000. The machine is expected to have a residual value of $2,000 at the end of its useful life in five years. Calculate depreciation expense using the straight-line method.
>
> **Answer:**
>
> The annual depreciation expense each year will be:
>
> $$\frac{\text{cost} - \text{residual}}{\text{useful life}} = \frac{(\$12,000 - \$2,000)}{5} = \$2,000$$

With an **accelerated depreciation** method, more depreciation expense is recognized in the early years of an asset's life and less depreciation expense in the later years. Thus, accelerated depreciation results in lower net income in the early years of an asset's life and higher net income in the later years, compared to straight-line depreciation. One often-used accelerated depreciation method is the **double-declining balance** (DDB) method:

DDB depreciation in year x =

$$\frac{2}{\text{depreciable life in years}} \times \text{book value at beginning of year } x$$

Note that salvage value is not in the formula for double-declining balance depreciation. However, once the carrying (book) value of the asset reaches the salvage value, no additional depreciation expense is recognized.

> **EXAMPLE: Calculating double-declining balance depreciation expense**
>
> Littlefield Company recently purchased a machine at a cost of $12,000. The machine is expected to have a residual value of $2,000 at the end of its useful life in five years. Calculate depreciation expense for all five years using the double-declining balance method.
>
> **Answer:**
>
> The depreciation expense using the double declining balance method is:
>
> - Year 1: (2 / 5)($12,000) = $4,800
> - Year 2: (2 / 5)($12,000 – $4,800) = $2,880
> - Year 3: (2 / 5)($12,000 – $7,680) = $1,728
>
> In years 1 through 3, the company has recognized cumulative depreciation expense of $9,408. Since the total depreciation expense is limited to $10,000 ($12,000 – $2,000 salvage value), the depreciation in year 4 is limited to $592, rather than the (2 / 5)($12,000 – $9,408) = $1,036.80 using the DDB formula.
>
> Year 5: Depreciation expense is $0, since the asset is fully depreciated.
>
> Note that the rate of depreciation is doubled (2 / 5) from straight-line, and the only thing that changes from year to year is the base amount (book value) used to calculate annual depreciation.

> **PROFESSOR'S NOTE**
>
> *We've been discussing the "double" declining balance method, which uses a factor of two times the straight-line rate. Firms can compute declining balance depreciation based on any factor (e.g., 1.5, double, triple).*

Depreciation under the **units-of-production method** is based on usage rather than time. Depreciation expense is higher in periods of high usage.

units-of-production depreciation =

$$\frac{\text{original cost } - \text{ salvage value}}{\text{life in output units}} \times \text{output units in the period}$$

PROFESSOR'S NOTE

The units-of-production method applied to natural resources is referred to as depletion.

Component Depreciation

IFRS requires firms to depreciate the components of an asset separately, thereby requiring useful life estimates for each component. For example, a building is made up of a roof, walls, flooring, electrical systems, plumbing, and many other components. Under **component depreciation**, the useful life of each component is estimated and depreciation expense is computed separately for each.

Component depreciation is allowed under U.S. GAAP but is seldom used.

> **EXAMPLE:** Component depreciation
>
> Global Airlines purchased a new airplane with an all-inclusive cost of $50 million. The estimated life of the airplane is 30 years and the estimated salvage value is $5 million. Global expects to replace the interior of the aircraft after 15 years. The component cost of the interior is estimated at $3 million.
>
> Calculate depreciation expense in Year 1 using the straight-line method, both assuming the interior is a separate component and assuming the component method is not used.
>
> **Answer:**
>
> **Straight-line depreciation using the component method:**
>
> | | |
> |---|---|
> | Total aircraft cost | $50,000,000 |
> | Interior cost | (3,000,000) |
> | Aircraft component | $47,000,000 |
>
> Depreciation expense:
>
> | | | |
> |---|---|---|
> | Aircraft component | $1,400,000 | ($47,000,000 − 5,000,000) / 30 years |
> | Interior component | 200,000 | ($3,000,000 / 15 years) |
> | Year 1 expense | $1,600,000 | |
>
> **Straight-line depreciation without the component method:**
>
> | | |
> |---|---|
> | Year 1 expense | ($50,000 − 5,000,000) / 30 years = $1,500,000 |
>
> Depreciation expense is lower by $100,000 each year ($1,600,000 − $1,500,000) for the first 15 years without the component method. However, at the end of Year 15, Global will spend $3,000,000 to replace the interior. Thus, additional depreciation expense of $3,000,000 / 15 years = $200,000 each year is required for the last 15 years of the asset's life.
>
> Under both scenarios, Global will have expended a total of $53,000,000 and recognized $48,000,000 of depreciation expense over the airplane's life:
>
> | | |
> |---|---|
> | Component method | $1,600,000 × 30 years = $48,000,000 |
> | Non-component method | ($1,500,000 × 30 years) + ($200,000 × 15 years) = $48,000,000 |

LOS 28.e: Describe how the choice of depreciation method and assumptions concerning useful life and residual value affect depreciation expense, financial statements, and ratios.

CFA® Program Curriculum, Volume 3, page 435

In the early years of an asset's life, compared to straight-line depreciation, using an accelerated depreciation method will result in higher depreciation expense and lower net income, total assets, and shareholders' equity. For a single long-lived asset, these effects reverse in the later years of its useful life. For a fast-growing firm, however, these effects will persist over time as long as the firm is acquiring more depreciable assets than it is derecognizing.

Return on assets and return on equity are higher with straight-line depreciation compared to accelerated methods. This is because the effect on the numerator (higher net income) is relatively larger than the effect on the denominators (higher assets and equity). Asset turnover ratios (revenue / average assets) are lower with straight-line depreciation. Assuming that the depreciation method for tax is unchanged, the choice of depreciation method for financial reporting will not affect cash flows.

Figure 28.2 summarizes the effects of depreciation methods on financial statements and ratios in the early years of an asset's useful life or for a fast-growing firm.

Figure 28.2: Effects of Depreciation Methods (Early Years or Fast-Growing Firm)

	Straight-Line	Accelerated
Depreciation expense	Lower	Higher
Net income	Higher	Lower
Total assets	Higher	Lower
Shareholders' equity	Higher	Lower
Return on assets	Higher	Lower
Return on equity	Higher	Lower
Asset turnover ratios	Lower	Higher
Cash flow	Same	Same

Useful Lives and Salvage Values

Calculating depreciation expense requires estimating an asset's useful life and its salvage (residual) value. Firms can manipulate depreciation expense, and therefore net income, by increasing or decreasing either of these estimates.

A longer estimated useful life decreases annual depreciation and increases reported net income, while a shorter estimated useful life will have the opposite effect. A higher estimate of the salvage value will also decrease depreciation and increase net income, while a lower estimate of the salvage value will increase depreciation and decrease net income.

A change in an accounting estimate, such as useful life or salvage value, is put into effect in the current period and prospectively. That is, the change in estimate is applied to the asset's carrying (book) value and depreciation is calculated going forward using the new estimate. The previous periods are not affected by the change.

> **EXAMPLE: Change in depreciation estimate**
>
> Alpine Company purchased machinery for $20,000 with an estimated useful life of four years and a salvage value of $4,000. Alpine uses the straight-line depreciation method. At the beginning of the third year, Alpine reduces its salvage value estimate to $1,600. Determine the depreciation expense for each year.
>
> **Answer:**
>
> For the first two years, straight-line depreciation expense is [($20,000 original cost − $4,000 salvage value) / 4-year life] = $4,000 each year. At the beginning of the third year, the asset's carrying value on the balance sheet is $20,000 original cost − $8,000 accumulated depreciation = $12,000.
>
> To calculate straight-line depreciation expense for the remaining years, simply begin with the carrying value and depreciate over the remaining useful life using the new salvage value estimate. Depreciation expense for the last two years is [($12,000 carrying value − $1,600 revised salvage value) / 2 years remaining life] = $5,200 each year.

Estimates are also involved when a manufacturing firm allocates depreciation expense between COGS and SG&A. While the allocation does not affect a firm's operating margin, it affects the firm's gross margin (which is computed before SG&A expense) and operating expenses.

LOS 28.f: Describe the different amortisation methods for intangible assets with finite lives and calculate amortisation expense.

CFA® Program Curriculum, Volume 3, page 443

Intangible assets with finite lives are amortized over their useful lives. Amortization is identical to the depreciation of tangible assets. The same methods, straight-line, accelerated, and units-of-production, are permitted. The calculation of amortization expense also requires estimates of useful lives and salvage values. However, estimating useful lives is complicated by many legal, regulatory, contractual, competitive, and economic factors that may limit the use of the intangible assets.

As with depreciation, the total amount of amortization is the same under all of the methods. Timing of the amortization expense in the income statement is the only difference.

Another example of an intangible asset with an indefinite life is a trademark that may have a specific expiration date, but can be renewed at minimal cost. In this case, the trademark is considered to have an indefinite life and no amortization is required.

EXAMPLE: Calculating amortization expense

At the beginning of this year, Brandon Corporation entered into business acquisition. As a result of the acquisition, Brandon reported the following intangible assets:

Patent	$480,000
Franchise agreement	$350,000
Copyright	$150,000
Goodwill	$550,000
	$1,530,000

The patent expires in 12 years. The franchise agreement expires in 7 years but can be renewed indefinitely at a minimal cost. The copyright is expected to be sold at the end of 20 years for $30,000. Use the straight-line amortization method to calculate the total carrying value of Brandon's intangible assets at the end of the year.

Answer:

Goodwill is an indefinite-lived asset and is not amortized. Because the franchise agreement can be renewed indefinitely at minimal cost, it is also considered an indefinite-lived asset and is not amortized.

Using the straight-line method, amortization expense is $46,000 as follows:

Patent	$40,000 = $480,000 / 12 years
Copyright	6,000 = ($150,000 − 30,000) / 20 years
Amortization expense	$46,000

Thus, the carrying value at the end of the first year is $1,484,000 as follows:

Intangible assets, at cost	$1,530,000
Accumulated amortization	(46,000)
Intangible assets, net	$1,484,000

LOS 28.g: Describe how the choice of amortisation method and assumptions concerning useful life and residual value affect amortisation expense, financial statements, and ratios.

CFA® Program Curriculum, Volume 3, page 443

The choice of amortization method will affect expenses, assets, equity, and financial ratios in exactly the same way that the choice of depreciation method will. Just as with the depreciation of tangible assets, increasing either the estimate of an asset's useful life or the estimate of its residual value will reduce annual amortization expense, which will increase net income, assets, ROE, and ROA for the typical firm.

MODULE QUIZ 28.2

To best evaluate your performance, enter your quiz answers online.

1. East Company purchased a new truck at the beginning of this year for $30,000. The truck has a useful life of eight years or 150,000 miles, and an estimated salvage value of $3,000. If the truck is driven 16,500 miles this year, how much depreciation will East report under the double-declining balance (DDB) method and the units-of-production (UOP) method?

DDB	UOP
A. $7,500	$2,970
B. $7,500	$3,300
C. $6,750	$2,970

2. In the early years of an asset's life, a firm using the double-declining balance method, as compared to a firm using straight-line depreciation, will report lower:
   A. depreciation expense.
   B. operating cash flow.
   C. retained earnings.

3. Which of the following statements about indefinite-lived intangible assets is *most accurate*?
   A. They are amortized on a straight-line basis over a period not to exceed 40 years.
   B. They are reported on the balance sheet indefinitely.
   C. They never appear on the balance sheet unless they are internally developed.

4. At the beginning of this year, Fairweather Corp. incurred $200,000 of research costs and $100,000 of development costs to create a new patent. The patent is expected to have a useful life of 40 years with no salvage value. Calculate the carrying value of the patent at the end of this year, assuming Fairweather follows U.S. GAAP.
   A. $0.
   B. $97,500.
   C. $292,500.

5. Which of the following is *least likely* considered in determining the useful life an intangible asset?
   A. Initial cost.
   B. Legal, regulatory, or contractual provisions.
   C. Provisions for renewal or extension.

Video covering this content is available online.

MODULE 28.3: IMPAIRMENT AND REVALUATION

LOS 28.h: Describe the revaluation model.

CFA® Program Curriculum, Volume 3, page 444

Under U.S. GAAP, most long-lived assets are reported on the balance sheet at depreciated cost (original cost less accumulated depreciation and any impairment charges).

There is no fair value alternative for asset reporting under U.S. GAAP. Under IFRS, most long-lived assets are also reported at depreciated cost (the *cost model*). IFRS provides an alternative, the **revaluation model**, that permits a long-lived asset to be reported at its fair value, as long as an active market exists for the asset so its fair value can be reliably (and somewhat objectively) estimated. Firms must choose the same treatment for similar assets (e.g., land and buildings) so they cannot revalue only specific assets that are more likely to increase than decrease in value. The revaluation model is rarely used in practice by IFRS reporting firms.

Under the revaluation model, an asset is carried at its depreciated cost, but at each revaluation date, the balance sheet value is adjusted to fair value. Between revaluation dates, depreciation is recorded for the asset. Revaluation to fair value must be done sufficiently often that the reported value is not significantly different from fair value. Whether a revaluation affects the income statement, rather than only affecting equity, depends on previous revaluations. Consider the following situations.

First Revaluation Date

When there have been no prior revaluations and fair value is less than the carrying value (cost minus accumulated depreciation as of the first revaluation date), a loss is recorded on the income statement, much like an impairment charge. If fair value at the first revaluation date is greater than the carrying value of the asset, the difference is recorded as **revaluation surplus**, a component of equity, so net income is not affected.

Subsequent Revaluation Dates

On a revaluation date after the first revaluation, if fair value is greater than the carrying value, a gain is first reported on the income statement to the extent it reverses any previously recorded loss from revaluation. If the revaluation gain is greater than prior losses reported in the income statement that have not been reversed, the excess is reported in the revaluation surplus account.

If fair value on a revaluation date after the first revaluation date is less than the carrying value, the difference first goes to reduce any existing balance in the revaluation surplus account. Any remaining difference in excess of the balance in the revaluation surplus account is reported on the income statement as a loss.

> **EXAMPLE: Revaluation model**
>
> On December 31, 20X1, Parsons Corp. reports a carrying value for an asset class as $30 million and a fair value of $29 million and reports a revaluation loss on the income statement of $1 million.
>
> On December 31, 20X2, Parsons determines that the fair market value of the asset class is $1.5 million above its carrying value. This upward revaluation will be reported as a $1 million gain on the income statement (to reverse the previously recorded loss on the income statement) and a $0.5 million increase in the revaluation surplus account that does not affect income, but increases equity directly.

> On December 31, 20X3, Parsons determines that the fair market value of the asset class is $1 million below its carrying value. This loss first goes to reduce the existing revaluation surplus of $0.5 million, and the other $0.5 million of the downward revaluation is reported as a loss on the income statement.

LOS 28.i: Explain the impairment of property, plant, and equipment and intangible assets.

CFA® Program Curriculum, Volume 3, page 448

Both IFRS and U.S. GAAP require firms to write down impaired assets by recognizing a loss in the income statement. However, there are differences in applying the standards.

PROFESSOR'S NOTE

The following discussion applies to both tangible and intangible long-lived assets with finite lives that are held for use.

Impairments Under IFRS

Under IFRS, the firm must annually assess whether events or circumstances indicate an **impairment** of an asset's value has occurred. For example, there may have been a significant decline in the market value of the asset or a significant change in the asset's physical condition. If so, the asset's value must be tested for impairment.

An asset is impaired when its carrying value (original cost less accumulated depreciation) exceeds the **recoverable amount**. The recoverable amount is the greater of its fair value less any selling costs and its **value in use**. The value in use is the present value of its future cash flow stream from continued use.

If impaired, the asset's value must be written down on the balance sheet to the recoverable amount. An impairment loss, equal to the excess of carrying value over the recoverable amount, is recognized in the income statement.

Under IFRS, an impairment loss on an identifiable long-lived asset can be reversed if the asset's value recovers in the future. However, the loss reversal is limited to the original impairment loss. Thus, the carrying value of the asset after reversal cannot exceed the carrying value before the impairment loss was recognized.

Impairments Under U.S. GAAP

Under U.S. GAAP, an asset is tested for impairment only when events and circumstances indicate the firm may not be able to recover the carrying value through future use.

Determining an impairment and calculating the loss potentially involves two steps. In the first step, the asset is tested for impairment by applying a **recoverability test**. If the asset is impaired, the second step involves measuring the loss.

Recoverability. An asset is considered impaired if the carrying value (original cost less accumulated depreciation) is greater than the asset's future *undiscounted* cash flow stream. Because the recoverability test is based on estimates of future undiscounted cash flows, tests for impairment involve considerable management discretion.

Loss measurement. If impaired, the asset's value is written down to fair value on the balance sheet and a loss, equal to the excess of carrying value over the fair value of the asset (or the *discounted* value of its future cash flows if the fair value is not known), is recognized in the income statement.

Under U.S. GAAP, loss recoveries are typically not permitted.

PROFESSOR'S NOTE

The difference between testing for impairment and measuring the impairment loss can be confusing. In testing for impairment, undiscounted cash flows are used. Once impairment has been detected, the loss is based on fair value or the discounted expected future cash flows. Using undiscounted cash flows to test for impairment keeps PP&E assets from becoming "impaired" by increases in the discount rate when interest rates increase.

EXAMPLE: Asset impairment

Information related to equipment owned by Brownfield Company follows:

Original cost	$900,000
Accumulated depreciation to date	$100,000
Expected future cash flows	$795,000
Fair value	$790,000
Value in use	$785,000
Selling costs	$30,000

Assuming Brownfield will continue to use the equipment, test the asset for impairment under both IFRS and U.S. GAAP and discuss the results.

Answer:

The carrying value of the equipment is $900,000 original cost – $100,000 accumulated depreciation = $800,000, and the recoverable amount under IFRS is $785,000 (greater of $785,000 value in use and $760,000 fair value less selling costs). Under IFRS, the asset is written down on the balance sheet to the $785,000 recoverable amount, and a $15,000 loss ($800,000 carrying value – $785,000 recoverable amount) is recognized in the income statement.

Under U.S. GAAP, the asset is impaired because the $795,000 expected future cash flows is less than the $800,000 carrying value. The asset is written down on the balance sheet to its $790,000 fair value, and a $10,000 loss ($800,000 carrying value – $790,000 fair value) is recognized on the income statement.

Intangible Assets With Indefinite Lives

Intangible assets with indefinite lives are not amortized; rather, they are tested for impairment at least annually. An impairment loss is recognized when the carrying amount exceeds fair value.

PROFESSOR'S NOTE

The details of impairment for indefinite-lived intangibles, such as goodwill, are covered at Level II.

Long-Lived Assets Held for Sale

If a firm reclassifies a long-lived asset from *held for use* to *held for sale* because management intends to sell it, the asset is tested for impairment. At this point, the asset is no longer depreciated or amortized. The held-for-sale asset is impaired if its carrying value exceeds its net realizable value (fair value less selling costs). If impaired, the asset is written down to net realizable value and the loss is recognized in the income statement.

For long-lived assets held for sale, the loss can be reversed under IFRS and U.S. GAAP if the value of the asset recovers in the future. However, the loss reversal is limited to the original impairment loss. Thus, the carrying value of the asset after reversal cannot exceed the carrying value before the impairment was recognized.

LOS 28.j: Explain the derecognition of property, plant, and equipment and intangible assets.

CFA® Program Curriculum, Volume 3, page 451

Eventually, long-lived assets are removed from the balance sheet. **Derecognition** occurs when assets are sold, exchanged, or abandoned.

When a long-lived asset is sold, the asset is removed from the balance sheet and the difference between the sale proceeds and the carrying value of the asset is reported as a gain or loss in the income statement. The carrying value is equal to original cost minus accumulated depreciation and any impairment charges.

The gain or loss is usually reported in the income statement as a part of other gains and losses, or reported separately if material. Also, if the firm presents its cash flow statement using the indirect method, the gain or loss is removed from net income to compute cash flow from operations because the proceeds from selling a long-lived asset are an investing cash inflow.

If a long-lived asset is abandoned, the treatment is similar to a sale, except there are no proceeds. In this case, the carrying value of the asset is removed from the balance sheet and a loss of that amount is recognized in the income statement.

If a long-lived asset is exchanged for another asset, a gain or loss is computed by comparing the carrying value of the old asset with fair value of the old asset (or the fair value of the new asset if that value is clearly more evident). The carrying value of the old asset is removed from the balance sheet and the new asset is recorded at its fair value.

LOS 28.k: Explain and evaluate how impairment, revaluation, and derecognition of property, plant, and equipment and intangible assets affect financial statements and ratios.

CFA® Program Curriculum, Volume 3, page 444

Impairment reduces an asset's carrying value on the balance sheet. An impairment charge is recognized as a loss in the income statement, reducing assets and equity (retained earnings). In the year of impairment, ROA and ROE will decrease because the impairment charge reduces net income.

In subsequent periods, net income will be higher than it would have been without the impairment charge because depreciation will be lower (the asset has a lower depreciable value). Both ROA and ROE will increase in periods after the impairment charge because both equity and assets will fall as a result of the impairment charge. Asset turnover will increase in the period in which the impairment charge is taken, and in subsequent periods as well.

Asset impairment has no impact on cash flow because the impairment does not reduce taxable income; it is an unrealized loss until the asset is disposed of.

Analysis of Impairments

An impairment loss is an indication that the firm has not recognized sufficient depreciation or amortization expense, and has overstated earnings as a result.

The judgment required in determining asset impairments gives management considerable discretion about the timing and amounts of impairment charges. Consequently, impairment decisions present an opportunity for management to manipulate earnings. Waiting to recognize an impairment loss until a period of relatively high earnings would tend to smooth earnings.

Alternatively, existing managements may take more impairment charges in periods when earnings will be poor due to external (macroeconomic or industry) factors. New managements may also choose to take more or greater impairment charges when they take over. In either case, the resulting low earnings might not be perceived as the "fault" of management, and lower values for assets and equity give a boost to ROA and ROE going forward.

Revaluation

Under U.S. GAAP, most long-lived assets are reported on the balance sheet at depreciated cost using the *cost model* (original cost less accumulated depreciation and impairment charges). Revaluing long-lived assets upward is generally prohibited. One exception relates to long-lived assets held for sale, for which prior impairment losses can be reversed.

Under IFRS, firms can choose to use the **revaluation model** and report long-lived assets at their fair values. Firms can choose depreciated cost for some asset classes and fair value for others.

PROFESSOR'S NOTE

Do not confuse the revaluation model with fair-value reporting of trading securities or some types of inventory, under which all gains and losses flow through the income statement.

Revaluing an asset's value upward will result in:

- Higher total assets and higher shareholders' equity.

- Lower leverage ratios as measured by the debt ratio (total debt / total assets) and the debt-to-equity ratio (higher denominators).

- Higher depreciation expense and thus lower profitability in periods after revaluation.

- Lower ROA and ROE in periods after revaluation (lower numerators and higher denominators). However, if the increase in the asset value is the result of higher operating capacity, such higher capacity should result in higher revenues and thus higher earnings.

An analyst should check the source of the appraisal that supports the revaluation. Appraisals from independent sources are usually more reliable than appraisals by management.

Derecognition of Assets

Derecognition of an asset refers to its disposal by sale, exchange for another asset, or abandonment. Under the cost model, the carrying (book) value of a long-lived asset is its historical cost minus accumulated depreciation or amortization, adjusted for any impairment charges taken. Under the revaluation model, the carrying value of an asset is its value as of the last revaluation date, less any subsequent depreciation or amortization.

The difference between the sale price and the carrying value is reported as a gain or loss on the income statement. Such gains and losses may be reported in *other income or losses* or as a separate line item if the amount is material. When an asset is abandoned, the treatment is the same, but the sale price is zero and the loss is equal to the carrying value.

If an asset is exchanged for another asset, the sale price is taken to be the fair value of the asset exchanged, or the value of the asset acquired if that value is more readily available. There are no cash flows with an exchange of assets, but gains or losses, based on the difference between the carrying value and the "price" received for the exchanged asset, are reported on the income statement (as they are with a sale). If the fair values of the assets cannot be reliably estimated, the price of the acquired asset is taken to be the carrying value of the exchanged asset and no gains or losses are recorded.

MODULE QUIZ 28.3

To best evaluate your performance, enter your quiz answers online.

1. Two years ago, Metcalf Corp. purchased machinery for $800,000. At the end of last year, the machinery had a fair value of $720,000. Assuming Metcalf uses the revaluation model, what amount, if any, is recognized in Metcalf's net income this year if the machinery's fair value is $810,000?
   A. $0.
   B. $80,000.
   C. $90,000.

2. According to U.S. GAAP, an asset is impaired when:
   A. the firm cannot fully recover the carrying amount of the asset through operations.
   B. accumulated depreciation plus salvage value exceeds acquisition cost.
   C. the present value of future cash flows from an asset exceeds its carrying value.

3. In the year after an impairment charge on a finite-lived identifiable intangible asset, compared to not taking the charge, net income is *most likely* to be:
   A. lower.
   B. higher.
   C. unaffected.

4. A firm recently recognized a $15,000 loss on the sale of machinery used in its manufacturing operation. The original cost of the machinery was $100,000 and the accumulated depreciation at the date of sale was $60,000. What amount did the firm receive from the sale?
   A. $25,000.
   B. $45,000.
   C. $85,000.

5. Other things equal, which of the following actions related to property, plant, and equipment will decrease a firm's return on assets in future periods?
   A. Impairment.
   B. Derecognition.
   C. Upward revaluation.

MODULE 28.4: LEASES AND FIXED ASSET DISCLOSURES

LOS 28.1: Describe the financial statement presentation of and disclosures relating to property, plant, and equipment and intangible assets.

CFA® Program Curriculum, Volume 3, page 453

IFRS Disclosures

Under IFRS, the firm must disclose the following for each class of property, plant, and equipment (PP&E):

■ Basis for measurement (usually historical cost).

■ Useful lives or depreciation rate.

■ Gross carrying value and accumulated depreciation.

■ Reconciliation of carrying amounts from the beginning of the period to the end of the period.

The firm must also disclose:

■ Title restrictions and assets pledged as collateral.

■ Agreements to acquire PP&E in the future.

If the revaluation (fair value) model is used, the firm must disclose:

■ The revaluation date.

■ How fair value was determined.

■ Carrying value using the historical cost model.

Under IFRS, the disclosure requirements for intangible assets are similar to those for PP&E, except that the firm must disclose whether the useful lives are finite or indefinite.

For impaired assets, the firm must disclose:

■ Amounts of impairment losses and reversals by asset class.

■ Where the losses and loss reversals are recognized in the income statement.

■ Circumstances that caused the impairment loss or reversal.

U.S. GAAP Disclosures

Under U.S. GAAP, the PP&E disclosures include:

■ Depreciation expense by period.

■ Balances of major classes of assets by nature and function, such as land, improvements, buildings, machinery, and furniture.

■ Accumulated depreciation by major classes or in total.

■ General description of depreciation methods used.

Under U.S. GAAP, the disclosure requirements for intangible assets are similar to those for PP&E. In addition, the firm must provide an estimate of amortization expense for the next five years.

For impaired assets, the firm must disclose:

- A description of the impaired asset.

- Circumstances that caused the impairment.

- How fair value was determined.

- The amount of loss.

- Where the loss is recognized in the income statement.

LOS 28.m: Analyze and interpret financial statement disclosures regarding property, plant, and equipment and intangible assets.

CFA® Program Curriculum, Volume 3, page 453

Financial statement disclosures provide an analyst considerable information about a company's fixed assets and depreciation (amortization) methods. An analyst can use these data to estimate the average age of the firm's assets. The average age is useful for two reasons:

1. Older, less-efficient assets may make a firm less competitive.

2. The average age of assets helps an analyst to estimate the timing of major capital expenditures and a firm's future financing requirements.

The level of detail provided in footnote disclosures regarding fixed assets and depreciation varies across firms. Because assets are often grouped by their useful lives, the following methods of estimating the average age, economic life, and remaining useful life of a firm's assets do not produce precise values, but they can highlight issues for further investigation.

Three useful calculations (in years) for an analyst are:

Average Age

$$\text{average age} = \frac{\text{accumulated depreciation}}{\text{annual depreciation expense}}$$

This calculation is more accurate for a firm that uses straight-line depreciation. The calculation can be significantly affected by the mix of assets.

Total Useful Life

$$\text{total useful life} = \frac{\text{historical cost}}{\text{annual depreciation expense}}$$

Historical cost is gross PP&E before deducting accumulated depreciation.

Remaining Useful Life

$$\text{remaining useful life} = \frac{\text{ending net PP\&E}}{\text{annual depreciation expense}}$$

Net PP&E is equal to original cost (gross PP&E) minus accumulated depreciation.

PROFESSOR'S NOTE

The remaining useful life can also be approximated by subtracting the average age from the average depreciable life.

EXAMPLE: Calculating average age and total useful life

At the end of 20X8, a company has gross PP&E of $3 million and accumulated depreciation of $1 million. During the year, depreciation expense was $500,000.

What is the average age, total useful life, and remaining useful life of the company's PP&E?

Answer:

$$\text{average age} = \frac{\text{accumulated depreciation}}{\text{depreciation expense}} = \frac{\$1,000,000}{\$500,000} = 2 \text{ years}$$

$$\text{total useful life} = \frac{\text{historical cost}}{\text{depreciation expense}} = \frac{\$3,000,000}{\$500,000} = 6 \text{ years}$$

$$\text{remaining useful life} = \frac{\text{ending net PP\&E}}{\text{depreciation expense}} = \frac{\$2,000,000}{\$500,000} = 4 \text{ years}$$

Another popular metric is the ratio of annual capital expenditures to depreciation expense. This ratio provides information about whether the firm is replacing its PP&E at the same rate as its assets are being depreciated.

LOS 28.n: Compare the financial reporting of investment property with that of property, plant, and equipment.

CFA® Program Curriculum, Volume 3, page 464

Under IFRS, property that a firm owns for the purpose of collecting rental income, earning capital appreciation, or both, is classified as **investment property**. U.S. GAAP does not distinguish investment property from other kinds of long-lived assets.

IFRS gives firms the choice of using a cost model or a fair value model when valuing investment property, if a fair value for the property can be established reliably. A firm generally must use the same valuation model (cost or fair value) for all of its investment properties.

The cost model for investment property is the same as the cost model for valuing property, plant, and equipment, but the fair value model is different from the revaluation model we described earlier. Recall that under the revaluation model, an increase in an asset's carrying value is recognized as revaluation surplus in owners' equity (unless it reverses a previously recognized loss). For investment property, however, an upward revaluation is recognized as a gain on the income statement.

Firms are required to disclose which valuation model they use for investment property. Firms that use the fair value model must state how they determine the fair value of investment property and reconcile its beginning and ending values. Firms that use the cost model must disclose the fair value of their investment property, along with the disclosures that are required for other types of long-lived assets (e.g., useful lives, depreciation methods used).

In some cases, a firm may change its use of a property such that it becomes investment property or is no longer classified as investment property. For example, a firm may move its offices out of a building it owns and begin renting the space to others. If the firm uses the fair value model, the financial statement treatment of the asset's value depends on the nature of the change, as summarized in Figure 28.3. If the firm uses the cost model, the property's carrying amount does not change when it is transferred into or out of investment property.

Figure 28.3: Transfers To or From Investment Property (Fair Value Model)

Transfer From	Transfer To	Financial Statement Treatment
Owner-occupied	Investment property	Treat as revaluation: recognize gain only if it reverses previously recognized loss
Inventory	Investment property	Recognize gain or loss if fair value is different from carrying amount
Investment property	Owner-occupied or inventory	Fair value of asset at date of transfer will be its cost under new classification

LOS 28.o: Explain and evaluate how leasing rather than purchasing assets affects financial statements and ratios.

LOS 28.p: Explain and evaluate how finance leases and operating leases affect financial statements and ratios from the perspective of both the lessor and the lessee.

CFA® Program Curriculum, Volume 3, page 467

PROFESSOR'S NOTE

We will revisit lease accounting, with additional detail, in the topic review of Non-Current (Long-Term) Liabilities.

A *lease* is a contractual arrangement whereby the **lessor**, the owner of an asset, allows a **lessee** to use the asset for a specified period of time in return for periodic payments.

Leases are classified as either finance leases or operating leases. In the United States, a finance lease is known as a **capital lease**.

A **finance lease** is, in substance, a purchase of an asset that is financed with debt. Accordingly, at the inception of the lease, the lessee will add equal amounts to both assets and liabilities on the balance sheet. Over the term of the lease, the lessee will recognize depreciation expense on the asset and interest expense on the liability. This is the same treatment as if the asset were purchased with borrowed funds at the same asset value and terms as the finance lease.

An **operating lease** is essentially a rental arrangement. No asset or liability is reported by the lessee and the periodic lease payments are simply recognized as rental expense in the income statement.

PROFESSOR'S NOTE

Accounting standards scheduled to take effect in 2019 will require operating leases to appear on the balance sheets of lessees.

Reporting by the Lessee

The treatment of a lease as either an operating lease or finance lease determines whether or not the lease is reported on the balance sheet, how the lease expense is recognized in the income statement, and the classification of the lease payments on the cash flow statement.

Operating lease. At the inception of the lease, no entry is made (though any related future obligations must be disclosed in the footnotes). During the term of the lease, *rent expense*, equal to the lease payment, is recognized in the lessee's income statement. In the cash flow statement, the lease payment is reported as an outflow from operating activities.

Finance lease. At the inception of the lease, the lower of the *present value* of future minimum lease payments or the fair value is recognized as an asset and as a liability on the lessee's balance sheet. Over the term of the lease, the asset is depreciated and *depreciation* expense as well as *interest* expense is reported in the income statement. Interest expense is equal to the lease liability at the beginning of the period multiplied by the interest rate implicit in the lease.

In the cash flow statement, the lease payment is allocated to interest expense and principal repayment, just as with an amortizing loan. The principal portion of the lease payment is equal to the total payment minus the interest expense for the period. Under U.S. GAAP, interest expense is reported in the cash flow statement as an outflow from operating activities and the principal payment is reported as an outflow from financing activities.

PROFESSOR'S NOTE

Under IFRS, firms can choose to report interest paid in the cash flow statement either as an operating or a financing activity.

Figure 28.4 and Figure 28.5 compare the impacts on a lessee of accounting for a lease as operating or financing.

Figure 28.4: Financial Statement Impact of Finance vs. Operating Leases

	Finance Lease	Operating Lease
Assets	Higher	Lower
Liabilities (current and long-term)	Higher	Lower
Net income (in the early years)	Lower	Higher
Net income (later years)	Higher	Lower
Total net income	Same	Same
EBIT (operating income)	Higher	Lower
Cash flow from operations	Higher	Lower
Cash flow from financing	Lower	Higher
Total cash flow	Same	Same

Figure 28.5: Ratio Impact of Finance vs. Operating Leases

	Finance Lease	Operating Lease
Current ratio (CA / CL)	Lower	Higher
Working capital (CA – CL)	Lower	Higher
Asset turnover (Revenue / TA)	Lower	Higher
Return on assets* (NI / TA)	Lower	Higher
Return on equity* (NI / SE)	Lower	Higher
Debt / Assets	Higher	Lower
Debt / Equity	Higher	Lower

* In the early years of the lease.

In sum, all the ratios in Figure 28.5 are worse when a lease is capitalized (i.e., treated as a finance lease). The only improvements from a finance lease are higher EBIT (because interest is not subtracted in calculating EBIT), higher CFO (because principal repayment is CFF), and higher net income in the later years of the lease (because interest plus depreciation is less than the lease payment in the later years).

Reporting by the Lessor

From the lessor's perspective, a lease is also classified as either an operating lease or a finance (capital) lease.

At the inception of a finance lease, the lessor will recognize a sale equal to the present value of the lease payments, and cost of goods sold equal to the carrying value of the asset. Just as with a normal sales transaction, the difference between the sales price and cost of goods sold is gross profit. If the lessor is not a manufacturer or dealer for the asset, but strictly offering financing in the form or a lease, the gross profit at the inception of the lease is zero (PV of the lease payments equals the carrying value of the leased asset).

The asset is removed from the balance sheet and a lease receivable, equal to the present value of the lease payments, is created. As the lease payments are received, the principal portion of the payment reduces the lease receivable. It is as if the lessor sold the asset for its fair market value, and loaned the lessee the purchase price.

The lessor also recognizes interest income over the term of the lease. The interest revenue is equal to the lease receivable at the beginning of each period multiplied by the interest rate.

In the cash flow statement, the interest revenue portion of the lease payment is reported as an inflow from operating activities and the principal reduction is reported as an inflow from investing activities, just as with any amortizing loan the lessor may make.

If a lease is treated as an operating lease, the lessor simply recognizes the lease payment as rental income. The lessor will keep the leased asset on its balance sheet and recognize depreciation expense over the asset's useful life.

Total income over the life of the lease is the same for an operating lease and a finance lease. However, in the early years of the lease, the income reported from the finance lease is higher than the income reported from the operating lease. Just like an amortizing loan, the interest is higher in the early years. This situation reverses in the later years of the lease.

Total cash flow is the same for an operating lease and a finance lease. However, cash flow from operations is higher with the operating lease. With a finance lease, the lease payment is separated into the interest portion (CFO) and principal portion (CFI).

PROFESSOR'S NOTE

From the lessee's perspective, principal is a financing outflow. From the lessor's perspective, principal is a return of capital invested in the lease. Thus, the principal is reported as an investing inflow.

MODULE QUIZ 28.4

To best evaluate your performance, enter your quiz answers online.

1. Which of the following disclosures would *least likely* be found in the financial statement footnotes of a firm?
   A. Accumulated depreciation.
   B. Carrying values by asset class.
   C. Average age of assets.

2. Metallurgy, Inc., reported depreciation expense of $15 million for the most recent year. Beginning-of-year gross PP&E and accumulated depreciation were $287 million and $77 million, respectively. If end-of year gross PP&E and accumulated depreciation were $300 million and $80 million, the estimated remaining useful life of PP&E is *closest* to:
   A. 10 years.
   B. 15 years.
   C. 20 years.

3. A firm owns a warehouse that it rents out. Under IFRS, the firm may report the value of this asset on its balance sheet using:
    A. the cost model or the fair value model.
    B. the cost model or the revaluation model.
    C. the revaluation model or the fair value model.

4. A firm is deciding whether to acquire an asset with a finance lease or purchase it with cash for its fair value. The present value of the lease payments is greater than the fair value of the asset. The firm uses straight-line depreciation for its long-lived assets. Compared to purchasing the asset, a finance lease will result in:
    A. higher depreciation.
    B. higher total expenses.
    C. lower book value of PP&E.

KEY CONCEPTS

LOS 28.a

When an asset is expected to provide benefits for only the current period, its cost is expensed on the income statement for the period. If an asset is expected to provide benefits over multiple periods, it is capitalized rather than expensed.

LOS 28.b

The cost of a purchased finite-lived intangible asset is amortized over its useful life. Indefinite-lived intangible assets are not amortized, but are tested for impairment at least annually. The cost of internally developed intangible assets is expensed.

Under IFRS, research costs are expensed but development costs may be capitalized. Under U.S. GAAP, both research and development costs are expensed as incurred, except in the case of software created for sale to others.

The acquisition method is used to account for assets acquired in a business combination. The purchase price is allocated to the fair value of identifiable assets of the acquired firm less its liabilities. Any excess of the purchase price above the fair value of the acquired firm's net assets is recorded as goodwill, an unidentifiable intangible asset that cannot be separated from the business itself.

LOS 28.c

With capitalization, the asset value is put on the balance sheet and the cost is expensed through the income statement over the asset's useful life through either depreciation or amortization. Compared to expensing the asset cost, capitalization results in:

- Lower expense and higher net income in period of acquisition, higher expense (depreciation or amortization) and lower net income in each of the remaining years of the asset's life.

- Higher assets and equity.

- Lower CFI and higher CFO because the cost of a capitalized asset is classified as an investing cash outflow.

- Higher ROE and ROA in the initial period, and lower ROE and ROA in subsequent periods because net income is lower and both assets and equity are higher.

- Lower debt-to-assets and debt-to-equity ratios because assets and equity are higher.

LOS 28.d

Depreciation methods:

- Straight-line: Equal amount of expense each period.

- Accelerated (declining balance): Higher depreciation expense in the early years and lower depreciation expense in the later years of an asset's life.

- Units-of-production: Expense based on percentage usage rather than time.

Straight-line method:

$$\text{depreciation expense} = \frac{\text{original cost} - \text{salvage value}}{\text{depreciable life}}$$

Double-declining balance (DDB), an accelerated depreciation method:

DDB depreciation in year $x =$

$$\frac{2}{\text{depreciable life in years}} \times \text{book value at beginning of year } x$$

Units of production method:

$$\frac{\text{original cost} - \text{salvage value}}{\text{life in output units}} \times \text{output units used in the period}$$

IFRS requires component depreciation, in which significant parts of an asset are identified and depreciated separately.

LOS 28.e

In the early years of an asset's life, accelerated depreciation results in higher depreciation expense, lower net income, and lower ROA and ROE compared to straight-line depreciation. Cash flow is the same assuming tax depreciation is unaffected by the choice of method for financial reporting.

Firms can reduce depreciation expense and increase net income by using longer useful lives and higher salvage values.

LOS 28.f

Amortization methods for intangible assets with finite lives are the same as those for depreciation: straight line, accelerated, or units of production. Calculation of amortization expense for such assets is the same as with depreciation expense.

LOS 28.g

The choice of amortization method will affect expenses, assets, equity, and financial ratios in exactly the same way that the choice of depreciation method will. Just as with the depreciation of tangible assets, increasing either the estimate of an asset's useful life or the estimate of its residual value will reduce annual amortization expense, which will increase net income, assets, ROE, and ROA for a typical firm.

LOS 28.h

Under IFRS, firms have the option to revalue assets based on fair value under the revaluation model. U.S. GAAP does not permit revaluation.

The impact of revaluation on the income statement depends on whether the initial revaluation resulted in a gain or loss. If the initial revaluation resulted in a loss (decrease in carrying value), the initial loss would be recognized in the income statement and any subsequent gain would be recognized in the income statement only to the extent of the previously reported loss. Revaluation gains beyond the initial loss bypass the income statement and are recognized in shareholders' equity as a revaluation surplus.

If the initial revaluation resulted in a gain (increase in carrying value), the initial gain would bypass the income statement and be reported as a revaluation surplus. Later revaluation losses would first reduce the revaluation surplus.

LOS 28.i

Under IFRS, an asset is impaired when its carrying value exceeds the recoverable amount. The recoverable amount is the greater of fair value less selling costs and the value in use (present value of expected cash flows). If impaired, the asset is written down to the recoverable amount. Loss recoveries are permitted, but not above historical cost.

Under U.S. GAAP, an asset is impaired if its carrying value is greater than the asset's undiscounted future cash flows. If impaired, the asset is written down to fair value. Subsequent recoveries are not allowed for assets held for use.

Asset impairments result in losses in the income statement. Impairments have no impact on cash flow as they have no tax or other cash flow effects until disposal of the asset.

LOS 28.j

When a long-lived asset is *sold*, the difference between the sale proceeds and the carrying (book) value of the asset is reported as a gain or loss in the income statement.

When a long-lived asset is *abandoned*, the carrying value is removed from the balance sheet and a loss is recognized in that amount.

If a long-lived asset is *exchanged* for another asset, a gain or loss is computed by comparing the carrying value of the old asset with fair value of the old asset (or fair value of the new asset if more clearly evident).

LOS 28.k

Impairment charges decrease net income, assets, and equity, which results in lower ROA and ROE and higher debt-to-equity and debt-to-assets ratios for a typical firm.

Upward revaluation increases assets and equity, and thereby decreases debt-to-assets and debt-to-equity ratios. A downward revaluation has opposite effects. The effect on net income and related ratios depends on whether the revaluation is to a value above or below cost.

Derecognition of assets can result in either a gain or loss on the income statement. A loss will reduce net income and assets, while a gain will increase net income and assets.

LOS 28.l

There are many differences in the disclosure requirements for tangible and intangible assets under IFRS and U.S. GAAP. However, firms are generally required to disclose:

- Carrying values for each class of asset.

- Accumulated depreciation and amortization.

- Title restrictions and assets pledged as collateral.

- For impaired assets, the loss amount and the circumstances that caused the loss.

- For revalued assets (IFRS only), the revaluation date, how fair value was determined, and the carrying value using the historical cost model.

LOS 28.m

Analysts can use disclosures of the historical cost, accumulated depreciation (amortization), and annual depreciation (amortization) expense to estimate average age of assets, total useful life of assets, and remaining useful life of assets. These estimates are more accurate for firms that use straight-line depreciation.

$$\text{Average age} = \frac{\text{accumulated depreciation}}{\text{annual depreciation expense}}$$

$$\text{Total useful life} = \frac{\text{historical cost}}{\text{annual depreciation expense}}$$

$$\text{Remaining useful life} = \frac{\text{ending net PP\&E}}{\text{annual depreciation expense}}$$

LOS 28.n

Under IFRS (but not U.S. GAAP), investment property is defined as property owned for the purpose of earning rent, capital appreciation, or both. Firms can account for investment property using the cost model or the fair value model. Unlike the revaluation model for property, plant, and equipment, increases in the fair value of investment property above its historical cost are recognized as gains on the income statement if the firm uses the fair value model.

LOS 28.o

For a lessee, the accounting treatment of a finance (capital) lease is like that of purchasing the asset with debt. The leased asset is recorded on the lessee's balance sheet and depreciated over its life. The present value of the lease payment is a liability that is amortized over the term of the lease. The interest portion of the lease payment and the depreciation of the asset are recorded as expenses on the income statement. On the cash flow statement, the interest portion of the lease payment is an operating cash outflow and the principal portion is a financing cash outflow.

With an operating lease, the full lease payment is reported as rental expense on the lessee's income statement and as an operating cash outflow. No asset or liability is reported on the balance sheet.

LOS 28.p

With an operating lease, the asset remains on the balance sheet of the lessor and is depreciated. The lease payments are rental income. For a finance lease, the lessor removes the asset from the balance sheet and replaces it with a lease receivable. The interest portion of the lease payment is interest income to the lessor and the remainder of the payment is a principal repayment that decreases the lease receivable on the lessor's balance sheet.

Compared to an operating lease, a finance lease adds the asset and the related lease liability to the lessee's balance sheet so that equity is initially unchanged. The leased asset is depreciated over the lease term. Depreciation and interest expense comprise the lease expenses recorded on the income statement and will exceed the lease payment in the early years of the lease and be less than the lease payment in the later years of the lease. This results in less profit for the lessee in the early years of a lease and greater profit in the later years.

ANSWER KEY FOR MODULE QUIZZES

Module Quiz 28.1

1. **A** If the future economic benefits of a purchase are highly uncertain, a company should expense the purchase in the period it is incurred. (LOS 28.a)

2. **A** The cost of an intangible asset is amortized if the asset has a finite life and was purchased or acquired in a business combination. Development costs for internally generated intangible assets may be capitalized under IFRS, but research costs are expensed as incurred. (LOS 28.b)

3. **C** As compared to a firm that capitalizes its expenditures, a firm that immediately expenses expenditures will report lower assets. Thus, asset turnover (revenue / average assets) will be higher for the expensing firm (lower denominator). (LOS 28.c)

Module Quiz 28.2

1. **A** Double-declining balance = $30,000 book value × (2/8) = $7,500.

   Units-of-production = ($30,000 cost – $3,000 salvage value) / 150,000 miles = $0.18 per mile.

   16,500 miles driven × $0.18 per mile = $2,970.

   (LOS 28.d)

2. **C** In the early years, accelerated depreciation will result in higher depreciation expense; thus, lower net income. Lower net income will result in lower retained earnings. (LOS 28.e)

3. **B** Indefinite-lived intangible assets are not amortized; rather, they are reported on the balance sheet indefinitely unless they are impaired. (LOS 28.f)

4. **A** Under U.S. GAAP, research and development costs are expensed as incurred. Thus, the entire $300,000 of R&D is expensed this year. The result is a zero carrying value. (LOS 28.f)

5. **A** Initial cost has nothing to do with the useful life of an intangible asset. (LOS 28.g)

Module Quiz 28.3

1. **B** Under the revaluation method, Metcalf reports the equipment on the balance sheet at fair value. At the end of last year, an $80,000 loss was recognized (from $800,000 to $720,000) in the income statement. Any recovery is recognized in the income statement to the extent of the loss. Any remainder is recognized in shareholders' equity as revaluation surplus.

Thus, at the end of this year, an $80,000 gain is recognized in the income statement, and a $10,000 revaluation surplus is recognized in shareholders' equity. (LOS 28.h)

2. **A** An asset is impaired when the firm cannot recover the carrying value. Under U.S. GAAP, recoverability is tested based on undiscounted future cash flows. (LOS 28.i)

3. **B** Because a finite-lived identifiable intangible asset would be amortized, amortization expense in the year after the reduction from the impairment charge would be lower (the carrying value of the asset would most likely be lower), increasing net income. (LOS 28.i)

4. **A** Gain or loss is equal to the sale proceeds minus the carrying value (cost minus accumulated depreciation) at the time of sale. Given the loss of $15,000 and carrying value of $40,000 ($100,000 – $60,000), we can solve for the proceeds of $25,000 (–15,000 + 40,000). (LOS 28.j)

5. **C** An upward revaluation will increase the book value of assets and increase depreciation expense in future periods (decreasing net income), both of which reduce ROA. Impairment would have the opposite effects, decreasing future depreciation and book values. Derecognizing a fully depreciated asset will have no effect on net income in future periods but will decrease assets, resulting in higher ROA. (LOS 28.k)

Module Quiz 28.4

1. **C** The average age is not a required disclosure. However, it can be calculated given other disclosures. (LOS 28.l)

2. **B** The remaining useful life can be estimated as ending net PP&E value divided by annual deprecation.

    $(300 – 80)/15 = 14.66$ years

    (LOS 28.m)

3. **A** Under IFRS, the warehouse is classified as investment property because it is owned primarily for rental income. Investment property may be reported using either the cost model or the fair value model. (LOS 28.n)

4. **B** With a finance lease, the firm will recognize a long-lived asset and a liability in the same amounts. That value is the lower of the asset's fair value or the present value of the minimum lease payments. In this case, the asset and liability would equal the fair value of the asset, so PP&E will be the same with either a purchase or a lease. The firm will recognize depreciation expense for either a purchase or a finance lease. Total expenses, however, will be higher with a finance lease because the firm will also recognize interest expense on the lease liability. (LOS 28.o, 28.p)

READING
29

Income Taxes

EXAM FOCUS

In many countries, financial reporting standards and tax reporting standards differ. Candidates should be aware of the terminology that relates to each set of standards, notably taxes payable, which are the taxes actually due to the government, and income tax expense, which is reported on the income statement and reflects taxes payable plus any deferred income tax expense. The timing of revenue and expense recognition in the income statement and the tax return may lead to the creation of deferred tax liabilities, which the company may have to pay in the future, or deferred tax assets, which may provide benefits in the future. For the exam, you should know that some differences between taxable and pretax income are temporary, while some are permanent and will never reverse. Be prepared to calculate taxes payable, tax expense, deferred tax liabilities and assets, and be able to make the necessary adjustments for analytical purposes.

MODULE 29.1: TAX TERMS

▶

Video covering this content is available online.

LOS 29.a: Describe the differences between accounting profit and taxable income and define key terms, including deferred tax assets, deferred tax liabilities, valuation allowance, taxes payable, and income tax expense.

CFA® Program Curriculum, Volume 3, page 508

Financial accounting standards (IFRS and U.S. GAAP) are often different than income tax laws and regulations. As a result, the amount of income tax expense recognized in the income statement may differ from the actual taxes owed to the taxing authorities.

Tax Return Terminology

- **Taxable income.** Income subject to tax based on the tax return.

- **Taxes payable.** The tax liability caused by *taxable income*. This is also known as current tax expense, but do not confuse this with *income tax expense* (see below).

- **Income tax paid.** The actual cash flow for income taxes including payments or refunds from other years.

- **Tax loss carryforward.** A current or past loss that can be used to reduce taxable income (thus, taxes payable) in the future. Can result in a deferred tax asset.

- **Tax base.** Net amount of an asset or liability used for tax reporting purposes.

Financial Reporting Terminology

- **Accounting profit.** Pretax financial income based on financial accounting standards. Also known as *income before tax* and *earnings before tax*.

- **Income tax expense.** Expense recognized in the income statement that includes taxes payable and *changes* in deferred tax assets and liabilities (DTA and DTL). The income tax expense equation is:

  income tax expense = taxes payable + ΔDTL − ΔDTA

- **Deferred tax liabilities.** Balance sheet amounts that result from an excess of income tax expense over taxes payable that are expected to result in future cash outflows.

- **Deferred tax assets.** Balance sheet amounts that result from an excess of taxes payable over income tax expense that are expected to be recovered from future operations. Can also result from tax loss carryforwards.

- **Valuation allowance.** Reduction of deferred tax assets based on the likelihood the assets will not be realized.

- **Carrying value.** Net balance sheet value of an asset or liability.

- **Permanent difference.** A difference between taxable income (tax return) and pretax income (income statement) that will not reverse in the future.

- **Temporary difference.** A difference between the tax base and the carrying value of an asset or liability that will result in either taxable amounts or deductible amounts in the future. Several examples of how temporary differences arise are presented later in this review.

MODULE 29.2: DEFERRED TAX LIABILITIES AND ASSETS

Video covering this content is available online.

LOS 29.b: Explain how deferred tax liabilities and assets are created and the factors that determine how a company's deferred tax liabilities and assets should be treated for the purposes of financial analysis.

CFA® Program Curriculum, Volume 3, page 510

Differences between the treatment of an accounting item for tax reporting and for financial reporting can occur when:

- The timing of revenue and expense recognition in the income statement and the tax return differ.
- Certain revenues and expenses are recognized in the income statement but never on the tax return or vice-versa.
- Assets and/or liabilities have different carrying amounts and tax bases.
- Gain or loss recognition in the income statement differs from the tax return.
- Tax losses from prior periods may offset future taxable income.
- Financial statement adjustments may not affect the tax return or may be recognized in different periods.

Deferred Tax Liabilities

A **deferred tax liability** is created when income tax expense (income statement) is greater than taxes payable (tax return) due to temporary differences. Deferred tax liabilities occur when:

- Revenues (or gains) are recognized in the income statement before they are included on the tax return due to temporary differences.
- Expenses (or losses) are tax deductible before they are recognized in the income statement.

Deferred tax liabilities are expected to reverse (i.e., they are caused by temporary differences) and result in future cash outflows when the taxes are paid.

A deferred tax liability is most often created when an accelerated depreciation method is used on the tax return and straight-line depreciation is used on the income statement.

Deferred Tax Assets

A **deferred tax asset** is created when taxes payable (tax return) are greater than income tax expense (income statement) due to temporary differences. Deferred tax assets occur when:

- Revenues (or gains) are taxable before they are recognized in the income statement.

■ Expenses (or losses) are recognized in the income statement before they are tax deductible.

■ Tax loss carryforwards are available to reduce future taxable income.

Similar to deferred tax liabilities, deferred tax assets are expected to reverse through future operations. However, deferred tax assets are expected to provide future tax savings, while deferred tax liabilities are expected to result in future cash outflows. A firm that has taxable losses in excess of its taxable income can carry those excess losses forward and use them to reduce taxable income (and taxes) in future periods.

Post-employment benefits, *warranty expenses*, and *tax loss carryforwards* are typical causes of deferred tax assets.

Treatment for Analytical Purposes

If deferred tax liabilities are expected to reverse in the future, they are best classified by an analyst as liabilities. If, however, they are not expected to reverse in the future, they are best classified as equity (DTL decreased and equity increased by the same amount). The key question is, "When or will the total deferred tax liability be reversed in the future?" In practice, the treatment of deferred taxes for analytical purposes varies. An analyst must decide on the appropriate treatment on a case-by-case basis.

LOS 29.c: Calculate the tax base of a company's assets and liabilities.

CFA® Program Curriculum, Volume 3, page 513

Tax Base of Assets

An asset's **tax base** is the amount that will be deducted (expensed) on the tax return in the future as the economic benefits of the asset are realized. The **carrying value** is the value of the asset reported on the financial statements, net of depreciation and amortization.

Following are a few examples of calculating the tax bases of various assets.

Depreciable equipment. The cost of equipment is $100,000. In the income statement, depreciation expense of $10,000 is recognized each year for ten years. On the tax return, the asset is depreciated at $20,000 per year for five years.

At the end of the first year, the tax base is $80,000 ($100,000 cost − $20,000 accumulated tax depreciation) and the carrying value is $90,000 ($100,000 cost − $10,000 accumulated financial depreciation). A deferred tax liability ($10,000 × tax rate) is created to account for the timing difference from different depreciation for tax and for financial reporting.

Sale of the machine for $100,000, for example, would result in a gain of $10,000 on the income statement and a gain of $20,000 on the tax return. This would reverse the deferred tax liability.

Research and development. At the beginning of this year, $75,000 of R&D was expensed in the income statement. On the tax return, the R&D was capitalized and is amortized on a straight-line basis over three years.

At the end of the first year, the tax base is $50,000 ($75,000 cost − $25,000 accumulated tax amortization) and the asset has no carrying value (does not appear on the balance sheet) because the entire cost was expensed. Note that amortization for tax here leads to a deferred tax asset, since earnings before tax are less than taxable income.

Accounts receivable. Gross receivables totaling $20,000 are outstanding at year-end. Because collection is uncertain, the firm recognizes bad debt expense of $1,500 in the income statement. For tax purposes, bad debt expense cannot be deducted until the receivables are deemed worthless.

At the end of the year, the tax base of the receivables is $20,000 since no bad debt expense has been deducted on the tax return. The carrying value is $18,500 ($20,000 − $1,500 bad debt expense). Again, a deferred tax asset is the result.

Tax Base of Liabilities

A liability's tax base is the carrying value of the liability minus any amounts that will be deductible on the tax return in the future. The tax base of revenue received in advance is the carrying value minus the amount of revenue that will *not* be taxed in the future.

Following are a few examples of calculating the tax bases of various liabilities.

Customer advance. At year-end, $10,000 was received from a customer for goods that will be shipped next year. On the tax return, revenue received in advance is taxable when collected.

The carrying value of the liability is $10,000. The carrying value will be reduced when the goods are shipped next year. For revenue received in advance, the tax base is equal to the carrying value minus any amounts that will *not* be taxed in the future. Since the customer advance has already been taxed, $10,000 will not be taxed in the future. Thus, the customer advance liability has a tax base of zero ($10,000 carrying value − $10,000 revenue not taxed in the future). Since the $10,000 has been taxed but not yet reported as revenue on the income statement, a deferred tax asset is created.

Warranty liability. At year-end, a firm estimates that $5,000 of warranty expense will be required on goods already sold. On the tax return, warranty expense is not deductible until the warranty work is actually performed. The warranty work will be performed next year.

The carrying value of the warranty liability is $5,000. The tax base is equal to the carrying value minus the amount deductible in the future. Thus, the warranty liability has a tax base of zero ($5,000 carrying value − $5,000 warranty expense deductible in the future). Delayed recognition of this expense for tax results in a deferred tax asset.

Note payable. The firm has an outstanding promissory note with a principal balance of $30,000. Interest accrues at 10% and is paid at the end of each quarter.

The promissory note is treated the same way on the tax return and in the financial statements. Thus, the carrying value and the tax base are both $30,000. Interest paid is included in both pre-tax income on the income statement and in taxable income on the tax return. With no timing difference, no deferred tax items are created.

MODULE QUIZ 29.1, 29.2

To best evaluate your performance, enter your quiz answers online.

1. Which of the following tax definitions is *least accurate*?
   A. Taxable income is income based on the rules of the tax authorities.
   B. Taxes payable are the amount due to the government.
   C. Pretax income is income tax expense divided by one minus the statutory tax rate.

2. Which of the following statements is *most accurate*? The difference between taxes payable for the period and the tax expense recognized on the financial statements results from differences:
   A. in management control.
   B. between basic and diluted earnings.
   C. between financial and tax accounting.

3. An analyst is comparing a firm to its competitors. The firm has a deferred tax liability that results from accelerated depreciation for tax purposes. The firm is expected to continue to grow in the foreseeable future. How should the liability be treated for analysis purposes?
   A. It should be treated as equity at its full value.
   B. It should be treated as a liability at its full value.
   C. The present value should be treated as a liability with the remainder being treated as equity.

4. If the tax base of an asset exceeds the asset's carrying value and a reversal is expected in the future:
   A. a deferred tax asset is created.
   B. a deferred tax liability is created.
   C. neither a deferred tax asset nor a deferred tax liability is created.

5. The author of a new textbook received a $100,000 advance from the publisher this year. $40,000 of income taxes were paid on the advance when received. The textbook will not be finished until next year. Determine the tax basis of the advance at the end of this year.
   A. $0.
   B. $40,000.
   C. $100,000.

MODULE 29.3: DEFERRED TAX EXAMPLES

Video covering this
content is available
online.

LOS 29.d: Calculate income tax expense, income taxes payable, deferred tax assets, and deferred tax liabilities, and calculate and interpret the adjustment to the financial statements related to a change in the income tax rate.

CFA® Program Curriculum, Volume 3, page 510

PROFESSOR'S NOTE

The effects of changing tax rates on deferred tax assets and liabilities are explained in the next LOS.

EXAMPLE: Deferred tax liabilities

Assume the original cost of an asset is $600,000. The asset has a 3-year life and no salvage value is expected. For tax purposes, the asset is depreciated using an accelerated depreciation method with tax return depreciation of $300,000 in year 1, $200,000 in year 2, and $100,000 in year 3. The firm recognizes straight-line (SL) depreciation expense of $200,000 each year in its income statements. Earnings before interest, taxes, depreciation, and amortization (EBITDA) is $500,000 each year. The firm's tax rate is 40%. Calculate the firm's income tax expense, taxes payable, and deferred tax liability for each year of the asset's life.

Answer:

The following tables illustrate the calculation of taxes payable reported on the tax return and income tax expense reported in the income statement.

Tax Return (40% Tax Rate, Accelerated Depreciation)

	Year 1	Year 2	Year 3	Total 1–3
EBITDA	$500,000	$500,000	$500,000	$1,500,000
Depreciation	$300,000	$200,000	$100,000	$600,000
Taxable income	$200,000	$300,000	$400,000	$900,000
Tax rate	× 0.40	× 0.40	× 0.40	× 0.40
Tax payable	$80,000	$120,000	$160,000	$360,000

Income Statement (40% Tax Rate, SL Depreciation)

	Year 1	Year 2	Year 3	Total 1–3
EBITDA	$500,000	$500,000	$500,000	$1,500,000
Depreciation	$200,000	$200,000	$200,000	$600,000
Pre-tax income	$300,000	$300,000	$300,000	$900,000
Tax rate	× 0.40	× 0.40	× 0.40	× 0.40
Income tax expense	$120,000	$120,000	$120,000	$360,000

In year 1, the firm recognizes $120,000 of income tax expense on the income statement but taxes payable (tax return) are only $80,000. So, income tax expense is *initially* higher than taxes payable. The $40,000 difference is deferred to a future period by using an accelerated depreciation method for tax purposes. The $40,000 is reported on the balance sheet by creating a DTL.

The tax base and the carrying value of the asset are used to calculate the *balance* of the DTL. At the end of year 1, the carrying value of the asset is $400,000 and the tax base of the asset is $300,000. By multiplying the $100,000 difference by the 40% tax rate, we get the *balance* of the DTL of $40,000.

We can reconcile income tax expense and taxes payable with the *change* in the DTL. In this example, the DTL increased $40,000 (from zero to $40,000) during year 1. Thus, income tax expense in year 1 is $120,000 ($80,000 taxes payable + $40,000 *change* in the DTL).

In year 2, depreciation expense is the same on the tax return and the income statement. Thus, taxable income is equal to pretax income and there is no change in the DTL. Income tax expense in year 2 is $120,000 ($120,000 taxes payable + zero *change* in the DTL).

In year 3, the firm recognizes income tax expense of $120,000 on the income statement but $160,000 in taxes payable (tax return). The $40,000 deferred tax liability recognized at the end of year 1 has reversed as a result of lower depreciation expense using the accelerated method on the tax return. In year 3, income tax expense is $120,000 [$160,000 taxes payable + (–$40,000 *change* in DTL)].

Note that over the useful life of the asset, total depreciation, total taxable (and pretax) income, and total taxes payable (and income tax expense) are the same on the financial statements and the tax return. Also, at the end of year 3, both the tax base and the carrying value of the asset are equal to zero. By using accelerated depreciation for tax purposes, the firm *deferred* $40,000 of taxes from year 1 to year 3.

EXAMPLE: Deferred tax assets

Consider warranty guarantees and associated expenses. Pretax income (financial reporting) includes an accrual for warranty expense, but warranty cost is not deductible for taxable income until the firm has made actual expenditures to meet warranty claims. Suppose:

- A firm has sales of $5,000 for each of two years.

- The firm estimates that warranty expense will be 2% of annual sales ($100).

- The actual expenditure of $200 to meet all warranty claims was not made until the second year.

- Assume a tax rate of 40%.

Calculate the firm's income tax expense, taxes payable, and deferred tax assets for year 1 and year 2.

Answer:

For tax reporting, taxable income and taxes payable for two years are:

Tax Reporting—Warranty Expense

	Year 1	Year 2
Revenue	$5,000	$5,000
Warranty expense	0	200
Taxable income	$5,000	$4,800
Taxes payable	2,000	1,920
Net income	$3,000	$2,880

For financial reporting, pretax income and tax expense are:

Financial Reporting—Warranty Expense

	Year 1	Year 2
Revenue	$5,000	$5,000
Warranty expense	100	100
Pretax income	$4,900	$4,900
Tax expense	1,960	1,960
Net income	$2,940	$2,940

In year 1, the firm reports $1,960 of tax expense in the income statement, but $2,000 of taxes payable are reported on the tax return. In this example, taxes payable are *initially* higher than tax expense and the $40 difference is reported on the balance sheet by creating a DTA.

The tax base and the carrying value of the warranty liability are used to calculate the *balance* of the DTA. At the end of year 1, the carrying value of the warranty liability is $100 (the warranty expense has been recognized in the income statement but it has not been paid), and the tax base of the liability is zero (the warranty expense has not been recognized on the tax return). By multiplying the $100 difference by the 40% tax rate, we get the *balance* of the DTA of $40 [($100 carrying value − zero tax base) × 40%].

We can reconcile income tax expense and taxes payable with the *change* in the DTA. In this example, the DTA increased $40 (from zero to $40) during year 1. Thus, income tax expense in year 1 is $1,960 ($2,000 taxes payable − $40 increase in the DTA).

In year 2, the firm recognizes $1,960 of tax expense in the income statement but only $1,920 is reported on the tax return (taxes payable). The $40 deferred tax asset recognized at the end of year 1 has reversed as a result of the warranty expense recognition on the tax return. So, in year 2, income tax expense is $1,960 ($1,920 taxes payable + $40 decrease in DTA).

PROFESSOR'S NOTE

To summarize, if taxable income (on the tax return) is less than pretax income (on the income statement) and the difference is expected to reverse in future years, a deferred tax liability is created. If taxable income is greater than pretax income and the difference is expected to reverse in future years, a deferred tax asset is created.

Video covering this content is available online.

MODULE 29.4: CHANGE IN TAX RATES

LOS 29.e: Evaluate the effect of tax rate changes on a company's financial statements and ratios.

CFA® Program Curriculum, Volume 3, page 517

When the income tax rate changes, deferred tax assets and liabilities are adjusted to reflect the new rate. The adjustment can also affect income tax expense.

An increase in the tax rate will increase both deferred tax liabilities and deferred tax assets. A decrease in the tax rate will decrease both deferred tax liabilities and deferred tax assets.

DTL and DTA values on the balance sheet must be changed because the new tax rate is the rate expected to be in force when the associated reversals occur. If there is an increase (decrease) in the tax rate, when previously deferred income is recognized for tax, the tax due will be higher (lower), and when expense items previously reported in the financial statements are recognized for tax, the benefit will be greater (less).

Changes in the balance sheet values of DTLs and DTAs to account for a change in the tax rate will affect income tax expense in the current period.

income tax expense = taxes payable + ΔDTL − ΔDTA

If tax rates increase, the increase in the DTL is added to taxes payable and the increase in the DTA is subtracted from taxes payable to arrive at income tax expense.

If tax rates decrease, the decrease in the DTL would result in lower income tax expense and the decrease in the DTA would result in higher income tax expense. In the case of the DTL we are adding a negative change, and in the case of the DTA we are subtracting a negative change.

The following example illustrates the effects of a change in the tax rate.

EXAMPLE: Accounting effects of a change in a firm's tax rate

A firm owns equipment with a carrying value of $200,000 and a tax base of $160,000 at year-end. The tax rate is 40%. In this case, the firm will report a DTL of $16,000 [($200,000 carrying value − $160,000 tax base) × 40%]. The firm has recognized a bad debt expense of $10,000 in its financial statements which is not yet deductible for tax purposes. The bad debt expense created a DTA of $4,000 [($10,000 tax base − zero carrying value) × 40%]. Calculate the effect on the firm's income tax expense if the tax rate decreases to 30%.

Answer:

As a result of the decrease in tax rate, the balance of the DTL is reduced to $12,000 [($200,000 carrying value − $160,000 tax base) × 30%]. Thus, due to the lower tax rate, the change in the DTL is −$4,000 ($16,000 reported DTL − $12,000 adjusted DTL).

The balance of the DTA is reduced to $3,000 [($10,000 tax base − zero carrying value) × 30%]. Thus, due to the lower tax rate, the DTA decreases by $1,000 ($4,000 reported DTA − $3,000 adjusted DTA).

Using the income tax equation, we can see that income tax expense decreases by $3,000 (income tax expense = taxes payable + ΔDTL − ΔDTA).

The effects of a change in the tax rate can also be calculated based on the difference between the tax base and carrying value for an asset or a liability, as in the following example.

EXAMPLE: Deferred tax liability with a change in the tax rate

A firm purchases equipment for $24,000 that has a three-year useful life. The firm depreciates the equipment using the straight-line method for financial reporting and double-declining balance for tax reporting. The tax rate is 40% in the first year, but in the second year, the expected tax rate decreases to 35%. Calculate the deferred tax liability in each year of the asset's life.

Answer:

The carrying value and tax base of the asset are shown in the following table:

	Year 1	Year 2	Year 3
Straight-line depreciation	$8,000	$8,000	$8,000
Carrying value	$16,000	$8,000	0
DDB depreciation	$16,000	$5,333	$2,667
Tax base	$8,000	$2,667	0
Carrying value minus tax base	$8,000	$5,333	0

The deferred tax liability is equal to the expected tax rate times the difference between the carrying value and the tax base. In Year 1, the expected tax rate was 40% and the DTL was 40% × $8,000 = $3,200. In Year 2, the expected tax rate changed to 35% and the DTL was 35% × $5,333 = $1,867. The DTL returns zero at the end of Year 3.

MODULE QUIZ 29.3, 29.4

To best evaluate your performance, enter your quiz answers online.

Use the following data to answer Questions 1 through 6.

- A firm acquires an asset for $120,000 with a 4-year useful life and no salvage value.

- The asset will generate $50,000 of cash flow for all four years.

- The tax rate is 40% each year.

- The firm will depreciate the asset over three years on a straight-line (SL) basis for tax purposes and over four years on a SL basis for financial reporting purposes.

1. Taxable income in year 1 is:
   A. $6,000.
   B. $10,000.
   C. $20,000.

2. Taxes payable in year 1 are:
   A. $4,000.
   B. $6,000.
   C. $8,000.

3. Pretax income in year 4 is:
   A. $6,000.
   B. $10,000.
   C. $20,000.

4. Income tax expense in year 4 is:
   A. $4,000.
   B. $6,000.
   C. $8,000.

5. Taxes payable in year 4 are:
   A. $4,000.
   B. $6,000.
   C. $20,000.

6. At the end of year 2, the firm's balance sheet will report a deferred tax:
   A. asset of $4,000.
   B. asset of $8,000.
   C. liability of $8,000.

7. An increase in the tax rate causes the balance sheet value of a deferred tax asset to:
   A. decrease.
   B. increase.
   C. remain unchanged.

8. Which one of the following statements is *most accurate*? Under the liability method of accounting for deferred taxes, a decrease in the tax rate at the beginning of the accounting period will:
   A. increase taxable income in the current period.
   B. increase a deferred tax asset.
   C. reduce a deferred tax liability.

MODULE 29.5: PERMANENT DIFFERENCES

Video covering this
content is available
online.

LOS 29.f: Distinguish between temporary and permanent differences in pre-tax accounting income and taxable income.

CFA® Program Curriculum, Volume 3, page 518

A **permanent difference** is a difference between taxable income and pretax income that will not reverse in the future. Permanent differences do not create deferred tax assets or deferred tax liabilities. Permanent differences can be caused by revenue that is not taxable, expenses that are not deductible, or tax credits that result in a direct reduction of taxes. For example, in the United States, interest received on municipal bonds is typically not taxable (but appears on the financial statements as pretax income), and the cost of life insurance on key company officers is typically not tax-deductible (but appears on the financial statements as a pretax expense).

Permanent differences will cause the firm's **effective tax rate** to differ from the **statutory tax rate**. The statutory rate is the tax rate of the jurisdiction where the firm operates. The effective tax rate is derived from the income statement.

$$\text{effective tax rate} = \frac{\text{income tax expense}}{\text{pretax income}}$$

The statutory rate and effective rate may also differ if the firm is operating in more than one tax jurisdiction.

A **temporary difference** refers to a difference between the tax base and the carrying value of an asset or liability that will result in taxable amounts or deductible amounts in the future. If the temporary difference is expected to reverse in the future and the balance sheet item is expected to provide future economic benefits, a DTA or DTL is created.

Temporary differences can be **taxable temporary differences** that result in expected future taxable income or **deductible temporary differences** that result in expected future tax deductions.

Temporary differences leading to DTLs can arise from an investment in another firm (e.g., subsidiaries, affiliates, branches, and joint ventures) when the parent company recognizes earnings from the investment before dividends are received. However, if the parent company can control the timing of the future reversal and it is probable the temporary difference will not reverse, no DTL is reported.

A temporary difference from an investment will result in a DTA only if the temporary difference is expected to reverse in the future, and sufficient taxable profits are expected to exist when the reversal occurs.

LOS 29.g: Describe the valuation allowance for deferred tax assets—when it is required and what effect it has on financial statements.

CFA® Program Curriculum, Volume 3, page 525

Although deferred taxes are created from temporary differences that are expected to reverse in the future, neither deferred tax assets nor deferred tax liabilities are carried on the balance sheet at their discounted present value. However, deferred tax assets are assessed at each balance sheet date to determine the likelihood of sufficient future taxable income to recover the tax assets. Without future taxable income, a DTA is worthless.

According to U.S. GAAP, if it is more likely than not (greater than a 50% probability) that some or all of a DTA will not be realized (insufficient future taxable income to recover the tax asset), then the DTA must be reduced by a **valuation allowance**. The valuation allowance is a contra account that reduces the net balance sheet value of the DTA. Increasing the valuation allowance will decrease the net balance sheet DTA, increasing income tax expense and decreasing net income.

If circumstances change, the net DTA can be increased by decreasing the valuation allowance. This would result in higher earnings.

It is up to management to defend the recognition of all deferred tax assets. If a company has order backlogs or existing contracts which are expected to generate future taxable income, a valuation allowance might not be necessary. However, if a company has cumulative losses over the past few years or a history of inability to use tax loss carryforwards, then the company would need to use a valuation allowance to reflect the likelihood that a deferred tax asset will never be realized.

Because an increase (decrease) in the valuation allowance will decrease (increase) earnings, management can manipulate earnings by changing the valuation allowance.

Whenever a company reports substantial deferred tax assets, an analyst should review the company's financial performance to determine the likelihood that those assets will be realized. Analysts should also scrutinize changes in the valuation allowance to determine whether those changes are economically justified.

PROFESSOR'S NOTE

A valuation allowance account is only used for deferred tax assets. Under U.S. GAAP, deferred tax assets and deferred tax liabilities appear separately on the balance sheet, and they are not typically netted.

LOS 29.h: Explain recognition and measurement of current and deferred tax items.

CFA® Program Curriculum, Volume 3, page 524

The measurement of deferred tax items depends on the tax rate expected to be in force when the underlying temporary difference reverses. We previously noted the effects of a change in the income tax rate on deferred tax assets and liabilities. In some circumstances, the applicable tax rate will depend on how the temporary difference will be settled. As an example, consider a tax jurisdiction that has a capital gains tax rate that is lower than the marginal tax rate. If, given its tax base, the currently unrealized gains on an asset will be taxed at the capital gains rate when the asset is disposed of, that rate should be used to calculate the deferred tax liability.

Another issue with the measurement of deferred tax items is whether a change in asset value is recorded on the income statement or taken directly to equity. In a case where the change that leads to a deferred tax item is taken directly to equity, the deferred tax item should also be taken directly to equity.

Consider a company reporting under IFRS that revalues PP&E upward. The revaluation gain is taken directly to equity without affecting either pretax income (on the income statement) or taxes payable (the gain is unrealized) so balance sheet deferred tax liabilities are not affected. Because the revaluation gain is taken directly to equity, the related future tax liability should be taken to equity as well. The adjustment is to reduce the amount of the gain added to revaluation surplus by the amount of the future tax liability on the revaluation gain.

The upward revaluation of the asset on the balance sheet will increase depreciation in subsequent periods, but will not affect the deferred tax liability. The tax liability on the increase in book value is incorporated into the recognition of the increase in revaluation surplus (rather than increasing the reported DTL). In each subsequent period, an amount equal to the additional depreciation from the upward revaluation of the asset, less the tax liability on that portion of the revaluation, is transferred from revaluation surplus to retained earnings. The previously unrealized gain in the asset's value is *realized* over time through use of the asset. The addition to retained earnings just offsets the after-tax decrease in net income (and retained earnings) from the additional depreciation resulting from the upward revaluation of the asset's carrying value.

LOS 29.i: Analyze disclosures relating to deferred tax items and the effective tax rate reconciliation and explain how information included in these disclosures affects a company's financial statements and financial ratios.

CFA® Program Curriculum, Volume 3, page 528

Companies are required to disclose details on the source of the temporary differences that cause the deferred tax assets and liabilities reported on the balance sheet. Changes in those balance sheet accounts are reflected in income tax expense on the income statement. Here are some common examples of temporary differences you may encounter:

■ A deferred tax liability results from using accelerated *depreciation* for tax purposes and straight-line depreciation for the financial statements. The analyst should consider the firm's growth rate and capital spending levels when determining whether the difference will actually reverse.

■ *Impairments* generally result in a deferred tax asset since the write-down is recognized immediately in the income statement, but the deduction on the tax return is generally not allowed until the asset is sold or disposed of.

■ *Restructuring* generates a deferred tax asset because the costs are recognized for financial reporting purposes when the restructuring is announced, but not deducted for tax purposes until actually paid. Note that restructuring usually results in significant cash outflows (net of the tax savings) in the years after the restructuring costs are reported.

■ In the United States, firms that use LIFO for their financial statements are required to use LIFO for tax purposes, so no temporary differences result. However, in countries where this is not a requirement, temporary differences can result from the *choice of inventory cost-flow method*.

■ *Post-employment benefits* and *deferred compensation* are both recognized for financial reporting when earned by the employee but not deducted for tax purposes until actually paid. These can result in a deferred tax asset that will be reversed when the benefits or compensation are paid.

■ A deferred tax adjustment is made to stockholders' equity to reflect the future tax impact of unrealized gains or losses on *available-for-sale marketable securities* that are taken directly to equity. No DTL is added to the balance sheet for the future tax liability when gains/losses are realized.

Typically, the following deferred tax information is disclosed:

■ Deferred tax liabilities, deferred tax assets, any valuation allowance, and the net change in the valuation allowance over the period.

■ Any unrecognized deferred tax liability for undistributed earnings of subsidiaries and joint ventures.

■ Current-year tax effect of each type of temporary difference.

■ Components of income tax expense.

■ Reconciliation of reported income tax expense and the tax expense based on the statutory rate.

■ Tax loss carryforwards and credits.

> **EXAMPLE: Analyzing deferred tax item disclosures**
>
> WCCO, Inc.'s income tax expense has consistently been larger than taxes payable over the last three years. WCCO disclosed in the footnotes to its 20X5 financial statements the major items recorded as deferred tax assets and liabilities (in millions of dollars), as shown in the following table.

Deferred Tax Disclosures in Footnotes to WCCO, Inc., Financial Statements

	20X5	20X4	20X3
Employee benefits	$278	$310	$290
International tax loss carryforwards	101	93	115
Subtotal	379	403	405
Valuation allowance	(24)	(57)	(64)
Deferred tax asset	355	346	341
Property, plant, and equipment	452	361	320
Unrealized gains on available-for-sale securities	67	44	23
Deferred tax liability	519	405	343
Deferred income taxes	$164	$59	$2

Use the table above to explain why income tax expense has exceeded taxes payable over the last three years. Also explain the effect of the change in the valuation allowance on WCCO's earnings for 20X5.

Answer:

The company's deferred tax asset balance results from international tax loss carryforwards and employee benefits (most likely pension and other post-retirement benefits), offset by a valuation allowance. The company's deferred tax liability balance results from property, plant, and equipment (most likely from using accelerated depreciation methods for tax purposes and straight-line on the financial statements) and unrealized gains on securities classified as available-for-sale (because the unrealized gain is not taxable until realized).

Income tax expense is equal to taxes payable plus deferred income tax expense. Because deferred tax liabilities have been growing faster than deferred tax assets, deferred income tax expense has been positive, resulting in income tax expense being higher than taxes payable.

Management decreased the valuation allowance by $33 million in 20X5. This resulted in a reduction in deferred income tax expense and an increase in reported earnings for 20X5.

Analyzing the Effective Tax Rate Reconciliation

Some firms' reported income tax expense differs from the amount based on the statutory income tax rate. Recall that the statutory rate is the tax rate of the jurisdiction where the firm operates. The differences are generally the result of:

- Different tax rates in different tax jurisdictions (countries).
- Permanent tax differences: tax credits, tax-exempt income, nondeductible expenses, and tax differences between capital gains and operating income.
- Changes in tax rates and legislation.

■ Deferred taxes provided on the reinvested earnings of foreign and unconsolidated domestic affiliates.

■ Tax holidays in some countries (watch for special conditions such as termination dates for the holiday or a requirement to pay the accumulated taxes at some point in the future).

Understanding the differences between reported income tax expense and the amount based on the statutory income tax rate will enable the analyst to better estimate future earnings and cash flow.

When estimating future earnings and cash flows, the analyst should understand each element of the reconciliation, including its relative impact, how it has changed with time, and how it is likely to change in the future.

In analyzing trends in tax rates, it is important to only include reconciliation items that are continuous in nature rather than those that are sporadic. Items including different rates in different countries, tax-exempt income, and non-deductible expenses tend to be continuous. Other items are almost always sporadic, such as the occurrence of large asset sales and tax holiday savings. The disclosures of each financial statement should be reviewed based on the footnotes and management discussion and analysis.

> **EXAMPLE:** Analyzing the tax rate reconciliation
>
> Novelty Distribution Company (NDC) does business in the United States and abroad. The company's reconciliation between effective and statutory tax rates for three years is provided in the following figure. Analyze the trend in effective tax rates over the three years shown.
>
> **Statutory U.S. Federal Income Tax Rate Reconciliation**
>
> | | 20X3 | 20X4 | 20X5 |
> |---|---|---|---|
> | Statutory U.S. federal income tax rate | 35.0% | 35.0% | 35.0% |
> | State income taxes, net of related federal income tax benefit | 2.1% | 2.2% | 2.3% |
> | Benefits and taxes related to foreign operations | (6.5%) | (6.3%) | (2.7%) |
> | Tax rate changes | 0.0% | 0.0% | (2.0%) |
> | Capital gains on sale of assets | 0.0% | (3.0%) | 0.0% |
> | Special items | (1.6%) | 8.7% | 2.5% |
> | Other, net | 0.8% | 0.7% | (1.4%) |
> | Effective income tax rates | 29.8% | 37.3% | 33.7% |
>
> **Answer:**
>
> For some trend analysis, the analyst may want to convert the reconciliation from percentages to absolute numbers. However, for this example, the trends can be analyzed simply by using the percentages.
>
> The effective tax rate is upward trending over the 3-year period. Contributing to the upward trend is an increase in the state income tax rate and the loss of benefits related to taxes on foreign income. In 20X4, a loss related to the sale of

assets partially offset an increase in taxes created by special items. In 20X3 and 20X5, the special items and the other items also offset each other. The fact that the special items and other items are so volatile over the 3-year period suggests that it will be difficult for an analyst to forecast the effective tax rate for NDC for the foreseeable future without additional information. This volatility also reduces comparability with other firms.

LOS 29.j: Identify the key provisions of and differences between income tax accounting under International Financial Reporting Standards (IFRS) and US generally accepted accounting principles (GAAP).

CFA® Program Curriculum, Volume 3, page 533

Accounting for income taxes under U.S. GAAP and IFRS is similar in most respects. However, there are some differences. Many differences relate to the different tax laws and regulations of the different countries. Figure 29.1 is a summary of a few of the more important differences.

Figure 29.1: Tax Accounting Differences, IFRS vs. U.S. GAAP

	U.S. GAAP	**IFRS**
Revaluation of fixed assets and intangible assets	Not applicable, no revaluation allowed.	Deferred taxes are recognized in equity.
Undistributed profit from an investment in a subsidiary	No deferred taxes for foreign subsidiaries that meet the indefinite reversal criterion. No deferred taxes for domestic subsidiaries if the amounts are tax free.	Deferred taxes are recognized unless the parent is able to control the distribution of profit and it is probable the temporary difference will not reverse in the future.
Undistributed profit from an investment in a joint venture (JV)	No deferred taxes for foreign corporate JVs that meet the indefinite reversal criterion.	Deferred taxes are recognized unless the venturer is able to control the sharing of profit and it is probable the temporary difference will not reverse in the future.
Undistributed profit from an investment in an associate firm	Deferred taxes are recognized from temporary differences.	Deferred taxes are recognized unless the investor is able to control the sharing of profit and it is probable the temporary difference will not reverse in the future.
Deferred tax asset recognition	Recognized in full and then reduced if "more likely than not" that some or all of the tax asset will not be realized.	Recognized if "probable" that sufficient taxable profit will be available to recover the tax asset.
Tax rate used to measure deferred taxes	Enacted tax rate only.	Enacted or substantively enacted tax rate.
Presentation of deferred taxes on the balance sheet	Classified as current or noncurrent based on the classification of the underlying asset or liability.	Classified as noncurrent.

MODULE QUIZ 29.5

To best evaluate your performance, enter your quiz answers online.

1. While reviewing a company, an analyst identifies a permanent difference between taxable income and pretax income. Which of the following statements *most accurately* identifies the appropriate financial statement adjustment?
   A. The amount of the tax implications of the difference should be added to the deferred tax liabilities.
   B. The present value of the amount of the tax implications of the difference should be added to the deferred tax liabilities.
   C. No financial statement adjustment is necessary.

2. A U.S. GAAP reporting firm reports an increased valuation allowance at the end of the current period. What effect will this have on the firm's income tax expense in the current period?
   A. Increase.
   B. Decrease.
   C. No effect.

3. KLH Company reported the following:

   - Gross DTA at the beginning of the year $10,500
   - Gross DTA at the end of the year $11,250
   - Valuation allowance at the beginning of the year $2,700
   - Valuation allowance at the end of the year $3,900

   Which of the following statements *best* describes the expected earnings of the firm? Earnings are expected to:
   A. increase.
   B. decrease.
   C. remain relatively stable.

4. According to IFRS, the deferred tax consequences of revaluing held-for-use equipment upward is reported on the balance sheet:
   A. as an asset.
   B. as a liability.
   C. in stockholders' equity.

KEY CONCEPTS

LOS 29.a

Deferred tax terminology:

- **Taxable income**. Income subject to tax based on the tax return.

- **Accounting profit**. Pretax income from the income statement based on financial accounting standards.

- **Deferred tax assets**. Balance sheet asset value that results when taxes payable (tax return) are greater than income tax expense (income statement) and the difference is expected to reverse in future periods.

- **Deferred tax liabilities**. Balance sheet liability value that results when income tax expense (income statement) is greater than taxes payable (tax return) and the difference is expected to reverse in future periods.

- **Valuation allowance**. Reduction of deferred tax assets (contra account) based on the likelihood that the future tax benefit will not be realized.

- **Taxes payable**. The tax liability from the tax return. Note that this term also refers to a liability that appears on the balance sheet for taxes due but not yet paid.

- **Income tax expense**. Expense recognized in the income statement that includes taxes payable and changes in deferred tax assets and liabilities.

LOS 29.b

A *deferred tax liability* is created when income tax expense (income statement) is higher than taxes payable (tax return). Deferred tax liabilities occur when revenues (or gains) are recognized in the income statement before they are taxable on the tax return, or expenses (or losses) are tax deductible before they are recognized in the income statement.

A *deferred tax asset* is created when taxes payable (tax return) are higher than income tax expense (income statement). Deferred tax assets are recorded when revenues (or gains) are taxable before they are recognized in the income statement, when expenses (or losses) are recognized in the income statement before they are tax deductible, or when tax loss carryforwards are available to reduce future taxable income.

Deferred tax liabilities that are not expected to reverse, typically because of expected continued growth in capital expenditures, should be treated for analytical purposes as equity. If deferred tax liabilities are expected to reverse, they should be treated for analytical purposes as liabilities.

LOS 29.c

An asset's tax base is its value for tax purposes. The tax base for a depreciable fixed asset is its cost minus any depreciation or amortization previously taken on the tax return. When an asset is sold, the taxable gain or loss on the sale is equal to the sale price minus the asset's tax base.

Study Session 8

A liability's tax base is its value for tax purposes. When there is a difference between the book value of a liability on a firm's financial statements and its tax base that will result in future taxable gains or losses when the liability is settled, the firm will recognize a deferred tax asset or liability to reflect this future tax or tax benefit.

LOS 29.d

If taxable income is less than pretax income and the cause of the difference is expected to reverse in future years, a DTL is created. If taxable income is greater than pretax income and the difference is expected to reverse in future years, a DTA is created.

The balance of the DTA or DTL is equal to the difference between the tax base and the carrying value of the asset or liability, multiplied by the tax rate.

Income tax expense and taxes payable are related through the change in the DTA and the change in the DTL:

income tax expense = taxes payable + ΔDTL – ΔDTA.

LOS 29.e

When a firm's income tax rate increases (decreases), deferred tax assets and deferred tax liabilities are both increased (decreased) to reflect the new rate. Changes in these values will also affect income tax expense.

An increase in the tax rate will increase both a firm's DTL and its income tax expense. A decrease in the tax rate will decrease both a firm's DTL and its income tax expense.

An increase in the tax rate will increase a firm's DTA and decrease its income tax expense. A decrease in the tax rate will decrease a firm's DTA and increase its income tax expense.

LOS 29.f

A temporary difference is a difference between the tax base and the carrying value of an asset or liability that will result in taxable amounts or deductible amounts in the future.

A permanent difference is a difference between taxable income and pretax income that will not reverse in the future. Permanent differences do not create DTAs or DTLs.

LOS 29.g

If it is more likely than not that some or all of a DTA will not be realized (because of insufficient future taxable income to recover the tax asset), then the DTA must be reduced by a valuation allowance. The valuation allowance is a contra account that reduces the DTA value on the balance sheet. Increasing the valuation allowance will increase income tax expense and reduce earnings. If circumstances change, the DTA can be revalued upward by decreasing the valuation allowance, which would increase earnings.

LOS 29.h

Measurement of deferred tax items depends on the tax rate expected to be in force when the underlying temporary difference reverses. The applicable tax may depend on how the temporary difference will be settled (e.g., if a capital gains tax rate will apply). If a change that leads to a deferred tax item is taken directly to equity, such as an upward revaluation, the deferred tax item should also be taken directly to equity.

LOS 29.i

Firms are required to reconcile their effective income tax rate with the applicable statutory rate in the country where the business is domiciled. Analyzing trends in individual reconciliation items can aid in understanding past earnings trends and in predicting future effective tax rates. Where adequate data is provided, they can also be helpful in predicting future earnings and cash flows or for adjusting financial ratios.

LOS 29.j

The accounting treatment of income taxes under U.S. GAAP and their treatment under IFRS are similar in most respects. One major difference relates to the revaluation of fixed assets and intangible assets. U.S. GAAP prohibits upward revaluations, but they are permitted under IFRS and any resulting effects on deferred tax are recognized in equity.

Study Session 8

ANSWER KEY FOR MODULE QUIZZES

Module Quiz 29.1, 29.2

1. **C** Pretax income and income tax expense are not always linked because of temporary and permanent differences. (Module 29.1, LOS 29.a)

2. **C** The difference between taxes payable for the period and the tax expense recognized on the financial statements results from differences between financial and tax accounting. (Module 29.2, LOS 29.b)

3. **A** The DTL is not expected to reverse in the foreseeable future because a growing firm is expected to continue to increase its investment in depreciable assets, and accelerated depreciation for tax on the newly acquired assets delays the reversal of the DTL. The liability should be treated as equity at its full value. (Module 29.2, LOS 29.b)

4. **A** If the tax base of an asset exceeds the carrying value, a deferred tax asset is created. Taxable income will be lower in the future when the reversal occurs. (Module 29.2, LOS 29.c)

5. **A** For revenue received in advance, the tax base is equal to the carrying value minus any amounts that will *not* be taxed in the future. Since the advance has already been taxed, $100,000 will *not* be taxed in the future. Thus, the textbook advance liability has a tax base of $0 ($100,000 carrying value – $100,000 revenue not taxed in the future). (Module 29.2, LOS 29.c)

Module Quiz 29.3, 29.4

1. **B** Annual depreciation expense for tax purposes is ($120,000 cost – $0 salvage value) / 3 years = $40,000. Taxable income is $50,000 – $40,000 = $10,000. (Module 29.3, LOS 29.d)

2. **A** Taxes payable is taxable income × tax rate = $10,000 × 40% = $4,000. (The $10,000 was calculated in question #1.) (Module 29.3, LOS 29.d)

3. **C** Annual depreciation expense for financial purposes is ($120,000 cost – $0 salvage value) / 4 years = $30,000. Pretax income is $50,000 – $30,000 = $20,000. (Module 29.3, LOS 29.d)

4. **C** Because there has been no change in the tax rate, income tax expense is pretax income × tax rate = $20,000 × 40% = $8,000. (The $20,000 was calculated in question #3.) (Module 29.3, LOS 29.d)

5. **C** Note that the asset was fully depreciated for tax purposes after year 3, so taxable income is $50,000. Taxes payable for year 4 = taxable income × tax rate = $50,000 × 40% = $20,000. (Module 29.3, LOS 29.d)

6. **C** At the end of year 2, the tax base is $40,000 ($120,000 cost – $80,000 accumulated tax depreciation) and the carrying value is $60,000 ($120,000 cost – $60,000 accumulated financial depreciation). Since the carrying value exceeds the tax base, a DTL of $8,000 [($60,000 carrying value – $40,000 tax base) × 40%] is reported. (Module 29.3, LOS 29.d)

7. **B** If tax rates increase, the balance sheet value of a deferred tax asset will also increase. (Module 29.4, LOS 29.e)

8. **C** If the tax rate decreases, balance sheet DTL and DTA are both reduced. Taxable income is unaffected. (Module 29.4, LOS 29.e)

Module Quiz 29.5

1. **C** No analyst adjustment is needed. If a permanent difference between taxable income and pretax income is identifiable, the difference will be reflected in the firm's effective tax rate. (LOS 29.f)

2. **A** Recognizing a greater valuation allowance reduces the net value of a deferred tax asset, which increases income tax expense in the current period. (LOS 29.g)

3. **B** The valuation allowance account increased from $2,700 to $3,900. The most likely explanation is the future earnings are expected to decrease, thereby reducing the value of the DTA. (LOS 29.i)

4. **C** The deferred tax consequences of revaluing an asset upward under IFRS are reported in stockholders' equity. (LOS 29.j)

READING 30

Non-Current (Long-Term) Liabilities

EXAM FOCUS

Candidates must understand the financial statement effects of issuing a bond at par, at a discount, or at a premium. You must be able to calculate the book value of the bond and interest expense at any point in time using the effective interest rate method. Also, be able to calculate the gain or loss from retiring a bond before its maturity date. You must thoroughly understand how the classification of a lease as either an operating or finance lease affects the balance sheet, income statement, and cash flow statement from both the lessee and lessor perspectives. Be able to distinguish between the two types of pension plans and identify the financial statement reporting of a defined benefit plan. Finally, be able to evaluate a firm's solvency using the various leverage and coverage ratios.

MODULE 30.1: BOND ISSUANCE

Video covering this content is available online.

A **bond** is a contractual promise between a borrower (the bond issuer) and a lender (the bondholder) that obligates the bond issuer to make payments to the bondholder over the term of the bond. Typically, two types of payments are involved: (1) periodic interest payments, and (2) repayment of principal at maturity.

Bond Terminology

- The **face value**, also known as the **maturity value** or **par value**, is the amount of principal that will be paid to the bondholder at maturity. The face value is used to calculate the coupon payments.

- The **coupon rate** is the interest rate stated in the bond that is used to calculate the coupon payments.

- The **coupon payments** are the periodic interest payments to the bondholders and are calculated by multiplying the face value by the coupon rate.

- The **effective rate of interest** is the interest rate that equates the present value of the future cash flows of the bond and the issue price. The effective rate is the market rate of interest required by bondholders and depends on the bond's risks (e.g., default risk, liquidity risk), as well as the overall structure of interest rates and the timing of the bond's cash flows. *Do not confuse the market rate of interest with the coupon rate.* The coupon rate is typically fixed for the term of the bond. The market rate of interest on a firm's bonds, however, will likely change over the bond's life, which changes the bond's market value as well.

- The **balance sheet liability** of a bond is equal to the present value of its remaining cash flows (coupon payments and face value), discounted at the market rate of interest *at issuance*. At maturity, the liability will equal the face value of the bond. The balance sheet liability is also known as the book value or carrying value of the bond.

- The **interest expense** reported in the income statement is calculated by multiplying the book value of the bond liability at the beginning of the period by the market rate of interest of the bond when it was issued.

At the date of issuance, the market rate of interest may be equal to, less than, or greater than the coupon rate.

- When the market rate is equal to the coupon rate, the bond is a par bond (priced at face value).

- When the market rate is greater than the coupon rate, the bond is a discount bond (priced below par).

- When the market rate is less than the coupon rate, the bond is a premium bond (priced above par).

LOS 30.a: Determine the initial recognition, initial measurement and subsequent measurement of bonds.

CFA® Program Curriculum, Volume 3, page 546

Bonds Issued at Par

When a bond is issued at par, the bond's yield at issuance is equal to the coupon rate. In this case, the present value of the coupon payments plus the present value of the face amount is equal to the par value. The effects on the financial statements are straightforward:

- On the balance sheet, assets and liabilities increase by the bond proceeds (face value). The book value of the bond liability will not change over the term of the bond.

- On the income statement, interest expense for the period is equal to the coupon payment because the yield at issuance and the coupon rate are the same.

- On the cash flow statement, the issue proceeds are reported as a cash inflow from financing activities and the coupon payments are reported as cash outflows from operating activities (under U.S. GAAP; they may be reported as CFO or CFF outflows under IFRS). At maturity, repayment of the face value is reported as a cash outflow from financing activities.

Bonds Issued at a Discount or Premium

When the bond's yield at issuance is not equal to the coupon rate, the proceeds received (the present value of the coupon payments plus the present value of the face value) are not equal to par value. In this case, the bond is issued at a *premium* or a *discount*. The premium or discount at the issue date is usually relatively small for coupon bonds.

If the coupon rate is less than the bond's yield, the proceeds received will be less than the face value. The difference is known as a discount. The coupon rate is lower than the coupon rate that would make the market price of the bond equal to its par value. Investors will pay less than face value because of the lower coupon rate. Such bonds are known as **discount bonds**.

If the coupon rate is greater than the bond's yield, the bond price and the proceeds received will be greater than face value. We refer to such bonds as **premium bonds**. In this case, investors will pay more for the above-market coupon payments.

Balance Sheet Measurement

When a company issues a bond, assets and liabilities both initially increase by the bond proceeds. At any point in time, the book value of the bond liability will equal the present value of the remaining future cash flows (coupon payments and face value) discounted at the bond's yield at issuance.

> **PROFESSOR'S NOTE**
>
> Interest expense and the book value of a bond liability are calculated using the bond's yield at the time it was issued, not its yield today. This is a critical point.

A premium bond is reported on the balance sheet at more than its face value. As the premium is amortized (reduced), the book value of the bond liability will decrease until it reaches the face value of the bond at maturity.

A discount bond is reported on the balance sheet at less than its face value. As the discount is amortized, the book value of the bond liability will increase until it reaches face value at maturity.

MODULE 30.2: DISCOUNT AND PREMIUM BONDS

Video covering this content is available online.

LOS 30.b: Describe the effective interest method and calculate interest expense, amortisation of bond discounts/premiums, and interest payments.

CFA® Program Curriculum, Volume 3, page 546

For a bond issued at a premium or discount, interest expense and coupon interest payments are not equal. Interest expense includes amortization of any discount or premium. Using the **effective interest rate method**, interest expense is equal to the book value of the bond liability at the beginning of the period, multiplied by the bond's yield at issuance.

■ For a premium bond, interest expense is less than the coupon payment (yield < coupon rate). The difference between interest expense and the coupon payment is the amortization of the premium. The premium amortization is subtracted each period from the bond liability on the balance sheet. Thus, interest expense will decrease over time as the bond liability decreases.

■ For a discount bond, interest expense is greater than the coupon payment (yield > coupon rate). The difference between interest expense and the coupon payment is the amortization of the discount. The amortization of the discount each period is added to the bond liability on the balance sheet. Therefore, interest expense will increase over time as the bond liability increases.

PROFESSOR'S NOTE

In the case of a discount bond, the coupon is too low relative to the required rate of return of the market. The purposes of amortizing the discount are to (1) increase the book value of the bond liability over time, and (2) increase interest expense so that the coupon payment plus discount amortization is approximately equal to the interest expense that would have prevailed had the bond been issued at par. Conversely, amortizing a premium decreases the book value of the bond liability over time and decreases interest expense.

The effective interest rate method of amortizing a discount or premium is required under IFRS. Under U.S. GAAP, the effective interest rate method is preferred, but the straight-line method is allowed if the results are not materially different. The straight-line method is similar to straight-line depreciation in that the total discount or premium at issuance is amortized by equal amounts each period over the life of the bond.

While coupon interest is paid in cash, amortization is a noncash item. When presenting the cash flow statement using the indirect method, net income must be adjusted to remove the effects of any amortization of a discount or premium in order to calculate cash flow from operations.

Firms that follow U.S. GAAP must report cash interest paid in the cash flow statement as an operating cash flow. Firms that follow IFRS can report cash interest paid as either an operating or financing cash flow. Therefore, it may be necessary to reclassify interest paid when comparing firms that follow different standards.

PROFESSOR'S NOTE

Some analysts believe classifying interest expense as an operating activity is inconsistent with treating the bond proceeds as a financing activity. In addition, treating interest expense as an operating activity incorrectly describes the economics of a bond issued at a premium or discount. For bonds issued at a discount, cash flow from operations is overstated. This is because the coupon payment is reported as an operating cash flow, while the discount, when paid (as part of a bond's maturity payment), is reported as a financing cash flow. Stated differently, had the firm issued the bond at par, the coupon payment would have been higher to match the market rate of interest. Reclassifying interest as a financing activity in the cash flow statement corrects this inconsistent treatment.

EXAMPLE: Book values and cash flows

On December 31, 20X2, a company issued a 3-year, 10% annual coupon bond with a face value of $100,000. Calculate the book value of the bond at year-end 20X2, 20X3, and 20X4, and the interest expense for 20X3, 20X4, and 20X5, assuming the bond was issued at a market rate of interest of (a) 10%, (b) 9%, and (c) 11%.

Answer:

(a) Bond issued at par. If the market rate of interest at issuance is 10%, the book value of the bonds will always be $100,000, and the interest expense will always be $10,000, which is equal to the coupon payment of 0.10 × $100,000. There is no discount or premium to amortize.

(b) Premium bond. If the market rate of interest is 9%, the present value of the cash payments (a 3-year annuity of $10,000 and a payment in three years of $100,000) is $102,531:

N = 3; PMT = 10,000; FV = 100,000; I/Y = 9; CPT → PV = −$102,531

 PROFESSOR'S NOTE

The present value computed in this manner will have a minus sign.

The following table shows the interest expense and book value at the end of each year.

Interest Expense and Book Value for a Premium Bond

Year	(1) Beginning Book Value	(2) Interest Expense (1) × 9%	(3) Coupon	(4) Ending Book Value (1) + (2) − (3)
20X3	$102,531	$9,228	$10,000	$101,759
20X4	101,759	9,158	10,000	100,917
20X5	100,917	9,083	10,000	100,000

The premium amortization for 20X3 is 10,000 − 9,228 = $772. For 20X4, the amortization is 10,000 − 9,158 = $842. Finally, for 20X5, premium amortization is $917. Note that the premium has been fully amortized upon maturity so that the book value of the bond equals par value.

(c) Discount bond.. If the market rate of interest is 11%, the present value of the cash payments (a 3-year annuity of $10,000 and a payment in three years of $100,000) is $97,556.

N = 3; PMT = 10,000; FV = 100,000; I/Y = 11; CPT → PV = $97,556

The following table shows the interest expense and book value at the end of each year.

Interest Expense and Book Value for a Discount Bond

Year	(1) Beginning Book Value	(2) Interest Expense (1) × 11%	(3) Coupon	(4) Ending Book Value (1) + (2) −(3)
20X3	$97,556	$10,731	$10,000	$98,287
20X4	98,287	10,812	10,000	99,099
20X5	99,099	10,901	10,000	100,000

Again, the pattern of discount amortization is such that the discount is fully amortized upon maturity, when the book value of the bond equals par value.

Zero-coupon bonds make no periodic interest payments. A zero-coupon bond, also known as a *pure-discount bond,* is issued at a discount from its par value and its annual interest expense is implied, but not explicitly paid. The actual interest payment is included in the face value that is paid at maturity. The effects of zero-coupon bonds on the financial statements are qualitatively the same as any discount bond, but the impact is larger because the discount is larger.

> **EXAMPLE: Accounting for a zero-coupon bond**
>
> On December 31, 20X0, Vine Corp. issues a three-year, zero-coupon bond with a par value of $1,000 when the market interest rate is 12%. Using the effective interest method and an annual periodicity, calculate interest expense and the book value of the bond liability at the end of 20X1, 20X2, and 20X3.
>
> **Answer:**
>
> Cash received at issuance—and the initial book value of the bond liability—is $711.78: N = 3; I/Y = 12; PMT = 0; FV = 1,000; CPT → PV = −711.78
>
> Interest expense each year is equal to market interest rate at issuance times the book value of the liability at the beginning of the year. Because the bond does not pay cash coupon interest, the entire amount of interest expense amortizes the discount.
>
> | | (1) Beginning Book Value | (2) Interest Expense (1) × 12% | (3) Ending Book Value (1) + (2) |
> |------|--------------------------|-------------------------------|---------------------------------|
> | 20X1 | $711.78 | $85.41 | $797.19 |
> | 20X2 | 797.19 | 95.66 | 892.85 |
> | 20X3 | 892.85 | 107.15 | 1,000.00 |

MODULE QUIZ 30.1, 30.2

To best evaluate your performance, enter your quiz answers online.

1. According to U.S. GAAP, the coupon payment on a bond is:
   A. reported as an operating cash outflow.
   B. reported as a financing cash outflow.
   C. reported as part operating cash outflow and part financing cash outflow.

2. Using the effective interest rate method, the reported interest expense of a bond issued at a premium will:
   A. decrease over the term of the bond.
   B. increase over the term of the bond.
   C. remain unchanged over the term of the bond.

Use the following data to answer Questions 3 through 10.

A firm issues a $10 million bond with a 6% coupon rate, 4-year maturity, and annual interest payments when market interest rates are 7%.

3. The bond can be classified as a:
   A. discount bond.
   B. par bond.
   C. premium bond.

4. The annual coupon payments will each be:
   A. $600,000.
   B. $676,290.
   C. $700,000.

5. Total of all cash payments to the bondholders is:
   A. $12,400,000.
   B. $12,738,721.
   C. $12,800,000.

6. The initial book value of the bonds is:
   A. $9,400,000.
   B. $9,661,279.
   C. $10,000,000.

7. For the first period the interest expense is:
   A. $600,000.
   B. $676,290.
   C. $700,000.

8. If the market rate changes to 8% and the bonds are carried at amortized cost, the book value of the bonds at the end of the first year will be:
   A. $9,484,581.
   B. $9,661,279.
   C. $9,737,568.

9. The total interest expense reported by the issuer over the life of the bond will be:
   A. $2,400,000.
   B. $2,738,721.
   C. $2,800,000.

10. For analytical purposes, what is the impact on the debt-to-equity ratio if the market rate of interest increases after the bond is issued?
    A. An increase.
    B. A decrease.
    C. No change.

Video covering this content is available online.

MODULE 30.3: ISSUANCE COST, DERECOGNITION, AND DISCLOSURES

Issuance Costs

Issuing a bond involves legal and accounting fees, printing costs, sales commissions, and other fees. Under IFRS and U.S. GAAP, the initial bond liability on the balance sheet (the proceeds from issuing the bond) is reduced by the amount of issuance costs, increasing the bond's effective interest rate. In effect, issuance costs are treated as unamortized discount.

Before 2016, under U.S. GAAP, issuance costs were capitalized as an asset and allocated to the income statement over the life of the bond. Although the treatment of issuance costs has now converged, U.S. GAAP still permits the earlier treatment.

Under both U.S. GAAP and IFRS, bond issuance costs (an outflow) are usually netted against the bond proceeds (an inflow) and reported on the cash flow statement as a financing cash flow.

Fair Value Reporting Option

Recall that the book value of a bond liability is based on its market yield *at issuance*. So, as long as the bond's yield does not change, the bond liability represents fair (market) value. However, if the yield changes, the balance sheet liability is no longer equal to fair value.

An *increase* in the bond's yield will result in a *decrease* in the fair value of the bond liability. Conversely, a *decrease* in the bond's yield *increases* its fair value. Changes in yield result in a divergence between the book value of the bond liability and the fair value of the bond. The fair value of the bond is the economic liability at a point in time.

IFRS and U.S. GAAP give firms the irrevocable option to report debt at fair value. Under this option, gains (decreases in bond liability) and losses (increases in bond liability) that result from changes in bonds' market yields are reported in the income statement.

For analysis, the market value of a firm's debt may be more appropriate than its book value. For example, a firm that issued a bond when interest rates were low is relatively better off when interest rates increase. This is because the firm could repurchase the bond at its now-lower market value. Decreasing the bond liability on the balance sheet to market value increases equity and decreases the debt-to-assets and debt-to-equity ratios. If interest rates have decreased since issuance, adjusting debt to its market value will have the opposite effects.

Summary of Financial Statement Effects of Issuing a Bond

Figure 30.1: Cash Flow Impact of Issuing a Bond

	Cash Flow From Financing	Cash Flow From Operations
Issuance of debt	Increased by cash received (Present value of the bond at the market interest rate)	No effect
Periodic interest payments	No effect	Decreased by interest paid [(coupon rate) × (face or par value)]
Payment at maturity	Decreased by face (par) value	No effect

Figure 30.2: Income Statement Impact of Issuing a Bond

$$\text{interest expense} = \left(\begin{array}{c}\text{market rate}\\\text{at issue}\end{array}\right) \times \left(\begin{array}{c}\text{balance sheet value of}\\\text{liability at beginning of period}\end{array}\right)$$

Issued at Par	Issued at a Premium	Issued at a Discount
Market rate = coupon rate	Market rate < coupon rate	Market rate > coupon rate
Interest expense = coupon rate × face value = cash paid	Interest expense = cash paid − amortization of premium	Interest expense = cash paid + amortization of discount
Interest expense is constant	Interest expense decreases over time	Interest expense increases over time

Figure 30.3: Balance Sheet Impact of Issuing a Bond

Long-term debt is carried at the present value of the remaining cash payments discounted at the market rate prevailing when the debt was issued.

Issued at Par	Issued at a Premium	Issued at a Discount
Carried at face value	Carried at face value plus premium	Carried at face value less discount
	The liability decreases as the premium is amortized to interest expense	The liability increases as the discount is amortized to interest expense

LOS 30.c: Explain the derecognition of debt.

CFA® Program Curriculum, Volume 3, page 557

When bonds mature, no gain or loss is recognized by the issuer. At maturity, any original discount or premium has been fully amortized; thus, the book value of a bond liability and its face value are the same. The cash outflow to repay a bond is reported in the cash flow statement as a financing cash flow.

A firm may choose to **redeem** bonds before maturity because interest rates have fallen, because the firm has generated surplus cash through operations, or because funds from the issuance of equity make it possible (and desirable).

When bonds are redeemed before maturity, a gain or loss is recognized by subtracting the redemption price from the book value of the bond liability at the reacquisition date. For example, consider a firm that reacquires $1 million face amount of bonds at 102% of par when the carrying value of the bond liability is $995,000. The firm will recognize a loss of $25,000 ($995,000 carrying value – $1,020,000 redemption price). Had the carrying value been greater than the redemption price, the firm would have recognized a gain.

If the redeemed bonds' issuance costs were capitalized, any remaining unamortized costs must be written off and included in the gain or loss calculation. No separate entry is necessary if the issuance costs were accounted for in the initial bond liability, because in that case no separate asset representing unamortized issuance costs would have been created.

Any gain or loss from redeeming debt is reported in the income statement, usually as a part of continuing operations, and additional information is disclosed separately. Redeeming debt is usually not a part of the firm's day-to-day operations; thus, analysts often eliminate the gain or loss from the income statement for analysis and forecasting.

When presenting the cash flow statement using the indirect method, any gain (loss) is subtracted from (added to) net income in calculating cash flow from operations. The redemption price is reported as an outflow from financing activities.

LOS 30.d: Describe the role of debt covenants in protecting creditors.

CFA® Program Curriculum, Volume 3, page 559

Debt covenants are restrictions imposed by the lender on the borrower to protect the lender's position. Debt covenants can reduce default risk and thus reduce borrowing costs. The restrictions can be in the form of affirmative covenants or negative covenants.

With **affirmative covenants**, the borrower promises to do certain things, such as:

- Make timely payments of principal and interest.
- Maintain certain ratios (such as the current, debt-to-equity, and interest coverage ratios) in accordance with specified levels.
- Maintain collateral, if any, in working order.

With **negative covenants**, the borrower promises to refrain from certain activities that might adversely affect its ability to repay the outstanding debt, such as:

- Increasing dividends or repurchasing shares.
- Issuing more debt.
- Engaging in mergers and acquisitions.

The bondholders can demand immediate repayment of principal if the firm violates a covenant (referred to as **technical default**). Analyzing the covenants is a necessary component of the credit analysis of a bond. Bond covenants are typically discussed in the financial statement footnotes.

Covenants protect bondholders from actions the firm may take that would harm the value of the bondholders' claims to the firm's assets and earnings (i.e., decrease credit quality). To the extent that covenants restrict, for example, the firm's ability to invest, take on additional debt, or pay dividends, analysis of covenants can be important when valuing the firm's equity (especially involving its growth prospects) as well as when analyzing and valuing its debt securities.

PROFESSOR'S NOTE

Debt covenants are described further in Fixed Income.

LOS 30.e: Describe the financial statement presentation of and disclosures relating to debt.

CFA® Program Curriculum, Volume 3, page 561

Firms will often report all of their outstanding long-term debt on a single line on the balance sheet. The portion that is due within the next year is reported as a current liability. The firm separately discloses more detail about its long-term debt in the footnotes. These disclosures are useful in determining the timing and amounts of future cash outflows. The footnote disclosure usually includes a discussion of:

- The nature of the liabilities.
- Maturity dates.
- Stated and effective interest rates.
- Call provisions and conversion privileges.
- Restrictions imposed by creditors.
- Assets pledged as security.
- The amount of debt maturing in each of the next five years.

A discussion of the firm's long-term debt is also found in the Management Discussion and Analysis section. This discussion is both quantitative, such as identifying obligations and commitments that are due in the future, and qualitative, such as discussing capital resource trends and material changes in the mix and cost of debt.

MODULE QUIZ 30.3

To best evaluate your performance, enter your quiz answers online.

1. A firm has bonds with a $10.0 million face value outstanding. The book value of the bond liability is $10.2 million when the firm redeems the bonds for face value. Redeeming the bonds will result in:
   A. a loss on the income statement and a financing cash outflow.
   B. a gain on the income statement and a financing cash outflow.
   C. a loss on the income statement and an operating cash outflow.

2. The purpose of debt covenants is *best* described as:
   A. limiting issuance costs.
   B. preventing technical default.
   C. protecting the interests of creditors.

3. Which of the following is *least likely* to be disclosed in the financial statements of a bond issuer?
   A. The amount of debt that matures in each of the next five years.
   B. Collateral pledged as security in the event of default.
   C. The market rate of interest on the balance sheet date.

MODULE 30.4: LESSEE ACCOUNTING

Video covering this content is available online.

LOS 30.f: Explain motivations for leasing assets instead of purchasing them.

CFA® Program Curriculum, Volume 3, page 564

A **lease** is a contractual arrangement whereby the **lessor**, the owner of the asset, allows the **lessee** to use the asset for a specified period of time in return for periodic payments.

Leases are classified as either finance leases or operating leases. In the United States, a finance lease is known as a *capital lease*.

A **finance lease** is, in substance, a purchase of an asset that is financed with debt. Accordingly, at the inception of the lease, the lessee will add equal amounts to both assets and liabilities on the balance sheet. Over the term of the lease, the lessee will recognize depreciation expense on the asset and interest expense on the liability.

An **operating lease** is essentially a rental arrangement. No asset or liability is reported by the lessee and the periodic lease payments are simply recognized as rental expense in the income statement.

 PROFESSOR'S NOTE
Accounting standards scheduled to take effect in 2019 will require operating leases to appear on the balance sheets of lessees.

Leasing can have certain benefits:

- *Less costly financing.* Typically, a lease requires no initial down payment. Thus, the lessee conserves cash.

- *Reduced risk of obsolescence.* At the end of the lease, the asset can be returned to the lessor.

- *Less restrictive provisions.* Leases can provide more flexibility than other forms of financing because the lease agreement can be negotiated to better suit the needs of each party.

- *Off-balance-sheet financing.* Entering into an operating lease does not result in a balance sheet liability, so reported leverage ratios are lower compared to borrowing the funds to purchase assets.

- *Tax reporting advantages.* In the United States, firms can create a **synthetic lease** whereby the lease is treated as an ownership position for tax reporting. This allows the lessee to deduct depreciation expense and interest expense for tax purposes. For financial reporting, the lease is treated as a rental agreement and the lessee does not report the lease liability on the balance sheet.

LOS 30.g: Distinguish between a finance lease and an operating lease from the perspectives of the lessor and the lessee.

CFA® Program Curriculum, Volume 3, page 565

Lessee's Perspective

Under current IFRS, the classification of a lease is determined by the economic substance of the transaction. If substantially all the rights and risks of ownership are transferred to the lessee, the lease is treated as a finance lease. Circumstances that require a lease to be treated as a finance lease include:

- Title to the leased asset is transferred to the lessee at the end of the lease.

- The lessee can purchase the leased asset for a price that is significantly lower than the fair value of the asset at some future date.

- The lease term covers a major portion of the asset's economic life.

- The present value of the lease payments is substantially equal to the fair value of the leased asset.

- The leased asset is so specialized that only the lessee can use the asset without significant modifications.

Note that IAS 16, effective for periods after January 1, 2019, requires IFRS reporting firms to recognize a lease asset and lease liability on the balance sheet for both operating and finance leases. That is, for IFRS going forward, the treatment on the financial statements will be the same for operating and finance leases.

Under U.S. GAAP, the criteria are conceptually similar, but are more specific than under IFRS. A lessee must treat a lease as a capital (finance) lease if *any* of the following criteria are met:

- Title to the leased asset is transferred to the lessee at the end of the lease period.

- A *bargain purchase option* permits the lessee to purchase the leased asset for a price that is significantly lower than the fair market value of the asset at some future date.

- The lease period is 75% or more of the asset's economic life.

- The present value of the lease payments is 90% or more of the fair value of the leased asset.

A lease not meeting any of these criteria is classified as an operating lease. Lessees often prefer operating leases because no liability is reported. Recall that with a finance lease, the lessee reports both an asset and a liability on the balance sheet.

Lessor's Perspective

From the lessor's perspective, the lease is also classified as either an operating lease or a finance (capital) lease.

Under IFRS, classification by the lessor is the same as the lessee's; that is, if substantially all the rights and risks of ownership are transferred to the lessee, the lease is treated as a finance lease. Otherwise, the lease is treated as an operating lease.

Under U.S. GAAP, if any one of the capital (finance) lease criteria for lessees is met, and the collectability of lease payments is reasonably certain, and the lessor has substantially completed performance, the lessor must treat the lease as a capital (finance) lease. Otherwise, the lessor will treat the lease as an operating lease.

With an operating lease, the lessor recognizes rental income and continues to report and depreciate the leased asset on its balance sheet. With a capital (finance) lease, the lessor removes the leased asset from the balance sheet and replaces it with a lease investment account (lease receivable).

LOS 30.h: Determine the initial recognition, initial measurement, and subsequent measurement of finance leases.

CFA® Program Curriculum, Volume 3, page 566

Reporting by the Lessee

The treatment of a lease as either an operating lease or finance lease determines whether the lease is reported on the balance sheet, how the lease expense is recognized in the income statement, and the classification of the lease payments on the cash flow statement.

Operating lease. At the inception of the lease, the balance sheet is unaffected. No asset or liability is reported by the lessee. During the term of the lease, *rent expense* equal to the lease payment is recognized in the lessee's income statement. In the cash flow statement, the lease payment is reported as an outflow from operating activities.

Finance lease. At the inception of the lease, the lower of the present value of future minimum lease payments or the fair value of the leased asset is recognized as both an asset and as a liability on the lessee's balance sheet. Over the term of the lease, the asset is depreciated in the income statement and interest expense is recognized. Interest expense is equal to the lease liability at the beginning of the period multiplied by the lease interest rate.

PROFESSOR'S NOTE

In a finance lease, the interest rate used by the lessee is the lower of the lessee's incremental borrowing rate and the lessor's implicit rate.

In the cash flow statement, the lease payment is separated into its interest and principal components. Just as with any amortizing loan, the principal portion of the lease payment is equal to the total payment minus the interest portion. Under U.S. GAAP, interest paid is reported in the cash flow statement as an outflow from operating activities and the principal payment is reported as an outflow from financing activities.

PROFESSOR'S NOTE

Under IFRS, firms can choose to report interest paid in the cash flow statement as an operating or financing cash flow.

EXAMPLE: Accounting for a finance lease

Affordable Company leases a machine for its own use for three years with annual payments of $10,000. At the end of the lease, the machine is returned to the lessor, who will sell it for its scrap value. The appropriate interest rate is 7%.

Calculate the impact of the lease on Affordable's balance sheet and income statement for each of the three years, including the immediate impact. Affordable depreciates all assets on a straight-line basis. Assume the lease payments are made at the end of the year.

Answer:

The lease is classified as a finance lease because the asset is being leased for 75% or more of its useful life (we know this because at the end of the lease term, the asset will be sold for scrap). The present value of the lease payments at 7% is $26,243.

N = 3; I/Y = 7; PMT = –10,000; FV = 0; CPT → PV = $26,243

This amount is immediately recorded as both an asset and a liability on the lessee's balance sheet.

 PROFESSOR'S NOTE

Here we are assuming the payments are made at the end of the year. Watch out on the exam. If the lease had called for beginning of the year payments, it would have been necessary to change the payment mode on your calculator in order to compute the present value.

Over the next three years, depreciation will be $26,243 / 3 = $8,748 per year. The book value of the asset will decline each year by the depreciation expense.

The interest expense and liability values are shown in the following table. Note that the *principal repayment amount each period is* equal to the lease payment minus the interest expense for the period (7% times the liability at the beginning of the period).

Affordable Company Example: Finance Lease Calculations

Year	(1) Beginning Leasehold Value	(2) Interest Expense (1) × 7%	(3) Lease Payment	(4) Lease Liability (1) + (2) − (3)	(5) Book Value of the Asset
0				$26,243	$26,243
1	$26,243	$1,837	10,000	18,080	17,495
2	18,080	1,266	10,000	9,346	8,747
3	9,346	654	10,000	0	0

Column 5 shows the ending book value of the leased asset each year. Note that, initially, depreciation is greater than the amortization (principal repayment) of the loan, so the asset's book value declines more rapidly than the lease liability. In the later years of the lease term, annual interest expense is less and the amortization of the lease liability is greater. The book value of the leased asset and the lease liability are again equal (both are zero) at the end of the lease term.

Financial Statement and Ratio Effects of Operating and Finance Leases

Balance sheet. A finance lease results in a reported asset and a liability. Consequently, turnover ratios that use total or fixed assets in their denominators will be lower when a lease is treated as a finance lease as compared to an operating lease. For the same reason, return on assets will also be lower for finance leases. Most importantly, leverage ratios, such as the debt-to-assets ratio and the debt-to-equity ratio, will be higher with finance leases than with operating leases because of the reported liability. The principal payment due within the next year is reported as a current liability on the lessee's balance sheet. This reduces the lessee's current ratio and working capital (current assets minus current liabilities).

Because the liability for an operating lease does not appear on the lessee's balance sheet, operating leases are sometimes referred to as *off-balance-sheet financing activities*.

Income statement. Operating income (EBIT) will be higher for companies that use finance leases relative to companies that use operating leases. With an operating lease, the entire lease payment is an operating expense, while for a finance lease, only the depreciation of the leased asset (not the interest portion of the lease payment) is treated as an operating expense.

In the previous example, assume Affordable Company can treat the lease as either an operating lease or a finance lease. Figure 30.4 compares the income statement effects.

Figure 30.4: Affordable Company: Impact of Lease Accounting Method on the Income Statement

	Operating Lease	Finance Lease		
Year	Rent Expense	Depreciation	Interest	Finance Lease Expense
1	$10,000	$8,748	$1,837	$10,585
2	10,000	8,748	1,266	10,014
3	10,000	8,747	654	9,401
	$30,000			$30,000

Total expense over the life of a lease will be the same whether it is accounted for as an operating lease or a finance (capital) lease because the sum of depreciation expense and interest expense will equal the total of the lease payments. In the early years of a finance lease, however, the interest expense is higher, so the sum of depreciation and interest expense is greater than the lease payment. Consequently, net income will be lower for a finance lease in its early years and higher in its later years, compared to an operating lease.

Cash flow statement. Total cash flow is unaffected by the accounting treatment of a lease. In our example, the total cash outflow is $10,000 per year. If the lease is treated as an operating lease (rent expense = $10,000), then the total cash payment reduces cash flow from operations. If the lease is treated as a finance lease, then only the portion of the lease payment that is considered interest expense reduces cash flow from operations. The part of the lease payment considered repayment of principal reduces cash flow from financing activities. Figure 30.5 illustrates that for a finance lease, cash flow from operations (CFO) is higher, and cash flow from financing (CFF) is lower, compared to an operating lease.

Figure 30.5: Affordable Company: Impact on Cash Flow

	Finance Lease		Operating Lease
Year	CF Operations	CF Financing	CF Operations
1	–$1,837	–$8,163	–$10,000
2	–1,266	–8,734	–10,000
3	–654	–9,346	–10,000

If Affordable treats the lease as a finance lease, operating cash outflow is $1,837 in Year 1, and if it treats the lease as an operating lease, operating cash outflow is $10,000. Companies with finance leases will show higher CFO relative to firms that use operating leases (all else the same).

Figure 30.6 and Figure 30.7 summarize the differences between the effects of finance leases and operating leases on the financial statements and ratios of the lessee.

Figure 30.6: Financial Statement Impact of Lease Accounting

	Finance Lease	Operating Lease
Assets	Higher	Lower
Liabilities (current and long-term)	Higher	Lower
Net income (in the early years)	Lower	Higher
Net income (later years)	Higher	Lower
Total net income	Same	Same
EBIT (operating income)	Higher	Lower
Cash flow from operations	Higher	Lower
Cash flow from financing	Lower	Higher
Total cash flow	Same	Same

Figure 30.7: Ratio Impact of Lease Accounting

	Finance Lease	Operating Lease
Current ratio (CA / CL)	Lower	Higher
Working capital (CA – CL)	Lower	Higher
Asset turnover (revenue / TA)	Lower	Higher
Return on assets* (NI / TA)	Lower	Higher
Return on equity* (NI / SE)	Lower	Higher
Debt / assets	Higher	Lower
Debt / equity	Higher	Lower

* In the early years of the lease.

In sum, all the ratios in Figure 30.7 are worse when the lease is capitalized. The only improvements from a finance lease are higher EBIT (because interest is not subtracted in calculating EBIT), higher CFO (because principal repayment is CFF), and higher net income in the later years of the lease (because interest plus depreciation is less than the lease payment in the later years).

PROFESSOR'S NOTE

There are two points that candidates often find confusing. First, interest payments are an operating *cash flow* but are not considered an operating *expenditure*. That is, they are not subtracted in calculating operating income (EBIT). Second, adding equal amounts to assets and liabilities will typically increase the debt-to-assets ratio. Because assets are typically larger than debt (liabilities), the numerator of the debt-to-assets ratio increases by a greater proportion than the denominator when equal amounts are added to each, so the ratio increases. With respect to the current ratio and working capital, the current year principal amortization for a finance lease is added to current liabilities, but there is no increase in current assets because the asset is long-lived.

Video covering this content is available online.

MODULE 30.5: LESSOR ACCOUNTING

From the lessor's perspective, a capital lease under U.S. GAAP is treated as either a *sales-type* lease or a *direct financing* lease. If the present value of the lease payments exceeds the carrying value of the asset, the lease is treated as a sales-type lease. If the present value of the lease payments is equal to the carrying value, the lease is treated as a direct financing lease.

IFRS does not distinguish between a sales-type lease and a direct financing lease. However, similar treatment to a sales-type lease is allowed under IFRS for finance leases originated by manufacturers or dealers. In this case, the present value of the lease payments likely exceeds the carrying value of the asset.

Sales-Type Lease

A **sales-type lease** is treated as if the lessor sold the asset for the present value of the lease payments and provided a loan to the buyer in the same amount. Sales-type leases are typical when the lessor is a manufacturer or dealer because the cost (balance sheet value) of the leased asset is usually less than its fair value.

At the inception of the lease, the lessor recognizes a sale equal to the present value of the lease payments, and cost of goods sold equal to the carrying value of the asset. Just as with a normal sales transaction, the difference between the sales price and cost of goods sold is gross profit. The asset is removed from the balance sheet and a **lease receivable** is created, equal to the present value of the lease payments. As the lease payments are received, the principal portion of the payment reduces the lease receivable and the interest portion of the lease payment is recognized as interest income. The interest portion of each lease payment is equal to the lease receivable at the beginning of the period multiplied by the lease interest rate.

In the cash flow statement, the interest portion of the lease payment is reported as an inflow from operating activities, and the principal reduction is reported as an inflow from investing activities, just as with an amortizing loan.

Direct Financing Lease

In a **direct financing lease**, no gross profit is recognized by the lessor at the inception of the lease. Because the present value of the lease payments is equal to the carrying value of the leased asset, the lessor is simply providing a financing function to the lessee. In this case, the lessor is not usually a manufacturer or dealer, but has purchased the asset from a third party.

At the inception of the lease, the lessor removes the asset from its balance sheet and creates a lease receivable in the same amount. As the lease payments are received, the principal portion of each payment reduces the lease receivable.

In the income statement, the lessor recognizes interest income over the term of the lease. The interest portion of each lease payment is equal to the lease receivable at the beginning of the period multiplied by the interest rate.

In the cash flow statement, the interest portion of the lease payment is reported as an inflow from operating activities and the principal reduction is reported as an inflow from investing activities.

> **EXAMPLE:** Direct financing lease
>
> Assume Rowlands, Inc. purchases an asset for $24,000 to lease to Carver, Inc. for three years with an annual lease payment of $10,000 at the end of each year. At the end of the lease, Carver will return the asset and Rowlands will sell it for $5,000. The implied interest rate in the lease is N = 3; PMT = 10,000; FV = 5,000; PV = –24,000; CPT I/Y = 19.897%. Determine how Rowlands should account for the lease payments from Carver.
>
> **Answer:**
>
> Since the present value of lease payments of $24,000 is equal to the carrying value of the asset, Rowlands treats the lease as a direct financing lease. Rowlands removes the leased asset from the balance sheet and records a lease receivable of $24,000. The lease payments are recorded as follows:
>
> | Year | (1) Beginning Lease Receivable | (2) Interest Income (1) × 19.897% | (3) Lease Payment | (4) Ending Lease Receivable (1) + (2) − (3) |
> |------|------|------|------|------|
> | 0 | | | | $24,000 |
> | 1 | $24,000 | $4,775 | $10,000 | 18,775 |
> | 2 | 18,775 | 3,736 | 10,000 | 12,511 |
> | 3 | 12,511 | 2,489 | 10,000 | 0 |
>
> Interest income received each year will increase earnings. In the cash flow statement, the interest income is reported as an inflow from operating activities. The principal reduction (column 3 – column 2) reduces the lease receivable and is treated in the cash flow statement as an inflow from investing activities.
>
> If Rowlands had manufactured the equipment with a cost of goods of $20,000, it would have recorded a gross profit of $24,000 – $20,000 = $4,000 at lease inception, put a lease receivable of $24,000 on its balance sheet, and then accounted for the interest income portion of the lease payments just as in the previous table.

Operating Lease

If the lease is treated as an operating lease, the lessor simply recognizes the lease payment as rental income. In addition, the lessor will keep the leased asset on its balance sheet and depreciate it over its useful life.

Returning to our example, if Rowlands treats the lease as an operating lease, $10,000 of rental income is recognized each year. In addition, a depreciation expense of $6,333 [($24,000 – $5,000) / 3 years] is also recognized. Figure 30.8 compares the income from a direct financing lease and an operating lease.

Figure 30.8: Income Comparison of a Direct Financing Lease and Operating Lease

	Direct Financing Lease	Operating Lease		
Year	Interest Income	Rental Income	Depreciation Expense	Operating Lease Income
1	$4,775	$10,000	$6,333	$3,667
2	3,736	10,000	6,333	3,667
3	2,489	10,000	6,334	3,666
	$11,000			$11,000

Total income over the life of the lease is the same for an operating lease and a direct financing lease. However, in the early years of the lease, the income reported from the direct financing lease is higher than the income reported from the operating lease. Just as with an amortizing loan, the interest is higher in the early years. This situation reverses in the later years of the lease.

In the cash flow statement, the lease classifications result in significant differences in cash flow from operations, as shown in Figure 30.9.

Figure 30.9: Cash Flow Comparison to the Lessor of a Direct Financing Lease and an Operating Lease

	Direct Financing Lease		Operating Lease
Year	CF Operations	CF Investing	CF Operations
1	$4,775	$5,225	$10,000
2	3,736	6,264	10,000
3	2,489	7,511	10,000

Total cash flow is the same for an operating lease and a direct financing lease. However, cash flow from operations is higher with the operating lease. With a direct financing lease, the lease payment is separated into the interest portion (CFO) and principal portion (CFI).

PROFESSOR'S NOTE

From the lessee's perspective, principal is a financing outflow. From the lessor's perspective, principal is a return of capital invested in the lease. Thus, the principal is reported as an investing inflow.

LOS 30.i: Compare the disclosures relating to finance and operating leases.

CFA® Program Curriculum, Volume 3, page 570

Both lessees and lessors are required to disclose useful information about finance leases and operating leases in the financial statements or in the footnotes, including:

- General description of the leasing arrangement.

- The nature, timing, and amount of payments to be paid or received in each of the next five years. Lease payments after five years can be aggregated.

- Amount of lease revenue and expense reported in the income statement for each period presented.

- Amounts receivable and unearned revenues from lease arrangements.

- Restrictions imposed by lease agreements.

For lessees, analysts often use the disclosures to estimate the off-balance-sheet liabilities of operating leases.

PROFESSOR'S NOTE

Unfortunately, the interest rate used in the lease calculations is not always disclosed. Thus, it may be necessary for an analyst to derive the interest rate in order to make adjustments for analytical purposes. Deriving the interest rate and carrying out the lease adjustments are beyond the scope of the Level I exam.

MODULE 30.6: PENSION PLAN ACCOUNTING

LOS 30.j: Compare the presentation and disclosure of defined contribution and defined benefit pension plans.

Video covering this content is available online.

CFA® Program Curriculum, Volume 3, page 583

A **pension** is a form of deferred compensation earned over time through employee service. The most common pension arrangements are defined contribution plans and defined benefit plans.

A **defined contribution plan** is a retirement plan in which the firm contributes a sum each period to the employee's retirement account. The firm's contribution can be based on any number of factors, including years of service, the employee's age, compensation, profitability, or even a percentage of the employee's contribution. In any event, the firm makes no promise to the employee regarding the future value of the plan assets. The investment decisions are left to the employee, who assumes all of the investment risk.

The financial reporting requirements for defined contribution plans are straightforward. Pension expense is simply equal to the employer's contribution. There is no future obligation to report on the balance sheet as a liability.

In a **defined benefit plan**, the firm promises to make periodic payments to employees after retirement. The benefit is usually based on the employee's years of service and the employee's compensation at, or near, retirement. For example, an employee might earn a retirement benefit of 2% of her final salary for each year of service. Consequently, an employee with 20 years of service and a final salary of $100,000, would receive $40,000 ($100,000 final salary × 2% × 20 years of service) each year upon retirement until death. Because the employee's future benefit is defined, the employer assumes the investment risk.

A company that offers defined pension benefits typically funds the plan by contributing assets to a separate legal entity, usually a trust. The plan assets are managed to generate the income and principal growth necessary to pay the pension benefits as they come due.

Financial reporting for a defined benefit plan is much more complicated than for a defined contribution plan because the employer must estimate the value of the future obligation to its employees. The obligation involves forecasting a number of variables, such as future compensation levels, employee turnover, average retirement age, mortality rates, and an appropriate discount rate.

For a defined benefit plan, the **net pension asset** or **net pension liability** is a key element for analysis. If the fair value of the plan's assets is greater than the estimated pension obligation, the plan is said to be *overfunded* and the sponsoring firm records a net pension asset on its balance sheet. If the fair value of the plan's assets is less than the estimated pension obligation, the plan is *underfunded* and the firm records a net pension liability.

The change in the net pension asset or liability is recognized on the firm's financial statements each year. Some components are included in net income while others are recorded as other comprehensive income. The treatments of these cost components are similar under IFRS and U.S. GAAP. Component costs that go directly to equity as other comprehensive income are amortized to the income statement under U.S. GAAP, but under IFRS they are not amortized.

 PROFESSOR'S NOTE
Accounting for defined benefit pension plans is addressed in more detail at Level II.

For manufacturing companies, under either IFRS or U.S. GAAP, pension expense is allocated to inventory and cost of goods sold for employees who provide direct labor to production and to salary or administrative expense for other employees. As a result, pension expense does not appear separately on the income statement for manufacturing companies. An analyst must examine the financial statement notes to find the details of these companies' pension expense.

LOS 30.k: Calculate and interpret leverage and coverage ratios.

CFA® Program Curriculum, Volume 3, page 586

Analysts use solvency ratios to measure a firm's ability to satisfy its long-term obligations. In evaluating solvency, analysts look at leverage ratios and coverage ratios.

Leverage Ratios

Leverage ratios focus on the balance sheet by measuring the amount of debt in a firm's capital structure. For calculating these ratios, "debt" refers to interest-bearing obligations. Non-interest bearing liabilities, such as accounts payable, accrued liabilities, and deferred taxes, are not considered debt.

- *Debt-to-assets ratio* = total debt / total assets.

  Measures the percentage of total assets financed with debt.

- *Debt-to-capital ratio* = total debt / (total debt + total equity).

  Measures the percentage of total capital financed with debt. Debt-to-capital is similar to the debt-to-assets ratio, except that total capital excludes non-interest bearing liabilities. Recall the balance sheet equation A = L + E. Thus, total assets and total capital differ by the firm's non-interest bearing liabilities.

- *Debt-to-equity ratio* = total debt / total equity.

  Measures the amount of debt financing relative to the firm's equity base. A firm whose debt-to-equity ratio is 1.0 has equal amounts of debt and equity. Stated differently, its debt-to-capital ratio is 50%.

- *Financial leverage ratio* = average total assets / average total equity.

  Measure of leverage used in the DuPont formula.

All of these leverage ratios are interpreted similarly; that is, the higher the ratio, the higher the leverage. When comparing firms, analysts must remember that in some countries, debt financing is more popular than equity financing. Firms in these countries will have higher leverage.

Coverage Ratios

Coverage ratios focus on the income statement by measuring the sufficiency of earnings to repay interest and other fixed charges when due. Two popular coverage ratios are the interest coverage ratio and the fixed charge coverage ratio.

- *Interest coverage* = EBIT / interest payments.

  A firm with lower interest coverage will have more difficulty meeting its interest payments.

- *Fixed charge coverage* = (EBIT + lease payments) / (interest payments + lease payments).

  Similar to interest coverage ratio but more inclusive because operating lease payments are added to the numerator and denominator. Significant operating lease payments will reduce this ratio as compared to interest coverage. Fixed charge coverage is more meaningful for firms that engage in significant operating leases.

EXAMPLE: Leverage and coverage ratios

Westcliff Corporation is a hardware wholesaler. The following table shows selected information from Westcliff's most recent financial statements.

Liabilities and Equity	20X9	20X8
Accounts payable	$360,000	$310,000
Notes payable	385,200	321,100
Current maturities of long-term debt	60,000	60,000
Accrued liabilities	90,800	117,600
Total current liabilities	$896,000	$808,700
Long-term debt	740,000	800,000
Shareholders' equity	727,600	588,700
Total liabilities and equity	$2,363,600	$2,197,400

Partial Income Statement	20X9	20X8
Gross profit	$610,500	$580,800
Administrative expense	187,000	177,200
Lease expense	24,000	22,800
Earnings before interest and taxes	$399,500	$380,800
Interest expense	$168,000	$116,100

Discuss Westcliff's solvency using the appropriate leverage and coverage ratios.

Answer:

When evaluating solvency, accounts payable and accrued liabilities are not considered debt. Debt only includes interest bearing obligations:

	20X9	20X8
Notes payable	$385,200	$321,100
Current maturities of long-term debt	60,000	60,000
Long-term debt	740,000	800,000
Total debt	$1,185,200	$1,181,100

Westcliff's leverage and coverage ratios are calculated as follows:

Debt-to-assets 2009: 1,185,200 debt / 2,363,600 assets = 50.1%
Debt-to-assets 2008: 1,181,100 debt / 2,197,400 assets = 53.7%

Debt-to-equity 2009: 1,185,200 debt / 727,600 equity = 1.6
Debt-to-equity 2008: 1,181,100 debt / 588,700 equity = 2.0

Debt-to-total capital 2009: 1,185,200 debt / 1,912,800 total capital = 62.0%
Debt-to-total capital 2008: 1,181,100 debt / 1,769,800 total capital = 66.7%

(Note: Total capital = total debt + shareholders' equity.)

Interest coverage 2009: 399,500 EBIT / 168,000 interest expense = 2.4
Interest coverage 2008: 380,800 EBIT / 116,100 interest expense = 3.3

Fixed charge coverage 2009:

(399,500 EBIT + 24,000 lease payments) / (168,000 interest expense + 24,000 lease payments) = 2.2

Fixed charge coverage 2008:

(380,800 EBIT + 22,800 lease payments) / (116,100 interest expense + 22,800 lease payments) = 2.9

Leverage declined in 20X9 using all three measures, mainly as a result of an increase in shareholders' equity. On the other hand, both coverage ratios declined in 20X9 as a result of higher interest expense. One possible explanation for the increase in interest expense, given lower leverage, is that interest rates are increasing.

MODULE QUIZ 30.4, 30.5, 30.6

To best evaluate your performance, enter your quiz answers online.

1. As compared to purchasing an asset, which of the following is *least likely* an incentive to structure a transaction as a finance lease?
   A. At the end of the lease, the asset is returned to the lessor.
   B. The terms of the lease terms can be negotiated to better meet each party's needs.
   C. The lease enhances the balance sheet by the lease liability.

2. Under IFRS 16, a lease for a period of more than one year may be classified as an operating lease by:
   A. lessors only.
   B. lessees only.
   C. both lessors and lessees.

3. At the beginning of 20X6, Cougar Corporation enters a finance lease requiring five annual payments of $10,000 each beginning on the first day of the lease. Assuming the lease interest rate is 8%, the amount of interest expense recognized by Cougar in 20X6 is *closest* to:
   A. $2,650.
   B. $3,194.
   C. $3,450.

4. A net pension asset or liability can be associated with:
   A. defined benefit pension plans only.
   B. defined contribution pension plans only.
   C. either defined benefit or defined contribution pension plans.

5. At the end of last year, Maui Corporation's assets and liabilities were as follows:

Total assets	$98,500
Accrued liabilities	$5,000
Short-term debt	$12,000
Bonds payable	$39,000

   Maui's debt-to-equity ratio is *closest* to:
   A. 1.2.
   B. 1.3.
   C. 1.4.

KEY CONCEPTS

LOS 30.a

When a bond is issued, assets and liabilities both initially increase by the bond proceeds. At any point in time, the book value of the bond liability is equal to the present value of the remaining future cash flows (coupon payments and maturity value) discounted at the market rate of interest at issuance. The proceeds are reported in the cash flow statement as an inflow from financing activities.

A premium bond (coupon rate > market yield at issuance) is reported on the balance sheet at a value greater than its face value. As the premium is amortized (reduced), the book value of the bond liability will decrease until it reaches its face value at maturity.

A discount bond (market yield at issuance > coupon rate) is reported on the balance sheet at less than its face value. As the discount is amortized, the book value of the bond liability will increase until it reaches its face value at maturity.

LOS 30.b

Interest expense includes amortization of any discount or premium at issuance. Using the effective interest rate method, interest expense is equal to the book value of the bond liability at the beginning of the period multiplied by the bond's yield at issuance.

For a premium bond, interest expense is less than the coupon payment (yield < coupon rate). The difference between interest expense and the coupon payment is subtracted from the bond liability on the balance sheet.

For a discount bond, interest expense is greater than the coupon payment (yield > coupon rate). The difference between interest expense and the coupon payment is added to the bond liability on the balance sheet.

LOS 30.c

When bonds are redeemed before maturity, a gain or loss is recognized equal to the difference between the redemption price and the carrying (book) value of the bond liability at the reacquisition date.

LOS 30.d

Debt covenants are restrictions on the borrower that protect the bondholders' interests, thereby reducing both default risk and borrowing costs. Covenants can include restrictions on dividend payments and share repurchases; mergers and acquisitions; sale, leaseback, and disposal of certain assets; and issuance of new debt in the future. Other covenants require the firm to maintain ratios or financial statement items at specific levels.

LOS 30.e

The firm separately discloses details about its long-term debt in the footnotes. These disclosures are useful for determining the timing and amount of future cash outflows. The disclosures usually include a discussion of the nature of the liabilities, maturity dates, stated and effective interest rates, call provisions and conversion privileges, restrictions imposed by creditors, assets pledged as security, and the amount of debt maturing in each of the next five years.

LOS 30.f

Compared to purchasing an asset, leasing may provide the lessee with less costly financing, reduce the risk of obsolescence, and include less restrictive provisions than a typical loan. Synthetic leases provide tax advantages and keep the lease liability off the balance sheet.

LOS 30.g

Under IFRS, if substantially all the rights and risks of ownership are transferred to the lessee, the lease is treated as a finance lease by both the lessee and lessor. Otherwise, the lease is an operating lease.

Under U.S. GAAP, the lessee must treat a lease as a capital (finance) lease if any one of the following criteria is met:

- Title to the leased asset is transferred to the lessee at the end of the lease period.

- A bargain purchase option exists.

- The lease period is 75% or more of the asset's economic life.

- The present value of the lease payments is 90% or more of the fair value of the leased asset.

Under U.S. GAAP, the lessor capitalizes the lease if any one of the finance lease criteria for lessees is met, collectability of lease payments is reasonably certain, and the lessor has substantially completed performance.

LOS 30.h

A finance lease is, in substance, a purchase of an asset that is financed with debt. At any point in time, the lease liability is equal to the present value of the remaining lease payments.

From the lessee's perspective, finance lease expense consists of depreciation of the asset and interest on the loan. The finance lease payment consists of an operating outflow of cash (interest expense) and a financing outflow of cash (principal reduction).

An operating lease is simply a rental arrangement; no asset or liability is reported by the lessee. The rental payment is reported as an expense and as an operating outflow of cash.

From the lessor's perspective, a finance lease is either a sales-type lease or a direct financing lease. In either case, a lease receivable is created at the inception of the lease, equal to the present value of the lease payments. The lease payments are treated as part interest income (CFO) and part principal reduction (CFI).

With a sales-type lease, the lessor recognizes gross profit at the inception of the lease and interest income over the life of the lease. With a direct financing lease, the lessor recognizes interest income only.

Study Session 8

LOS 30.i

Both lessees and lessors are required to disclose useful information about finance leases and operating leases in the financial statements or in the footnotes, including:

- General description of the leasing arrangement.

- The nature, timing, and amount of payments to be paid or received in each of the next five years. Lease payments after five years can be aggregated.

- Amount of lease revenue and expense reported in the income statement for each period presented.

- Amounts receivable and unearned revenues from lease arrangements.

- Restrictions imposed by lease agreements.

LOS 30.j

A firm reports a net pension liability on its balance sheet if the fair value of a defined benefit plan's assets is less than the estimated pension obligation, or a net pension asset if the fair value of the plan's assets is greater than the estimated pension obligation. The change in the net pension asset or liability is reflected in a firm's comprehensive income each year.

Pension expense for a defined contribution pension plan is equal to the employer's contributions.

LOS 30.k

Analysts use solvency ratios to measure a firm's ability to satisfy its long-term obligations. In evaluating solvency, analysts look at leverage ratios and coverage ratios.

Leverage ratios, such as debt-to-assets, debt-to-capital, debt-to-equity, and the financial leverage ratio, focus on the balance sheet.

Debt-to-assets ratio = total debt / total assets

Debt-to-capital ratio = total debt / (total debt + total equity)

Debt-to-equity ratio = total debt / total equity

Financial leverage ratio = average total assets / average total equity

Coverage ratios, such as interest coverage and fixed charge coverage, focus on the income statement.

Interest coverage = EBIT / interest payments

Fixed charge coverage = (EBIT + lease payments) / (interest payments + lease payments)

ANSWER KEY FOR MODULE QUIZZES

Module Quiz 30.1, 30.2

1. **A** The actual coupon payment on a bond is reported as operating cash outflow under U.S. GAAP. (Module 30.1, LOS 30.a)

2. **A** Interest expense is based on the book value of the bond. As the premium is amortized, the book value of the bond decreases until it reaches face value. (Module 30.2, LOS 30.b)

3. **A** This bond is issued at a discount since the coupon rate < market rate. (Module 30.1, LOS 30.a)

4. **A** Coupon payment = (coupon rate × face value of bond) = 6% × $10,000,000 = $600,000. (Module 30.1, LOS 30.b)

5. **A** Four coupon payments and the face value = ($600,000 × 4) + $10,000,000 = $12,400,000. (Module 30.1, LOS 30.b)

6. **B** The present value of a 4-year annuity of $600,000 plus a 4-year lump sum of $10 million, all valued at a discount rate of 7%, equals $9,661,279. Choice C can be eliminated because the bond was issued at a discount. (Module 30.2, LOS 30.b)

7. **B** Market interest rate × book value = 7% × $9,661,279 = $676,290. (Module 30.2, LOS 30.b)

8. **C** The new book value = beginning book value + interest expense – coupon payment = $9,661,279 + $676,290 – $600,000 = $9,737,569. The interest expense was calculated in question 7. Alternatively, changing N from 4 to 3 and calculating the PV will yield the same result. The change in market rates will not affect amortized costs. (Module 30.2, LOS 30.b)

9. **B** Coupon payments + discount interest = coupon payments + (face value – issue value) = $2,400,000 + ($10,000,000 – $9,661,279) = $2,738,721. (Module 30.2, LOS 30.b)

10. **B** An increase in the market rate will decrease the price of a bond. For analytical purposes, adjusting the bond liability to its economic value will result in a lower debt-to-equity ratio (lower numerator and higher denominator). (Module 30.2, LOS 30.b)

Module Quiz 30.3

1. **B** The cash paid to redeem the bonds is a CFF outflow. Because the redemption price is less than the book value of the liability, the firm will recognize a gain. (LOS 30.c)

2. **C**   Debt covenants exist to protect the interests of creditors. A bond is considered to be in "technical" default if the borrower violates the bond's covenants. (LOS 30.d)

3. **C**   The market rate on the balance sheet date is not typically disclosed. The amount of debt principal scheduled to be repaid over the next five years and collateral pledged (if any) are generally included in the footnotes to the financial statements. (LOS 30.e)

Module Quiz 30.4, 30.5, 30.6

1. **C**   Operating leases enhance the balance sheet by excluding any lease liability. With a finance lease, an asset and a liability are reported on the balance sheet as with purchase made with debt. (Module 30.4, LOS 30.f)

2. **A**   Under IFRS 16, lessors may classify leases as operating or finance leases, but lessees must treat all leases longer than one year as finance leases. (Module 30.5, LOS 30.h)

3. **A**   At the inception of the lease, the present value of the lease payments is $43,121 (BGN mode: N = 5, I = 8, PMT = 10,000, FV = 0, solve for PV). After the first payment is made, the balance of the lease liability is $43,121 – 10,000 principal payment = $33,121. Interest expense for the first year is $33,121 × 8% = $2,650. (Module 30.4, LOS 30.h)

4. **A**   Defined benefit pension plans can be overfunded and result in a net pension asset, or they can be underfunded and result in a net pension liability. Defined contribution plans do not result in balance sheet assets or liabilities because they are neither owned by the sponsoring firm or obligations of the sponsoring firm. (Module 30.6, LOS 30.j)

5. **A**   Because A – L = E, shareholders' equity is 98,500 assets – 5,000 accrued liabilities – 12,000 short-term debt – 39,000 bonds payable = $42,500. Thus, debt-to-equity is (12,000 short-term debt + 39,000 bonds payable) / 42,500 equity = 1.2. Only interest-bearing liabilities are considered debt. Accrued liabilities are not interest bearing. (Module 30.6, LOS 30.k)

READING
31

Financial Reporting Quality

EXAM FOCUS

Here we cover the quality of a firm's financial statements, which, together with the quality of reported earnings, determines what is defined as the overall quality of the firm's financial reports. Candidates must understand how choices about several accounting methods and estimates can affect reported earnings, financial position, and the classification of cash flows. You should learn the additional disclosures required when non-GAAP measures are reported and the warning signs that management may be manipulating financial reports through biased reporting choices and estimates.

MODULE 31.1: REPORTING QUALITY

LOS 31.a: Distinguish between financial reporting quality and quality of reported results (including quality of earnings, cash flow, and balance sheet items).

Video covering this content is available online.

CFA® Program Curriculum, Volume 3, page 609

Financial reporting quality refers to the characteristics of a firm's financial statements. The primary criterion for judging financial reporting quality is adherence to generally accepted accounting principles (GAAP) in the jurisdiction in which the firm operates. However, given that GAAP provide choices of methods, estimates, and specific treatment of many items, compliance with GAAP by itself does not necessarily result in financial reporting of the highest quality.

High quality financial reporting must be *decision useful*. Two characteristics of decision-useful financial reporting are *relevance* and *faithful representation*. Relevance refers to the fact that information presented in the financial statements is useful to users of financial statements in making decisions. Relevant information must also be *material* in that knowledge of it would likely affect the decisions of users of financial statements. Faithful representation encompasses the qualities of *completeness*, *neutrality*, and the absence of errors. We develop the concept of neutrality of financial reports later in this topic review.

The **quality of earnings** is, in many respects, a separate issue. The quality of reported earnings (not the quality of earnings reports) can be judged based on the sustainability of the earnings as well as on their level. Sustainability can be evaluated by determining the proportion of reported earnings that can be expected to continue in the future. Increases in reported earnings resulting from changes in exchange rates or by sales of assets that have appreciated over many periods are not typically sustainable, whereas higher profits from increased efficiency or increasing market share would generally be considered sustainable.

One dollar of high-quality earnings is expected to add more value to a company than one dollar of low-quality earnings, based on the criterion of sustainability. The higher probability that high-quality earnings will continue in future periods increases their impact on the value of the firm, calculated as the present value of expected future earnings. At the other end of the sustainability spectrum, a one-time gain of a dollar from favorable currency exchange rate movements is not likely to be repeated and, therefore, has a smaller impact on estimates of a company's value.

The importance of the level of earnings is that reported earnings must be high enough to sustain the company's operations and existence over time, as well as high enough to provide an adequate return to the company's investors. Both of these concerns are important in determining the quality of a company's reported earnings. Sustainability of reported cash flows is also a consideration in determining the quality of reported earnings, as are the value of items reported on the balance sheet. Inadequate accruals for probable liabilities and overstatement of asset values can both decrease the quality of reported earnings and bring sustainability into question.

From our discussion here, we can see that it is quite possible that a firm has high financial reporting quality but a low quality of reported earnings. Reported earnings may be GAAP-compliant and relevant, represent the company's economic activities faithfully, and be decision useful as a result, but have low sustainability or be low enough in amount that the provision of adequate investor returns or the sustainability of the company itself are called into question.

LOS 31.b: Describe a spectrum for assessing financial reporting quality.

CFA® Program Curriculum, Volume 3, page 610

Combining both financial reporting quality and the quality of reported earnings, we can categorize the quality of financial reports along a spectrum from best to worst. At the high-quality end of the spectrum, we have financial reports that are compliant with GAAP, decision useful, and report earnings that are sustainable and represent an adequate return on invested capital. At the opposite end of the spectrum are financial reports that are essentially fictitious (fraudulent). When reporting quality is that low, the quality of the reported earnings themselves is impossible to assess. We can identify several levels of quality between these two extremes.

Here is one possible categorization of the quality levels of financial reports, from best to worst:

1. Reporting is compliant with GAAP and decision useful; earnings are sustainable and adequate.

2. Reporting is compliant with GAAP and decision useful, but earnings quality is low (earnings are not sustainable or not adequate).

3. Reporting is compliant with GAAP, but earnings quality is low and reporting choices and estimates are biased.

4. Reporting is compliant with GAAP, but the amount of earnings is actively managed to increase, decrease, or smooth reported earnings.

5. Reporting is not compliant with GAAP, although the numbers presented are based on the company's actual economic activities.

6. Reporting is not compliant and includes numbers that are essentially fictitious or fraudulent.

LOS 31.c: Distinguish between conservative and aggressive accounting.

CFA® Program Curriculum, Volume 3, page 620

Ideally, financial statements should be neutral or unbiased in order to offer the most value to analysts. In general, we describe the choices made within GAAP with respect to reported earnings as **conservative accounting** if they tend to decrease the company's reported earnings and financial position (on the balance sheet) for the current period. We describe choices that increase reported earnings or improve the financial position for the current period as **aggressive accounting**.

Aggressive accounting often results in decreased earnings in future periods, while conservative accounting will tend to increase future period earnings. Both these types of bias are sometimes used by management, for different periods, in an attempt to smooth earnings over time because greater earnings volatility tends to reduce the value of a company's shares. Often **earnings smoothing** is accomplished through adjustment of accrued liabilities that are based on management estimates. During periods of higher-than-expected earnings, management may employ a conservative bias by adjusting an accrued liability upward to reduce reported earnings for that period. This effectively allows deferral of the recognition of these earnings to a future period for which earnings are less than expected. In such a future period, the accrued liability is adjusted downward to increase reported earnings in that period, perhaps to meet market expectations. Deferral of reported earnings through conservative bias in financial reporting so they can be used opportunistically in a future period is sometimes referred to as putting earnings in the "cookie jar" (presumably to be "enjoyed" later).

Some examples of conservative versus aggressive financial reporting based on management choices and estimates are shown in Figure 31.1.

Figure 31.1: Aggressive and Conservative Accounting

Aggressive	Conservative
Capitalizing current period costs	Expensing current period costs
Longer estimates of the lives of depreciable assets	Shorter estimates of the lives of depreciable assets
Higher estimates of salvage values	Lower estimates of salvage values
Straight-line depreciation	Accelerated depreciation
Delayed recognition of impairments	Early recognition of impairments
Less accrual of reserves for bad debt	More accrual of reserves for bad debt
Smaller valuation allowances on deferred tax assets	Larger valuation allowances on deferred tax assets

Bias can also be present in the way that financial results are presented. A company may present transparent financial statements that help analysts and investors to understand the results and the activities that led to them. Alternatively, a company may provide minimal disclosure in an attempt to emphasize positive developments and obscure information about negative developments.

We should avoid thinking about conservatism in financial reporting as "good" and aggressive reporting as "bad." Conservative bias can also be considered as a deviation from neutral reporting or faithful representation that reduces the usefulness of financial statements to analysts and investors.

Sometimes GAAP themselves can introduce conservatism by imposing a higher standard of verification for revenue and profit than for expenses and accrual of liabilities. For example:

- Research costs are typically expensed in the period incurred because of the uncertainty about the future benefits to be provided from research activities, while the associated revenue is not recognized until some future period.

- Accruals for legal liabilities are recorded when a future payment becomes "probable," while the standard for recognizing increasing accrued asset value is stricter.

- Under U.S. GAAP, write-downs of inventory values are required when their future value is likely impaired, but increases in inventory value may not be recorded until the inventory is actually sold.

While conservative bias in financial reporting is not ideal for users of financial statements, it may be beneficial in reducing the probability of future litigation from users claiming they were misled, in reducing current period tax liability (when deductions for tax must also be deducted in the financial statements), and in protecting the interests of those who have less complete information than company management, such as buyers of the company's debt.

LOS 31.d: Describe motivations that might cause management to issue financial reports that are not high quality.

CFA® Program Curriculum, Volume 3, page 625

One important motivation for aggressive accounting choices is to meet or exceed a benchmark number for earnings per share. Specifically, managers may be motivated to report earnings that are greater than:

■ Earnings guidance offered earlier by management.

■ Consensus analyst expectations.

■ Those of the same period in the prior year.

The manager's motivation here may be career oriented, seeking to enhance her reputation and improve future career opportunities. Because beating certain benchmarks is very important to subsequent stock price movements, managers may be motivated by incentive compensation (bonuses) that depends on stock returns. Other possible motivations are to gain credibility with equity market investors or improve the way the company is viewed by its customers and suppliers.

For companies that are highly leveraged and unprofitable, aggressive accounting may be motivated by a desire to avoid violating debt covenants.

When earnings exceed benchmark levels, managers may make conservative accounting choices in ways that allow these earnings to be shown in future periods, increasing the probability that future period earnings will meet or exceed the relevant benchmark amount.

LOS 31.e: Describe conditions that are conducive to issuing low-quality, or even fraudulent, financial reports.

CFA® Program Curriculum, Volume 3, page 626

Three factors that typically exist in cases where management provides low-quality financial reporting are motivation, opportunity, and a rationalization of the behavior. So to the sources of *motivation* previously listed, we can add conditions that increase the *opportunity* to present low-quality financial reports. Circumstances in which low-quality, or even fraudulent, financial reporting is more probable are:

■ The company has weak internal controls.

■ The board of directors provides inadequate oversight.

■ Applicable accounting standards provide a large range of acceptable accounting treatments, provide for inconsequential penalties in the case of accounting fraud, or both.

The third likely element of low-quality financial reporting is *rationalization* by management for less-than-ethical actions. Most people who do something they know is wrong tell themselves a story that seems (at least to them) to justify breaking the rules. Whether the story is "I'll fix it next period" or "I have to do it to get my bonus and pay for my parents' care," the resulting behavior is the same.

LOS 31.f: Describe mechanisms that discipline financial reporting quality and the potential limitations of those mechanisms.

CFA® Program Curriculum, Volume 3, page 626

Each country has its own regulatory body responsible for publicly traded securities and the markets in which they trade. For example, in the United States, the regulatory body is the Securities and Exchange Commission (SEC). In the U.K., it is the Financial Conduct Authority (FCA). The International Organization of Securities Commissions (IOSCO) coordinates securities regulation on an international basis with over 200 members, such as national securities regulators, stock exchanges, and regional authorities. One such regional authority, the European Securities and Markets Authority (ESMA), coordinates policy among the securities regulators of countries in the European Union.

Securities regulations typically require:

- A registration process for the issuance of new publicly traded securities.

- Specific disclosure and reporting requirements, including periodic financial statements and accompanying notes.

- An independent audit of financial reports.

- A statement of financial condition (or management commentary) made by management.

- A signed statement by the person responsible for the preparation of the financial reports.

- A review process for newly registered securities and periodic reviews after registration.

Enforcement actions by securities regulators may include fines, suspension of participation in issuance and trading of securities, and public disclosure of the results of disciplinary proceedings. Regulators may also pursue criminal prosecution of fraudulent or otherwise illegal activities.

In addition to the audit opinion, a requirement for securities that trade in the United States is that management must include an assessment of the effectiveness of the firm's internal controls.

Note that an unqualified or "clean" audit opinion is not a guarantee that no fraud has occurred but only offers reasonable assurance that the financial reports (prepared the under the direction of management) have been "fairly reported" with respect to the applicable GAAP. The auditor is selected and paid by the firm being audited.

Another source of discipline on financial reporting quality is private contracts, such as those with lenders. Such contracts will often specify how financial measures referenced in the loan covenants will be calculated. The counterparties to private contracts with the firm have an incentive to see that the firm produces high-quality financial reports.

LOS 31.g: Describe presentation choices, including non-GAAP measures, that could be used to influence an analyst's opinion.

CFA® Program Curriculum, Volume 3, page 632

Firms will sometimes report accounting measures that are not defined or required under GAAP. Such **non-GAAP measures** typically exclude some items in order to make the firm's performance look better than it would using measures defined and required by GAAP. The claim is often made that certain items are excluded because they are one-time or nonoperating costs that will not affect operating earnings going forward, because the items are non-cash charges, or to "improve comparability with companies that use different accounting methods" for depreciation or restructuring charges.

In the United States, companies that report non-GAAP measures in their financial statements are required to:

■ Display the most comparable GAAP measure with equal prominence.

■ Provide an explanation by management as to why the non-GAAP measure is thought to be useful.

■ Reconcile the differences between the non-GAAP measure and the most comparable GAAP measure.

■ Disclose other purposes for which the firm uses the non-GAAP measure.

■ Include, in any non-GAAP measure, any items that are likely to recur in the future, even those treated as nonrecurring, unusual, or infrequent in the financial statements.

IFRS require that firms using non-IFRS measures in financial reports must:

■ Define and explain the relevance of such non-IFRS measures.

■ Reconcile the differences between the non-IFRS measure and the most comparable IFRS measure.

Overall, the supposition is that firms use non-GAAP measures in an attempt to control the metrics on which they are evaluated and to reduce the focus of analysts and investors on GAAP measures.

MODULE QUIZ 31.1

To best evaluate your performance, enter your quiz answers online.

1. A firm reports net income of $40 million. The firm's financial statements disclose in management's discussion and analysis that $30 million of net income is attributable to a gain on the sale of assets. Based only on this information, for this period, the firm is *best* described as having high quality of:
   A. financial reporting only.
   B. both earnings and financial reporting.
   C. neither earnings nor financial reporting.

2. Which of the following financial reports are considered to be of the lowest quality? Financial reports that reflect:
   A. unsustainable earnings.
   B. biased accounting choices.
   C. departures from accounting principles.

3. Financial reporting is *most likely* to be decision useful when management's accounting choices are:
   A. neutral.
   B. aggressive.
   C. conservative.

4. Which of the following is *least likely* to be a motivation to overreport earnings?
   A. Reduce tax obligations.
   B. Meet analyst expectations.
   C. Remain in compliance with bond covenants.

5. With respect to conditions that may lead to low-quality financial reporting, ineffective internal controls are *best* described as a(n):
   A. motivation.
   B. opportunity.
   C. rationalization.

6. A limitation on the effectiveness of auditing in ensuring financial reporting quality is that:
   A. detecting fraud is not the objective of audits.
   B. public firms are not required to obtain audit opinions.
   C. auditors may only issue a qualified or unqualified opinion but do not explain why.

7. Under IFRS, a firm that presents a nonstandard financial measure is *least likely* required to:
   A. provide the same measure for at least two prior periods.
   B. explain the reasons for presenting the nonstandard measure.
   C. reconcile the nonstandard measure to a comparable standard measure.

Video covering this content is available online.

MODULE 31.2: ACCOUNTING CHOICES AND ESTIMATES

LOS 31.h: Describe accounting methods (choices and estimates) that could be used to manage earnings, cash flow, and balance sheet items.

CFA® Program Curriculum, Volume 3, page 638

Revenue Recognition

One example of how a firm's choices affect the timing of revenue recognition is the choice of where in the shipping process the customer actually takes title to the goods. A firm may choose terms with their customer of **free-on-board** (FOB) at the shipping point (the firm's loading dock) or FOB at the destination (the customer's location). Choosing terms of FOB at the shipping point will mean that revenue is recognized earlier compared to FOB at the destination.

Firms can also manage the timing of revenue recognition by accelerating or delaying the shipment of goods. If additional revenue is required to meet targets, firms can offer discounts or special financing terms to increase orders in the current period, or ship goods to distributors without receiving an order. Overloading a distribution channel with more goods than would normally be sold during a period is referred to as **channel stuffing**. In periods where high earnings are expected, management may wish to delay recognition of revenue to the next period and hold or delay customer shipments to achieve this.

In a **bill-and-hold transaction**, the customer buys the goods and receives an invoice but requests that the firm keep the goods at their location for a period of time. The use of fictitious bill-and-hold transactions can increase earnings in the current period by recognizing revenue for goods that are actually still in inventory. Revenue for future periods will be decreased as real customer orders for these bill-and-hold items are filled but not recognized in revenue, offsetting the previous overstatement of revenue.

Estimates of Credit Losses

One example of accounting choices that affect financial reports is the estimation of losses from uncollectable customer credit accounts. On the balance sheet, the reserve for uncollectible debt is an offset to accounts receivable. If management determines the probability that accounts receivable will be uncollectible is lower than their current estimate, a decrease in the reserve for uncollectible accounts will increase net receivables reported on the balance sheet, reduce expenses on the income statement, and increase net income. An increase in the allowance for bad debt would have the opposite effect, decreasing net receivables on the balance sheet, increasing expenses, and decreasing net income.

A firm that simply underestimates the percentage of receivables that will be uncollectible will report higher receivables and higher net income as a result. At some point, when actual uncollectible accounts exceed the low estimate, the firm will report an additional expense that will reduce net income and net receivables.

Management can adjust the bad-debt reserve in order to smooth earnings. In periods of high earnings, the allowance for bad debt is increased to reduce reported earnings, in effect storing these earnings for later use. In subsequent periods, if earnings are below benchmark values, the bad-debt reserve can be reduced to meet earnings targets.

Other reserves recorded by a company, such as a reserve for warranty expense, can also be changed to manage reported earnings. A decrease in the estimated warranty expense as a percentage of sales will increase earnings, while an increase in the reserve for warranty expense will decrease earnings for the period.

Valuation Allowance

Another example of a contra account that can be used to manage earnings is a valuation allowance. Recall that a valuation allowance reduces the carrying value of a deferred tax asset based on the probability it will not be realized. Similar to the effects of an allowance for bad debt, increasing a valuation allowance will decrease the net deferred tax asset on the balance sheet and reduce net income for the period, while a decrease in the valuation allowance will increase the net deferred tax asset and increase net income for the period.

As with the contra account for bad debt, the valuation allowance can be understated to show higher asset values and it can also be adjusted over time to smooth earnings.

Depreciation Methods and Estimates

Compared to straight-line depreciation, using an accelerated method of depreciation increases expenses, and decreases net income, in the early years of an asset's life. In the later years of an asset's life, expenses are lower and net income higher when an accelerated depreciation method is used. The carrying value of a depreciable asset on the balance sheet will decrease more rapidly with accelerated depreciation than with straight-line depreciation.

Estimates of the useful life of a depreciable asset and its salvage value upon disposal can also affect net income and the carrying value of the asset. A greater salvage value will slow depreciation so the carrying value of the asset is greater, depreciation expense is less, and net income is higher. A smaller salvage value will have the opposite effects. If the salvage value of an asset is set higher than the actual sale price at the end of the asset's life, a loss on the sale of the asset will decrease net income in the period in which the asset is sold.

Using a longer estimated useful life of a depreciable asset decreases the periodic depreciation expense and increases net income in the early years of the asset's life compared to using a shorter estimated useful life.

Amortization and Impairment

Management choices and estimates regarding amortization of purchased intangible assets are similar to those for depreciation of tangible assets. The intangible asset *goodwill* is not amortized but is subject to a test for impairment. By ignoring or delaying recognition of an impairment charge for goodwill, management can increase earnings in the current period.

Inventory Method

The choice of inventory cost flow methods can have significant effects on both reported earnings and the balance sheet value of inventory. Consider the choice between FIFO and weighted-average inventory costing methods. During periods of rising prices, COGS under the FIFO method will be less than COGS under the weighted-average costing method. Gross profit, gross margin, and earnings will all be greater under the FIFO method than under the weighted-average method as a result. Balance sheet inventory value will be greater under FIFO than under the weighted-average method.

During periods of decreasing prices, the opposite is true; FIFO COGS are greater than weighted-average COGS and FIFO gross profits, gross margin, and earnings less than under the weighted-average method. With decreasing prices, balance sheet inventory will be less under FIFO than under the weighted-average cost method.

In terms of relevance, in an environment of either increasing or decreasing prices, FIFO results in more accurate balance sheet inventory values because inventory value is closer to current replacement cost than under the weighted average cost method. Conversely, COGS are closer to current (replacement) cost under the weighted-average cost method so that gross profit and margin better reflect economic reality. Gross profit under FIFO is distorted in that it includes gains from rising prices (or losses from decreasing prices), so the weighted-average cost method produces "better" information on the income statement. Financial reports that are transparent and provide users with the information needed to understand how the choice of inventory costing method affects income statement and balance sheet values are considered to be higher quality.

Related-Party Transactions

If a public firm does business with a supplier that is private and controlled by management, adjusting the price of goods supplied can shift profits either to or from the private company to manage the earnings reported by the public company.

Capitalization

Any expense that can be capitalized creates an asset on the balance sheet, and the impact of the expense on net income can be spread over many years. Consider a firm that has a marketing expense of $1.5 million and chooses to capitalize this expense and amortize it over three years. In the period in which the expense is incurred, capitalization will reduce the expense on the income statement from $1.5 million to $0.5 million, increasing pretax income by $1 million. At the end of the year, the related balance sheet asset is $1 million, and an amortization expense of $0.5 million will be taken (and reduce net income) in each of the following two years. Greater capitalization of research and development costs will shift net income into the current period in the same way.

Capitalization also affects cash flow classifications. If an expense is capitalized, the entire amount is classified as an investing cash outflow so that operating cash flow is increased by that amount.

Other Cash Flow Effects

Management can affect the classification of cash flows through other methods, primarily with the goal of increasing reported cash flow from operations. Taking longer to pay suppliers increases operating cash flows and is referred to as **stretching payables**. Delaying payments that would normally be made near the end of a reporting period until the beginning of the next accounting period will increase operating cash flow in the current period and reduce it in the subsequent period. There is no effect on reported earnings in the current period from stretching payables.

Capitalizing interest expense will decrease cash flow from investing and increase cash flow from operations, along with its effects on the pattern of earnings from depreciating the interest expense over time rather than expensing it all in the current period. More generally, the ability under IFRS to classify interest and dividends paid as either CFO or CFF, and interest and dividends received as either CFO or CFI, gives management an additional way to manage reported operating cash flow.

Video covering this content is available online.

MODULE 31.3: WARNING SIGNS

LOS 31.i: Describe accounting warning signs and methods for detecting manipulation of information in financial reports.

CFA® Program Curriculum, Volume 3, page 655

Below is a list of several warning signs that analysts should look for. The presence of these issues does not indicate fraud or even earnings manipulation, but in each case, the presence of one or more warning signs requires more analysis in order to determine whether there is a real business reason for the item or if earnings manipulation or fraud is driving the decisions and results. Avoiding investment in the company is one alternative when analysts and investors cannot obtain satisfactory answers to the questions raised when multiple warning signs are present.

Revenue Recognition

- Changes in revenue recognition methods.
- Use of bill-and-hold transactions.
- Use of barter transactions.
- Use of rebate programs that require estimation of the impact of rebates on net revenue.
- Lack of transparency with regard to how the various components of a customer order are recorded as revenue.
- Revenue growth out of line with peer companies.
- Receivables turnover is decreasing over multiple periods.
- Decreases in total asset turnover, especially when a company is growing through acquisition of other companies.
- Inclusion of nonoperating items or significant one-time sales in revenue.

Inventories

- Declining inventory turnover ratio.
- LIFO liquidations—drawing down inventory levels when LIFO (U.S. GAAP only) inventory costing is used so that COGS reflects the lower costs of items acquired in past periods, which increases current period earnings.

Capitalization Policies

- Firm capitalizes costs that are not typically capitalized by firms in their industry.

Relationship of Revenue and Cash Flow

- The ratio of operating cash flow to net income is persistently less than one or declining over time.

Other Warning Signs

- Depreciation methods, estimated asset lives, or estimates of salvage values are out of line with those of peer companies in the industry.
- Fourth-quarter earnings show a pattern (either high or low) compared to the seasonality of earnings in the industry or seasonality of revenue for the firm.
- The firm has significant transactions with related parties (entities controlled by management).
- Certain expenses are classified as nonrecurring but appear regularly in financial reports.
- Gross or operating profit margins are noticeably higher than are typical for the industry and peer companies.
- Management typically provides only minimal financial reporting information and disclosure.
- Management typically emphasizes non-GAAP earnings measures and uses special or nonrecurring designations aggressively for charges.
- Growth by purchasing a large number of businesses can provide many opportunities to manipulate asset values and future depreciation and amortization and make comparisons to prior period earnings problematic.

Analysts should consider adjusting prior-period earnings when large restructuring or impairment charges are recognized. Analysts sometimes take such events to be good news because they anticipate better firm performance going forward when poorly performing assets are disposed of. Because the charges represent, to some extent, "corrections" of previously understated expenses and overstated asset values, analysts should consider spreading these costs across prior periods and restating prior earnings to give a more realistic picture of true earnings trends.

MODULE QUIZ 31.2, 31.3

To best evaluate your performance, enter your quiz answers online.

1. For the current period, inappropriate capitalization is *most likely* to:
   A. overstate revenues.
   B. understate liabilities.
   C. understate expenses.

2. A potential warning sign that a firm is engaging in channel stuffing is an unusual increase in the firm's:
   A. receivables turnover.
   B. days of sales outstanding.
   C. number of days of payables.

KEY CONCEPTS

LOS 31.a

Financial reporting quality refers to the characteristics of a firm's financial statements. High-quality financial reporting adheres to generally accepted accounting principles (GAAP) and is decision useful in terms of relevance and faithful representation.

Quality of reported results refers to the level and sustainability of a firm's earnings, cash flows, and balance sheet items. High-quality earnings are high enough to provide the firm's investors with an adequate return and are sustainable in future periods.

LOS 31.b

A spectrum for assessing financial reporting quality considers both the quality of a firm's financial statements and the quality of its earnings. One such spectrum, from highest quality to lowest, is the following:

- Reporting is compliant with GAAP and decision useful; earnings are sustainable and adequate.

- Reporting is compliant and decision useful, but earnings quality is low.

- Reporting is compliant, but earnings quality is low and reporting choices and estimates are biased.

- Reporting is compliant, but earnings are actively managed.

- Reporting is not compliant, but the numbers presented are based on the company's actual economic activities.

- Reporting is not compliant and includes numbers that are fictitious or fraudulent.

LOS 31.c

Biased accounting choices that can be made within GAAP include conservative and aggressive accounting. Conservative accounting choices tend to decrease the company's reported earnings and financial position for the current period. Aggressive accounting choices tend to increase reported earnings or improve the financial position for the current period.

Some managers employ conservative bias during periods when earnings are above target and aggressive bias during poor periods of below-target earnings to artificially smooth earnings.

LOS 31.d

Motivations for firm managers to issue low-quality financial reports may include pressure to meet or exceed earnings targets, career considerations, increasing their compensation, improving perceptions of the firm among customers and suppliers, or meeting the terms of debt covenants.

LOS 31.e

Conditions that are often present when managers issue low-quality financial reports include motivations, opportunities, and rationalizations. Weak internal controls, inadequate oversight by the board of directors, and wide ranges of acceptable accounting treatments are among the factors that may provide opportunities for low-quality reporting.

LOS 31.f

Mechanisms that help to discipline financial reporting quality include regulation, auditing, and private contracts. Regulators typically require public companies to provide periodic financial statements and notes, including management commentary, and obtain independent audits.

A clean audit opinion offers reasonable assurance that financial statements are free from material errors but does not guarantee the absence of error or fraud. The fact that firms select and pay their auditors may limit the effectiveness of auditing to discipline financial reporting quality.

LOS 31.g

Firms may attempt to influence analysts' valuations by presenting non-GAAP measures, such as earnings that exclude certain nonrecurring items. IFRS requires firms to define and explain the relevance of any non-GAAP measures and reconcile them to the most comparable IFRS measure. Similar requirements apply to U.S. public firms.

LOS 31.h

Accounting choices and estimates that can be used to manage earnings include:

- Revenue recognition choices such as shipping terms (FOB shipping point versus FOB destination), accelerating shipments (channel stuffing), and bill-and-hold transactions.
- Estimates of reserves for uncollectible accounts or warranty expenses.
- Valuation allowances on deferred tax assets.
- Depreciation methods, estimates of useful lives and salvage values, and recognition of impairments.
- Inventory cost flow methods.
- Capitalization of expenses.
- Related-party transactions.

LOS 31.i

Accounting warning signs that indicate a need for closer analysis may include:

- Revenue growth out of line with comparable firms, changes in revenue recognition methods, or lack of transparency about revenue recognition.
- Decreases over time in turnover ratios (receivables, inventory, total asset).
- Bill-and-hold, barter, or related-party transactions.
- Net income not supported by operating cash flows.

- Capitalization decisions, depreciation methods, useful lives, salvage values out of line with comparable firms.

- Fourth-quarter earnings patterns not caused by seasonality.

- Frequent appearance of nonrecurring items.

- Emphasis on non-GAAP measures, minimal information and disclosure in financial reports.

Study Session 9

ANSWER KEY FOR MODULE QUIZZES

Module Quiz 31.1

1. **A** Because a large proportion of net income is due to a one-time gain, this period's earnings are likely not sustainable and the firm may be said to have low quality of earnings for the period. Clear disclosure of this fact in the financial statements suggests high quality of financial reporting. (LOS 31.a)

2. **C** In the spectrum of financial reporting quality, financial reports that depart from generally accepted accounting principles are considered to be of lower quality than those that reflect biased accounting choices. Financial reports that reflect unsustainable earnings, such as one-time gains, can still be of high quality if they state the situation clearly. (LOS 31.b)

3. **A** Financial reporting is most likely to be decision useful when accounting choices are neutral. Either aggressive or conservative accounting choices by management may be viewed as biases. (LOS 31.c)

4. **A** Reducing tax obligations would be a reason to *underreport* earnings. The other choices are motivations to overreport earnings. (LOS 31.d)

5. **B** Ineffective internal controls are a condition that provides an opportunity for low-quality financial reporting. (LOS 31.e)

6. **A** The objective of audits is to provide reasonable assurance that financial statements are presented fairly. A firm that is engaging in accounting fraud may deceive its auditor. Regulators in most countries require publicly traded firms to obtain independent audits of their financial statements. Auditors may issue a qualified opinion noting certain aspects of financial statements that are inconsistent with accounting principles or an adverse opinion if they find that financial statements are materially misstated and do not conform with GAAP. (LOS 31.f)

7. **A** IFRS require a firm that presents a nonstandard financial measure to reconcile that measure to an IFRS measure and explain why the firm believes the nonstandard measure is relevant to users of the financial statements. Presenting the nonstandard measure for prior periods is not a requirement. (LOS 31.g)

Module Quiz 31.2, 31.3

1. **C** Management may make inappropriate capitalization decisions to understate expenses by creating balance sheet assets for items that should instead be recognized as expenses in the current period, increasing net income in the current period. Revenues and liabilities are unlikely to be affected by capitalization decisions. (Module 31.2, LOS 31.h)

2. **B**   Channel stuffing, which includes activities such as accelerating deliveries to distributors or sending customers unordered merchandise, would likely increase accounts receivable as a percentage of revenues. This would decrease the receivables turnover ratio and increase days of sales outstanding. Payables would not be affected. (Module 31.3, LOS 31.i)

The following is a review of the Financial Reporting and Analysis (4) principles designed to address the learning outcome statements set forth by CFA Institute. Cross-Reference to CFA Institute Assigned Reading #32.

READING

32

Financial Statement Analysis: Applications

EXAM FOCUS

In this topic review, we will apply the analytic methods detailed in the topic review of Financial Analysis Techniques. Pay special attention to the method outlined for forecasting cash flows. Memorize the four types of items important in the determination of credit quality. Lastly, analyst adjustments to financial statements are covered one more time. Understand the reasons for all the adjustments covered and how the adjustments will affect financial ratios used for valuation and credit analysis.

MODULE 32.1: FORECASTING

LOS 32.a: **Evaluate a company's past financial performance and explain how a company's strategy is reflected in past financial performance.**

Video covering this content is available online.

CFA® Program Curriculum, Volume 3, page 673

In the review of Financial Analysis Techniques, we introduced a number of financial ratios that can be used to assess a company's profitability, leverage, solvency, and operational efficiency. The analyst can evaluate trends in these ratios, as well as their levels, to evaluate how the company has performed in these areas.

Trends in financial ratios and differences between a firm's financial ratios and those of its competitors or industry averages can indicate important aspects of a firm's business strategy. Consider two firms in the personal computer business. One builds relatively high-end computers with cutting-edge features, and one competes primarily on price and produces computers with various configurations using readily available technology. What differences in their financial statements would we expect to find?

Premium products are usually sold at higher gross margins than less differentiated commodity-like products, so we should expect cost of goods sold to be a higher proportion of sales for the latter. We might also expect the company with cutting-edge features and high quality to spend a higher proportion of sales on research and development, which may be quite minimal for a firm purchasing improved components from suppliers rather than developing new features and capabilities in-house. The ratio of gross profits to operating profits will be larger for a firm that spends highly on research and development or on advertising.

In general, it is important for an analyst to understand a subject firm's business strategy. If the firm claims it is going to improve earnings per share by cutting costs, examination of operating ratios and gross margins over time will reveal whether the firm has actually been able to implement such a strategy and whether sales have suffered as a result.

LOS 32.b: Forecast a company's future net income and cash flow.

CFA® Program Curriculum, Volume 3, page 681

A forecast of future net income and cash flow often begins with a forecast of future sales. Over shorter horizons, the "top down" approach to forecasting sales is used. The analyst begins with a forecast of GDP growth, often supplied by outside research or an in-house economics group. Historical relationships can be used to estimate the relationship between GDP growth and the growth of industry sales. If the subject firm's market share is expected to remain the same, the growth of firm sales will be the same as the growth in industry sales. If the analyst has reason to believe the firm's market share will increase or decrease next period, the market share can be adjusted for this change and then multiplied by estimated industry sales for the next period to get the forecast of firm sales for the period.

In a simple forecasting model, some historical average or trend-adjusted measure of profitability (operating margin, EBT margin, or net margin) can be used to forecast earnings. In complex forecasting models, each item on an income statement and balance sheet can be estimated based on separate assumptions about its growth in relation to revenue growth. For multi-period forecasts, the analyst typically employs a single estimate of sales growth at some point that is expected to continue indefinitely.

To estimate cash flows, the analyst must make assumptions about future sources and uses of cash. The most important of these will be increases in working capital, capital expenditures on new fixed assets, issuance or repayments of debt, and issuance or repurchase of stock. A typical assumption is that noncash working capital as a percentage of sales remains constant. A first-pass model might indicate a need for cash in future periods, and these cash requirements can then be met by projecting necessary borrowing in future periods. For consistency, interest expense in future periods must also be adjusted for any increase in debt.

Figure 32.1 illustrates this method. This projection assumes the company's sales increase 5% per year, its cost of goods sold is 35% of sales, and operating expenses are 55% of sales. It also assumes noncash working capital stays constant at 85% of sales, and fixed capital requirements will be 5% of sales in each year. Net income is projected to increase over the forecast period, but the analysis reveals that cash is expected to decrease, suggesting a need for financing.

Figure 32.1: Income and Cash Flow Projection

	20X0	20X1	20X2
Sales @ +5% per year	86,145	90,452	94,975
Cost of goods sold @ 35% of sales	30,151	31,658	33,241
Operating expenses @ 55% of sales	47,380	49,749	52,236
Pretax income	8,614	9,045	9,497
Taxes @ 35%	3,015	3,166	3,324
Net income	5,599	5,879	6,173
Cash	8,615	6,311	3,891
Noncash working capital @ 85% of sales	73,223	76,884	80,729
Current assets	81,838	83,195	84,620
Net income	5,599	5,879	6,173
– Investment in working capital	3,478	3,661	3,844
– Investment in fixed capital @ 5% of sales	4,307	4,523	4,749
Change in cash	(2,186)	(2,304)	(2,420)
Beginning cash	10,801	8,615	6,311
Ending cash	8,615	6,311	3,891

MODULE 32.2: CREDIT AND EQUITY ANALYSIS

LOS 32.c: Describe the role of financial statement analysis in assessing the credit quality of a potential debt investment.

Video covering this content is available online.

CFA® Program Curriculum, Volume 3, page 690

Traditionally, credit analysts have spoken of the "three Cs," "four Cs," or even the "five Cs" of credit analysis. One version of the three Cs includes: Character, Collateral, and Capacity to repay. Character refers to the firm management's professional reputation and the firm's history of debt repayment. The ability to pledge specific collateral reduces lender risk. It is the third C, the capacity to repay, that requires close examination of a firm's financial statements and ratios. Since some debt is for periods of 30 years or longer, the credit analyst must take a very long-term view of the firm's prospects.

Credit rating agencies such as Moody's and Standard and Poor's employ formulas that are essentially weighted averages of several specific accounting ratios and business characteristics. The specific items used in the formula and their weights vary from industry to industry, but the types of items considered can be separated into four general categories:

1. *Scale and diversification.* Larger companies and those with a wider variety of product lines and greater geographic diversification are better credit risks.

2. *Operational efficiency.* Such items as operating ROA, operating margins, and EBITDA margins fall into this category. Along with greater vertical diversification, high operating efficiency is associated with better debt ratings.

3. *Margin stability.* Stability of the relevant profitability margins indicates a higher probability of repayment (leads to a better debt rating and a lower interest rate). Highly variable operating results make lenders nervous.

4. *Leverage.* Ratios of operating earnings, EBITDA, or some measure of free cash flow to interest expense or total debt make up the most important part of the credit rating formula. Firms with greater earnings in relation to their debt and in relation to their interest expense are better credit risks.

PROFESSOR'S NOTE

We discuss credit quality in more detail in our topic review of "Fundamentals of Credit Analysis" in Fixed Income.

LOS 32.d: Describe the use of financial statement analysis in screening for potential equity investments.

CFA® Program Curriculum, Volume 3, page 694

In many cases, an analyst must select portfolio stocks from the large universe of potential equity investments. Whether the object is to select growth stocks, income stocks, or value stocks, accounting items and ratios can be used to identify a manageable subset of available stocks for further analysis.

Some investment strategies even have financial ratios in their names, such as low price/earnings and low price/sales investing. Multiple criteria are used because a screen based on a single factor can include firms with other undesirable characteristics. For example, a company with a low price/earnings ratio may also have operating losses, declining sales prospects, or very high leverage.

Analysts should be aware that their equity screens will likely include and exclude many or all of the firms in particular industries. A screen to identify firms with low P/E ratios will likely exclude growth companies from the sample. A low price-to-book or high dividend screen will likely include an inordinate proportion of financial services companies.

Backtesting refers to using a specific set of criteria to screen historical data to determine how portfolios based on those criteria would have performed. There is, of course, no guarantee that screening criteria that have identified stocks that outperformed in the past will continue to do so. Analysts must also pay special attention to the potential effects of survivorship bias, data-mining bias, and look-ahead bias (see the topic review of Sampling and Estimation) when evaluating the results of backtesting.

LOS 32.e: Explain appropriate analyst adjustments to a company's financial statements to facilitate comparison with another company.

CFA® Program Curriculum, Volume 3, page 697

Because different companies choose different accounting methods, an analyst must be prepared to adjust the financial statements of one company to make them comparable to those of another company or group of companies. Differences in accounting methods chosen by firms subject to the same standards, as well as differences in accounting methods due to differences in local accounting standards, can make comparisons between companies problematic.

Consider two companies in the same industry that have different depreciation schedules. One company has selected straight-line depreciation even though physical assets in its industry tend to lose most of their productive value early in their economic lives. The analyst would need to adjust the depreciation of that firm so that the net income figures for the firms are comparable. A change in a firm's financial statement depreciation would lead to changes in gross profit, operating profit, and so on, down to net profit and earnings per share.

Differences between U.S. GAAP and IFRS require an analyst to adjust the financial statements of firms from different countries before comparing their financial results. Important differences between the two include their treatments of the effect of exchange rate changes, certain securities held by the firm, and inventory cost flows.

Several adjustments to improve the comparability of firms' financial statements and ratios are as follows.

Investments in Securities

Because the classification of a firm's investment securities affects how changes in their values are recorded, it can significantly affect reported earnings and assets. Recall that unrealized gains and losses on held-for-trading securities are recorded in income, while those on available-for-sale or held-to-maturity securities are not. Additionally, while unrealized gains and losses on held-for-trading and available-for-sale securities are reflected in balance sheet asset values, for held-to-maturity securities they are not.

When these differences in classifications lead to significant differences in reported net income or balance sheet asset values for otherwise comparable companies, an analyst can use disclosures to adjust net income and assets of one firm to what they would have been had their classifications been the same.

Inventory Accounting Differences

As we covered in the topic review on inventory accounting, a firm using LIFO (permitted only under U.S. GAAP) will report higher cost of goods sold, lower income, and lower inventory compared to FIFO inventory accounting when costs are rising. The **LIFO reserve**, which all LIFO firms must report, can be used to adjust LIFO cost of goods and inventory to their FIFO-equivalent values.

Differences in Depreciation Methods and Estimates

Disclosures related to depreciation are not specific enough to permit adjustments to ensure comparability. However, some qualitative information for comparing companies' methods can be obtained.

Over an asset's life, differences between depreciation methods, estimates of useful lives, and estimates of salvage values used by otherwise comparable firms can lead to significant differences in reported income and balance sheet asset values. A firm that is aggressive in using higher estimates of useful asset lives or asset salvage values will report lower annual depreciation expense and higher net income, compared to a more conservative firm that uses lower estimates of useful lives or salvage values. If the analyst concludes that a firm's aggressive assumptions regarding asset lives, for example, are increasing balance sheet net asset values and reported net income, an adjustment to net income and fixed asset carrying values may be appropriate.

Note as well that upward revaluation of fixed asset values is permitted under IFRS but not under U.S. GAAP. Such a revaluation will increase assets and equity, and in a case where the upward revaluation reverses a previous downward revaluation, the increase in value is also reported on the income statement.

An analyst can estimate the number of years' worth of depreciation a firm has recognized by dividing accumulated depreciation from the balance sheet by depreciation expense from the income statement. The result can be interpreted as the **average age** of the firm's assets. Similarly, an analyst can estimate the **average useful life** of a firm's assets (gross property, plant, and equipment divided by depreciation expense) and their **average remaining useful life** (net property, plant, and equipment divided by depreciation expense). Comparing average ages and useful lives of assets within an industry may reveal differences in firms' future capital spending needs.

Off-Balance-Sheet Financing

Debt ratios should include liabilities for both capital (finance) leases and operating leases. Firms include the estimated present value of future capital lease payments with their financials, so that part is straightforward. Although firms must report payments due under operating leases (each year for five years, and total beyond five years), the present value of these is not a required item. To estimate the present value of operating lease liabilities, an analyst can use the ratio of the present value of capital lease obligations to the sum of these future payments, or make some assumption about the timing of operating lease payments beyond five years and calculate a discount rate to use when calculating the present value of operating lease payments.

Goodwill

Two companies with identical assets, but where one has grown through acquisition of some business units while the other has grown internally by creating such business units, will show different balance sheet values for the same assets. For the company that has grown through acquisition:

- Tangible assets of the acquired units will be recorded at fair value as of the acquisition date, rather than at historical cost net of accumulated depreciation.

- Identifiable intangible assets of the acquired units will be valued at their acquisition cost, rather than not being included in balance sheet assets.

- Goodwill, the excess of acquisition price over the fair value of acquired net assets, will be shown on the balance sheet.

Two adjustments are typically made to goodwill to improve comparability in such a case. First, goodwill should be subtracted from assets when calculating financial ratios. Second, any income statement expense from impairment of goodwill in the current period should be reversed, increasing reported net income.

In calculating price to book value of equity per share, an analyst can remove goodwill from assets and recalculate a lower adjusted book value, resulting in a price to adjusted book value ratio that is greater.

Other Intangible Assets

Additional adjustment may be required for IFRS firms that revalue intangible assets upward, which is not permitted under U.S. GAAP. As revaluations that do not reverse previously reported impairment are taken directly to equity, an analyst can improve comparability of financial ratios by reducing intangible asset values (and thereby equity) by the cumulative amount of any such upward revaluations.

An alternative ratio, **price to tangible book value**, removes both goodwill and intangible assets from equity to get tangible book value. This adjustment will reduce assets and equity and produce a ratio that is not affected by differences in intangible asset values resulting from differences in how the assets were acquired.

Analysts should also note that a firm's pre- and post-acquisition financial statements may lack comparability when the acquisition method is used. The acquisition method combines fair value estimates of identifiable assets with historical asset costs on the balance sheet and adds the earnings of the purchased firm with no restatement of prior results.

MODULE QUIZ 32.1, 32.2

To best evaluate your performance, enter your quiz answers online.

1. The table below shows selected data from a company's financial statements.

	20X6	20X7	20X8	20X9
Sales	8,614	9,217	9,862	10,553
COGS	5,304	5,622	6,072	6,679
Purchases	5,257	5,572	6,018	6,620
Inventory	2,525	2,475	2,421	2,362
Accounts receivable	3,491	3,728	3,928	4,352
Accounts payable	1,913	2,102	2,311	2,539

Based on these results, what was this company's *most likely* strategy for improving its operating activity during this period?
   A. Improve its inventory management.
   B. Change its credit and collections policies with its customers.
   C. Change the degree to which it uses trade credit from suppliers.

2. An analyst who is projecting a company's net income and cash flows is *least likely* to assume a constant relationship between the company's sales and its:
   A. interest expenses.
   B. cost of goods sold.
   C. noncash working capital.

3. Credit analysts are likely to consider a company's credit quality to be improving if the company reduces its:
   A. scale and diversification.
   B. margin stability.
   C. leverage.

4. Which of the following stock screens is *most likely* to identify stocks with high earnings growth rates?
   A. Dividend payout ratio greater than 30%.
   B. Price to cash flow per share ratio less than 12.
   C. Book value to market value ratio less than 25%.

5. An analyst needs to compare the financial statements of Firm X and Firm Y. Which of the following differences in the two firms' financial reporting is *least likely* to require the analyst to make an adjustment?

Firm X	Firm Y
A. Straight-line depreciation	Accelerated depreciation
B. Direct method cash flows	Indirect method cash flows
C. IFRS financial reporting	U.S. GAAP financial reporting

6. When comparing a firm that uses LIFO inventory accounting to firms that use FIFO, an analyst should:
   A. subtract the LIFO reserve from cost of sales.
   B. add the change in the LIFO reserve to inventories.
   C. subtract the change in the LIFO reserve from cost of sales.

7. The ratio of a firm's property, plant, and equipment, net of accumulated depreciation, to its annual depreciation expense is *best* interpreted as an estimate of the:
   A. average age of the firm's assets.
   B. average useful life of the firm's assets.
   C. remaining useful life of the firm's assets.

8. How should an analyst *most appropriately* adjust the financial statements of a firm that uses operating leases to finance its plant and equipment?
   A. Increase liabilities.
   B. Decrease long-lived assets.
   C. Decrease shareholders' equity.

KEY CONCEPTS

LOS 32.a

Trends in a company's financial ratios and differences between its financial ratios and those of its competitors or industry average ratios can reveal important aspects of its business strategy.

LOS 32.b

A company's future income and cash flows can be projected by forecasting sales growth and using estimates of profit margins and the increases in working capital and fixed assets necessary to support the forecast sales growth.

LOS 32.c

Credit analysis uses a firm's financial statements to assess its credit quality. Indicators of a firm's creditworthiness include its scale and diversification, operational efficiency, margin stability, and use of financial leverage.

LOS 32.d

Potentially attractive equity investments can be identified by screening a universe of stocks, using minimum or maximum values of one or more ratios. Which (and how many) ratios to use, what minimum or maximum values to use, and how much importance to give each ratio all present challenges to the analyst.

LOS 32.e

When companies use different accounting methods or estimates relating to areas such as inventory accounting, depreciation, capitalization, and off-balance-sheet financing, analysts must adjust the financial statements for comparability.

LIFO ending inventory can be adjusted to a FIFO basis by adding the LIFO reserve. LIFO cost of goods sold can be adjusted to a FIFO basis by subtracting the change in the LIFO reserve.

When calculating solvency ratios, analysts should estimate the present value of operating lease obligations and add it to the firm's liabilities.

ANSWER KEY FOR MODULE QUIZ

Module Quiz 32.1, 32.2

1. **A**   To analyze this company's operating strategy, calculate its activity ratios:

	20X7	20X8	20X9
Inventory turnover	2.25	2.48	2.79
Receivables turnover	2.55	2.58	2.55
Payables turnover	2.78	2.73	2.73
Days of inventory on hand	162	147	131
Days of sales outstanding	143	142	143
Number of days of payables	132	134	134

   The ratios that have changed most significantly are the ones related to inventory. Receivables and payables performance has remained steady, suggesting no change in the company's use of supplier credit or extension of customer credit. (Module 32.1, LOS 32.a)

2. **A**   Projections of net income and cash flows are typically based on assumptions that cost of goods sold, operating expenses, and noncash working capital remain a constant percentage of sales. The projections then show whether additional borrowing is needed during the forecast period. If so, the analyst will adjust the interest expense to reflect the additional debt. (Module 32.1, LOS 32.b)

3. **C**   Lower leverage improves a company's creditworthiness. Larger scale, more diversification, higher operating efficiency, and more stable margins also tend to indicate better credit quality. (Module 32.2, LOS 32.c)

4. **C**   Firms with high growth rates will tend to have high market values relative to the book value of their equity. Low price to cash flow ratios would tend to identify value stocks rather than growth stocks. Screening for high dividend payout ratios would tend to identify mature firms with relatively few growth opportunities. (Module 32.2, LOS 32.d)

5. **B**   Cash flows are the same under either method. Differences in depreciation methods and IFRS versus U.S. GAAP reporting can require an analyst to adjust financial statements to make them comparable. (Module 32.2, LOS 32.e)

6. **C**   To adjust LIFO financial statement data to a FIFO basis, add the LIFO reserve to inventories on the balance sheet and subtract the change in the LIFO reserve from cost of sales on the income statement. Remember that the balance sheet is cumulative (use the full LIFO reserve) while the income statement refers to the most recent period (use the change for the period in the LIFO reserve). (Module 32.2, LOS 32.e)

7. **C** Remaining useful life = net PP&E / depreciation expense.

Average age of assets = accumulated depreciation / depreciation expense.

Average useful life = gross PP&E / depreciation expense.

(Module 32.2, LOS 32.e)

8. **A** The appropriate adjustment for operating leases is to treat them as if they were capital leases by estimating the present value of the future lease obligations and adding that value to the firm's liabilities and long-lived assets. (Module 32.2, LOS 32.e)

TOPIC ASSESSMENT: FINANCIAL REPORTING AND ANALYSIS

You have now finished the Financial Reporting and Analysis topic section. The following Topic Assessment provides immediate feedback on how effective your study has been for this material. The number of questions on this test is equal to the number of questions for the topic on one-half of the actual Level I CFA exam. Questions are more exam-like than typical Module Quiz or QBank questions; a score of less than 70% indicates that your study likely needs improvement. These tests are best taken timed; allow 1.5 minutes per question.

After you've completed this Topic Assessment, you may additionally log in to your Schweser.com online account and enter your answers in the Topic Assessments product. Select "Performance Tracker" to view a breakdown of your score. Select "Compare with Others" to display how your score on the Topic Assessment compares to the scores of others who entered their answers.

1. The fundamental qualitative characteristics of financial statements as described by the IASB conceptual framework *least likely* include:
   A. relevance.
   B. reliability.
   C. faithful representation.

2. A decrease in a firm's inventory turnover ratio is *most likely* to result from:
   A. a write-down of inventory.
   B. goods in inventory becoming obsolete.
   C. decreasing purchases in a period of stable sales.

3. Two firms are identical except that the first pays higher interest charges and lower dividends, while the second pays higher dividends and lower interest charges. Both prepare their financial statements under U.S. GAAP. Compared to the first, the second will have cash flow from financing (CFF) and earnings per share (EPS) that are:

	CFF	EPS
A.	The same	Higher
B.	Lower	Higher
C.	Lower	The same

4. The following information is summarized from Famous, Inc.'s financial statements for the year, which ended December 31, 20X0:

   ▪ Sales were $800,000.

   ▪ Net profit margin was 20%.

   ▪ Sales to assets was 50%.

   ▪ Equity multiplier was 1.6.

   ▪ Interest expense was $30,000.

   ▪ Dividends declared were $32,000.

   Famous, Inc.'s sustainable growth rate based on results from this period is *closest* to:
   A. 3.2%.
   B. 8.0%.
   C. 12.8%.

5. On January 1, Orange Computers issued employee stock options for 400,000 shares. Options on 200,000 shares have an exercise price of $18, and options on the other 200,000 shares have an exercise price of $22. The year-end stock price was $24, and the average stock price over the year was $20. The change in the number of shares used to calculate diluted earnings per share for the year due to these options is *closest* to:
   A. 20,000 shares.
   B. 67,000 shares.
   C. 100,000 shares.

6. A snowmobile manufacturer that uses LIFO begins the year with an inventory of 3,000 snowmobiles, at a carrying cost of $4,000 each. In January, the company sells 2,000 snowmobiles at a price of $10,000 each. In July, the company adds 4,000 snowmobiles to inventory at a cost of $5,000 each. Compared to using a perpetual inventory system, using a periodic system for the firm's annual financial statements would:
   A. increase COGS by $2,000,000.
   B. leave ending inventory unchanged.
   C. decrease gross profit by $4,000,000.

7. Which of the following is *least likely* to result in low-quality financial statements?
   A. Unsustainable cash flows.
   B. Activities that manage earnings.
   C. Conservative accounting choices.

8. Train Company paid $8,000,000 to acquire a franchise at the beginning of 20X5 that was expensed in 20X5. If Train had elected to capitalize the franchise as an intangible asset and amortize the cost of the franchise over eight years, what effect would this decision have on Train's 20X5 cash flow from operations (CFO) and 20X6 debt-to-assets ratio?
   A. Both would be higher with capitalization.
   B. Both would be lower with capitalization.
   C. One would be higher and one would be lower with capitalization.

9. Graphics, Inc. has a deferred tax asset of $4,000,000 on its books. As of December 31, it is probable that $2,000,000 of the deferred tax asset's value will never be realized because of the uncertainty about future income. Under U.S. GAAP, Graphics, Inc. should:
   A. reduce the deferred tax asset account by $2,000,000.
   B. establish a valuation allowance of $2,000,000.
   C. establish an offsetting deferred tax liability of $2,000,000.

10. Long-lived assets cease to be depreciated when the firm's management decides to dispose of the assets by:
    A. sale.
    B. abandonment.
    C. exchange for another asset.

11. If Lizard Inc., a lessee, treats a 5-year lease as a finance lease with straight-line depreciation rather than as an operating lease:
    A. it will have greater equity at lease inception.
    B. its operating income will be less in the first year of the lease.
    C. its CFO will be greater and CFF will be less in the second year of the lease.

12. In the notes to its financial statements, Gilbert Company discloses a €400,000 reversal of an earlier write-down of inventory values, which increases this inventory's carrying value to €2,000,000. It is *most likely* that:
    A. the reasons for this reversal are also disclosed.
    B. a gain of €400,000 appears on the income statement.
    C. the net realizable value of this inventory is €2,000,000.

13. If a firm's management wishes to use its discretion to increase operating cash flows, it is *most likely* to:
    A. capitalize an expense.
    B. decrease the allowance for uncollectible accounts.
    C. change delivery terms from FOB destination to FOB shipping point.

14. A firm that purchases a building that it intends to rent out for income would report this asset as investment property under:
    A. U.S. GAAP only.
    B. IFRS only.
    C. both U.S. GAAP and IFRS.

15. When a company redeems bonds before they mature, the gain or loss on debt extinguishment is calculated as the bonds' carrying amount minus the:
    A. face or par value of the bonds.
    B. amount required to redeem the bonds.
    C. amortized historical cost of the bonds.

16. Which of the following terms from the extended DuPont equation would an analyst *least likely* be able to obtain, given only a company's common-size income statement and common-size balance sheet? The company's:
    A. EBIT margin.
    B. asset turnover.
    C. financial leverage.

17. An analyst is comparing two firms, one that reports under IFRS and one that reports under U.S. GAAP. An analyst is *least likely* to do which of the following to facilitate a comparison of the companies?
    A. Add the LIFO reserve to inventory for a United States-based firm that uses LIFO.
    B. Add the present values of each firm's future minimum operating lease payments to both assets and liabilities.
    C. Adjust the income statement of one of the firms if both have significant unrealized gains or losses from changes in the fair values of trading securities.

18. An analyst wants to compare the cash flows of two United States companies, one that reports cash flow using the direct method and one that reports it using the indirect method. The analyst is *most likely* to:
    A. convert the indirect statement to the direct method to compare the firms' cash expenditures.
    B. adjust the reported CFO of the firm that reports under the direct method for depreciation and amortization expense.
    C. increase CFI for any dividends reported as investing cash flows by the firm reporting cash flow by the direct method.

TOPIC ASSESSMENT ANSWERS: FINANCIAL REPORTING AND ANALYSIS

1. **B** The fundamental qualitative characteristics of financial statements according to the IASB are relevance and faithful representation. (Study Session 6, Module 22.2, LOS 22.d)

2. **B** Obsolescence can cause goods in inventory to remain unsold, which tends to reduce the inventory turnover ratio (COGS / average inventory). Write-downs of inventory increase the inventory turnover ratio by decreasing the denominator. If purchases decrease while sales remain stable, inventory decreases, which increases the inventory turnover ratio. (Study Session 7, Module 26.2, LOS 26.b)

3. **B** Interest paid is an operating cash flow, and dividends paid are a financing cash flow, so the firm that pays higher dividends will have lower CFF. The firm with lower interest expense will have higher EPS. (Study Session 7, Module 25.1, LOS 25.e)

4. **C** Famous, Inc.'s sustainable growth rate = (retention rate)(ROE).

   ROE = 0.20(800,000) / [(800,000 / 0.5)(1 / 1.6)] = 160,000 / 1,000,000 = 16%.

   Alternatively:

   ROE = (0.20)(0.50)(1.6) = 0.16 = 16%

   Retention rate = (1 − dividend payout ratio) = 1 − {32,000 / [(0.20)(800,000)]} = 0.80.

   Sustainable growth = 0.80(16%) = 12.8%.

   (Study Session 7, Module 26.5, LOS 26.e)

5. **A** Based on the average stock price, only the options at 18 are in the money (and therefore dilutive). Using the treasury stock method, the average shares outstanding for calculating diluted EPS would increase by [(20 − 18) / 20]200,000 = 20,000 shares. (Study Session 7, Module 23.5, LOS 23.h)

6. **A** Under a perpetual inventory system, the snowmobiles sold in January are associated with the $4,000 cost of the beginning inventory. Cost of sales is $8,000,000, gross profit is $12,000,000, and end-of-year inventory is $24,000,000. Under a periodic inventory system, the snowmobiles sold in January would be associated with the $5,000 cost of the snowmobiles manufactured in July. Cost of sales would be higher by $2,000,000, gross profit would be lower by $2,000,000, and ending inventory would be lower by $2,000,000. (Study Session 8, Module 27.2, LOS 27.c)

7. **A** Even if earnings or cash flows are unsustainable (i.e., low quality), the firm's financial statements can still be high quality. Conservative accounting choices are considered to be biased compared to the ideal of neutral accounting choices. Earnings management is viewed as reducing the quality of a firm's financial statements. (Study Session 9, Module 31.1, LOS 31.a)

8. **C**   If the cost was amortized rather than expensed, the $8,000,000 cost of the franchise would be classified as an investing cash flow rather than an operating cash flow, so CFO would increase (and CFI decrease). The asset created by capitalizing the cost would increase assets, so the debt-to-assets ratio would decrease. (Study Session 8, Module 28.1, LOS 28.c)

9. **B**   If it becomes probable that a portion of a deferred tax asset will not be realized, a valuation allowance should be established. A valuation allowance serves to reduce the value of a deferred tax asset for the probability that it will not be realized (the difference between tax payable and income tax expense will not reverse in future periods). (Study Session 8, Module 29.5, LOS 29.g)

10. **A**   Under both IFRS and U.S. GAAP, long-lived assets that are reclassified as *held for sale* cease to be depreciated. Long-lived assets that are to be abandoned or exchanged are classified as *held for use* until disposal and continue to be depreciated. (Study Session 8, Module 28.3, LOS 28.j)

11. **C**   With a finance lease, only the interest portion of the lease payment is classified as CFO, so CFO will be greater than it would be with an equivalent operating lease. CFF will be less for a finance lease because the principal portion of each lease payment is classified as a financing cash outflow. Operating income (EBIT) will be reduced only by the (equal) annual depreciation expense with a finance lease, so operating income will be greater for a finance lease than for an operating lease (for which the entire lease payment will be an operating expense). At inception, a finance lease will increase assets and liabilities by the same amount so there is no effect on equity. (Study Session 8, Module 30.4, LOS 30.g)

12. **A**   Required disclosures related to inventories under IFRS include the amount of any reversal of previous write-downs and the circumstances that led to the reversal. Under IFRS, the reversal of an inventory write-down is not recognized as a gain, but instead as a reduction in the cost of sales for the period. From only the information given, we cannot conclude that the net realizable value of the inventory is €2,000,000. This value may be the original cost of the inventory. (Study Session 8, Module 27.4, LOS 27.i)

13. **A**   By capitalizing a purchase instead of recognizing it as an expense in the current period, a firm increases operating cash flow by classifying the cash outflow as CFI rather than CFO. Decreasing the allowance for uncollectible accounts or changing delivery terms for shipments from FOB destination to FOB shipping point would increase earnings but would not affect operating cash flows. (Study Session 9, Module 31.2, LOS 31.h)

14. **B**   Under IFRS, the building is classified as investment property. U.S. GAAP does not distinguish investment property from other types of long-lived assets. (Study Session 8, Module 28.4, LOS 28.n)

15. **B**   Under IFRS, when a company redeems bonds before they mature, the company records a gain or loss equal to the bonds' carrying amount minus the cash amount required to redeem the bonds. (Study Session 8, Module 30.3, LOS 30.c)

16. **B** Asset turnover—revenue/assets —requires an item from the income statement and an item from the balance sheet, so this ratio cannot be obtained from the common-size statements. The EBIT margin—EBIT/revenue (or sales)—would be on a common-size income statement. Financial leverage—assets/equity—is the reciprocal of equity/assets, which would be shown on a common-size balance sheet.(Study Session 7, Modules 23.6, 24.7, 26.4, LOS 23.j, 24.g, 26.d)

17. **C** Unrealized gains and losses on trading securities are reported in the income statement under both U.S. and IFRS standards. Since LIFO is not permitted under IFRS, adjusting the inventory amount for a LIFO firm is a likely adjustment. To account for differences in how companies report leases, adding the present value of future minimum operating lease payments to both the assets and liabilities of a firm will remove the effects of lease reporting methods from solvency and leverage ratios. (Study Session 9, Module 32.2, LOS 32.e)

18. **A** By converting a cash flow statement to the direct method, an analyst can view cash expenses and receipts by category, which will facilitate a comparison of two firms' cash outlays and receipts. CFO is correct under either method and requires no adjustment. Neither dividends received nor dividends paid are classified as CFI under U.S. GAAP. (Study Session 7, Module 25.3, LOS 25.g)

FORMULAS

Activity Ratios:

$$\text{receivables turnover} = \frac{\text{annual sales}}{\text{average receivables}}$$

$$\text{days of sales outstanding} = \frac{365}{\text{receivables turnover}}$$

$$\text{inventory turnover} = \frac{\text{cost of goods sold}}{\text{average inventory}}$$

$$\text{days of inventory on hand} = \frac{365}{\text{inventory turnover}}$$

$$\text{payables turnover} = \frac{\text{purchases}}{\text{average trade payables}}$$

$$\text{number of days of payables} = \frac{365}{\text{payables turnover ratio}}$$

$$\text{total asset turnover} = \frac{\text{revenue}}{\text{average total assets}}$$

$$\text{fixed asset turnover} = \frac{\text{revenue}}{\text{average net fixed assets}}$$

$$\text{working capital turnover} = \frac{\text{revenue}}{\text{average working capital}}$$

Liquidity Ratios:

$$\text{current ratio} = \frac{\text{current assets}}{\text{current liabilities}}$$

$$\text{quick ratio} = \frac{\text{cash + marketable securities + receivables}}{\text{current liabilities}}$$

$$\text{cash ratio} = \frac{\text{cash + marketable securities}}{\text{current liabilities}}$$

$$\text{defensive interval} = \frac{\text{cash + marketable securities + receivables}}{\text{average daily expenditures}}$$

$$\text{cash conversion cycle} = \left(\begin{array}{c}\text{days sales}\\\text{outstanding}\end{array}\right) + \left(\begin{array}{c}\text{days of inventory}\\\text{on hand}\end{array}\right) - \left(\begin{array}{c}\text{number of days}\\\text{of payables}\end{array}\right)$$

Solvency Ratios:

$$\text{debt-to-equity} = \frac{\text{total debt}}{\text{total shareholders' equity}}$$

$$\text{debt-to-capital} = \frac{\text{total debt}}{\text{total debt + total shareholders' equity}}$$

$$\text{debt-to-assets} = \frac{\text{total debt}}{\text{total assets}}$$

$$\text{financial leverage} = \frac{\text{average total assets}}{\text{average total equity}}$$

$$\text{interest coverage} = \frac{\text{earnings before interest and taxes}}{\text{interest payments}}$$

$$\text{fixed charge coverage} = \frac{\text{earnings before interest and taxes} + \text{lease payments}}{\text{interest payments} + \text{lease payments}}$$

Profitability Ratios:

$$\text{net profit margin} = \frac{\text{net income}}{\text{revenue}}$$

$$\text{gross profit margin} = \frac{\text{gross profit}}{\text{revenue}}$$

$$\text{operating profit margin} = \frac{\text{operating income}}{\text{revenue}} \text{ or } \frac{\text{EBIT}}{\text{revenue}}$$

$$\text{pretax margin} = \frac{\text{EBT}}{\text{revenue}}$$

$$\text{return on assets (ROA)} = \frac{\text{net income}}{\text{average total assets}}$$

$$\text{return on assets (ROA)} = \frac{\text{net income} + \text{interest expense} (1 - \text{tax rate})}{\text{average total assets}}$$

$$\text{operating return on assets} = \frac{\text{operating income}}{\text{average total assets}} \text{ or } \frac{\text{EBIT}}{\text{average total assets}}$$

$$\text{return on total capital} = \frac{\text{EBIT}}{\text{average total capital}}$$

$$\text{return on equity} = \frac{\text{net income}}{\text{average total equity}}$$

$$\text{return on common equity} = \frac{\text{net income} - \text{preferred dividends}}{\text{average common equity}}$$

$$= \frac{\text{net income available to common}}{\text{average common equity}}$$

Free Cash Flow to the Firm:

FCFF = net income + noncash charges + [cash interest paid × (1 − tax rate)] − fixed capital investment − working capital investment

FCFF = cash flow from operations + [cash interest paid × (1 − tax rate)] − fixed capital investment

Free Cash Flow to Equity:

$$FCFE = \text{cash flow from operations} - \text{fixed capital investment} + \text{net borrowing}$$

$$\text{common-size income statement ratios} = \frac{\text{income statement account}}{\text{sales}}$$

$$\text{common-size balance sheet ratios} = \frac{\text{balance sheet account}}{\text{total assets}}$$

$$\text{common-size cash flow ratios} = \frac{\text{cash flow statement account}}{\text{revenues}}$$

$$\text{original DuPont equation: ROE} = \left(\begin{array}{c}\text{net profit}\\\text{margin}\end{array}\right)\left(\begin{array}{c}\text{asset}\\\text{turnover}\end{array}\right)\left(\begin{array}{c}\text{leverage}\\\text{ratio}\end{array}\right)$$

extended DuPont equation:

$$ROE = \left(\frac{\text{net income}}{EBT}\right)\left(\frac{EBT}{EBIT}\right)\left(\frac{EBIT}{\text{revenue}}\right)\left(\frac{\text{revenue}}{\text{total assets}}\right)\left(\frac{\text{total assets}}{\text{total equity}}\right)$$

$$\text{basic EPS} = \frac{\text{net income} - \text{preferred dividends}}{\text{weighted average number of common shares outstanding}}$$

diluted EPS =

$$\frac{\left[\text{net income} - \begin{array}{c}\text{preferred}\\\text{dividends}\end{array}\right] + \left[\begin{array}{c}\text{convertible}\\\text{preferred}\\\text{dividends}\end{array}\right] + \left(\begin{array}{c}\text{convertible}\\\text{debt}\\\text{interest}\end{array}\right)(1-t)}{\left(\begin{array}{c}\text{weighted}\\\text{average}\\\text{shares}\end{array}\right) + \left(\begin{array}{c}\text{shares from}\\\text{conversion of}\\\text{conv. pfd. shares}\end{array}\right) + \left(\begin{array}{c}\text{shares from}\\\text{conversion of}\\\text{conv. debt}\end{array}\right) + \left(\begin{array}{c}\text{shares}\\\text{issuable from}\\\text{stock options}\end{array}\right)}$$

Coefficients of Variation:

$$CV_{\text{sales}} = \frac{\text{standard deviation of sales}}{\text{mean sales}}$$

$$CV_{\text{operating income}} = \frac{\text{standard deviation of operating income}}{\text{mean operating income}}$$

$$CV_{\text{net income}} = \frac{\text{standard deviation of net income}}{\text{mean net income}}$$

Inventories:

ending inventory = beginning inventory + purchases − COGS

FIFO COGS = LIFO COGS − (ending LIFO reserve − beginning LIFO reserve)

Long-Lived Assets:

$$\text{straight-line depreciation} = \frac{\text{cost} - \text{salvage value}}{\text{useful life}}$$

$$\text{DDB depreciation} = \left(\frac{2}{\text{useful life}}\right)(\text{cost} - \text{accumulated depreciation})$$

$$\text{units-of-production depreciation} =$$

$$\frac{\text{original cost} - \text{salvage value}}{\text{life in output units}} \times \text{output units in the period}$$

$$\text{average age} = \frac{\text{accumulated depreciation}}{\text{annual depreciation expense}}$$

$$\text{total useful life} = \frac{\text{historical cost}}{\text{annual depreciation expense}}$$

$$\text{remaining useful life} = \frac{\text{ending net PP\&E}}{\text{annual depreciation expense}}$$

Deferred Taxes:

$$\text{income tax expense} = \text{taxes payable} + \Delta\text{DTL} - \Delta\text{DTA}$$

Debt Liabilities:

$$\text{interest expense} = \left(\begin{array}{c}\text{the market rate} \\ \text{at issue}\end{array}\right) \times \left(\begin{array}{c}\text{the balance sheet value} \\ \text{of the liability at} \\ \text{the beginning of the period}\end{array}\right)$$

Performance Ratios:

$$\text{cash flow-to-revenue} = \frac{\text{CFO}}{\text{net revenue}}$$

$$\text{cash return-on-assets} = \frac{\text{CFO}}{\text{average total assets}}$$

$$\text{cash return-on-equity} = \frac{\text{CFO}}{\text{average total equity}}$$

$$\text{cash-to-income} = \frac{\text{CFO}}{\text{operating income}}$$

$$\text{cash flow per share} = \frac{\text{CFO} - \text{preferred dividends}}{\text{weighted average number of common shares}}$$

Coverage Ratios:

$$\text{debt coverage} = \frac{\text{CFO}}{\text{total debt}}$$

$$\text{interest coverage} = \frac{\text{CFO} + \text{interest paid} + \text{taxes paid}}{\text{interest paid}}$$

$$\text{reinvestment} = \frac{\text{CFO}}{\text{cash paid for long-term assets}}$$

$$\text{debt payment} = \frac{\text{CFO}}{\text{cash long-term debt repayment}}$$

$$\text{dividend payment} = \frac{\text{CFO}}{\text{dividends paid}}$$

$$\text{investing and financing} = \frac{\text{CFO}}{\text{cash outflows from investing and financing activities}}$$

INDEX

Notes